The LIVING DEAD Revival Guide

VITAL INFORMATION FOR LIVING IN CHRIST

Talon Schneider

Copyright © 2020 by Talon Schneider
ISBN: 9798695312966
Library of Congress Registration:
Published in the United States of America

All rights reserved. No part of this book may be used or reproduced by any means, graphic, electronic, or mechanical, including photocopying, recording, taping or by any information storage retrieval system without the written permission of the publisher except in the case of brief quotations embodied in critical articles and reviews.

Scripture quotations marked (NASB), are taken from the *NEW AMERICAN STANDARD BIBLE*, Copyright © 1960,1962,1963,1968,1971,1972,1973,1975,1977, 1995 by The Lockman Foundation. Used by permission.

Scripture quotations marked (NIV), are taken from *THE HOLY BIBLE, NEW INTERNATIONAL VERSION*, NIV' Copyright © 1973, 1978, 1984, 2011 by Biblica, Inc.' Used by permission. All rights reserved worldwide.

Scripture quotations marked (AMP) are taken from *THE AMPLIFIED BIBLE*. Copyright © 2015 by The Lockman Foundation, La Habra, CA 90631.

Scripture quotations marked (ESV) are taken from *THE ESV' BIBLE* (The Holy Bible, English Standard Version'). ESV' Text Edition: 2016. Copyright © 2001 by Crossway, a publishing ministry of Good News Publishers.

Scripture quotations marked (NET) are taken from *THE NET BIBLE*, New English Translation. Copyright © 1996 BY Biblical Studies Press, L.L.C.

Burkhart Books
www.BurkhartBooks.com
Bedford, Texas

DEDICATION

To Erika, I will love you always and in all ways.

To my children, be wise and innocent, strong and gentle.

To my family and friends, thank you for your continual love and support through the good times and the bad times.

All of you share in this with me in ways we will only fully know when we rejoice together at the marriage feast of the Lamb and His Bride.

ACKNOWLEDGMENTS

During the writing of this book, there were many times it felt as though the Darkness of the Zombie Apocalypse was nearly too much to endure. I want to urge anyone who has been called out of the Darkness and into the Light of Christ to find a Living Hope by exploring the music of these very dear friends in the family of the faith. Their songs draw us near to the Lord and are exceedingly vital to life in Christ. Seek them out, and you will find that God is there with them, ready to strengthen, confirm, and establish you so that you would never be shaken.

My brother Lovkn first and foremost, has shared his heart of worship with me in person, and he continues to press forward the advancement of the gospel with the resolve of a man who knows the undying love of Christ. His encouraging words came to me at a time of great need, and I will never forget how he helped me continue to Walk in the purpose for which God made me.

Furthermore, many other brothers and sisters should be relied upon in these last days. Josh Garrells has long been a pioneer of the wondrous creativity that comes from knowing the Creator intimately. Anyone who worships according to the music, Josh, makes Walks into a deeper faith and joy.

Josh White has also been an incredible benefit to the faith in how he expounds on the profound through simplicity and somehow opens our hearts to how the simple truths of Yahweh are also deeply profound. His worship is often heard in the voices of me, my wife, and children.

Allie Paige has shared an intimacy with the Lord that is such a tremendous blessing that I am often left ruminating on the wonderful words of life she sings about. I hope that her heart leads many other sisters to share the kind of worship of those who know how necessary it is to sit at the feet of the Lord and let all our temporary worries pass away.

Many other brothers and sisters are rising and can be found keeping the Worthy Walker motivated even though we Walk through the Valley of the shadow of Death. Look for them and fellowship with them because we all are being built up like Living Stones into a spiritual house to offer spiritual sacrifices of worship to the Lord our God.

CONTENTS

DEDICATION
ACKNOWLEDGMENTS
PREFACE 9

CHAPTER ONE: DAWN OF THE DEAD 13
INTRODUCTION TO ZOMBIES 13
TESTIMONY: A MATTER OF LIFE AND DEATH 14
THE GENESIS ACCOUNT 16
    ADAM AND EVE 16
    THE SERPENT 17
    CAIN AND ABEL 18
    DEATH SENTENCE 20
    WHAT IS DEATH? 20
    WHERE DID DEATH ORIGINATE? 21
    WHY DOES DEATH LIVE? 21
    THE CATALYSTS 22
    THE DEVIL 24
    CASE FILE 24
    GARDEN CONNECTION 26
    THE FLESH 27
    CASE FILE 29
    GARDEN CONNECTION 29
    THE WORLD 30
    CASE FILE 30
    GARDEN CONNECTION 31
    DARKEST BEFORE THE DAWN 32
    DAWN OF LIFE 32
    CASE FILE 33
    THE DEVIL 34
    THE FLESH 34
    THE WORLD 36
    WHEN CATALYSTS CONCLUDE 36

CHAPTER TWO: THE WALK 39
DEAD WALKER 39
    IDENTITY CRISIS 39
ZOMBIE MYTHS 43
ACTS OF THE FLESH 45

UNDENIABLE	48
UNDOING	49
UNWILLING	51
UNVEILING	52
UNLOVING	53
DEPRAVITY OF THE DEAD	55
THE UNDEAD DILEMMA	60
UNDEAD	61
UNREASONABLE	63
DEATH THREAT	65
DEAD END	67
PERILOUS	69
SLEEPWALKER	71
IENTIFICATION CRISIS	71
DREAMERS	72
DREAMS NOT AS THEY SEEM	72
IDENTITY CRISIS	73
THROUGH A GLASS DIMLY	79
IDENTIFYING WHO'S WHO	81
WOLVES AND SHEEP	84
JESUS IS LORD?	87
THE THIN GRAY LINE	88
LIBERTY OR DEATH?	89
RIPE OR RUIN?	91
DRIFTING OFF TO DEATH	93
IDENTIFYING DRIFTERS	94
UNALARMED	96
NUGHT TERRORS	97
BEYOND THE BASICS	99
AWAKENING	106
ALARM!	111
WORTHY WALKER	112
IDENTITY IN CHRIST	112
TASTE DEATH	113
WALK IN THE LIGHT	115
FRUIT OF THE SPIRIT	117
RECOGNIZING RESULTS	120
FRUITFUL RESISTANCE	123
TENACITY OF LIFE	124
THE MEANING OF LIFE	128
PREPARE TO DIE	131

Participation of the Saints	135
Hope of Glory	137
The Hopeless	140

CHAPTER THREE: ZOMBIE APOCALYPSE — 143

Living in the Zombie Apocalypse	143
The Fallout and the Hall of Faith	147
Dead Walkers	149
Sleep Walkers	149
Worthy Walkers	149
The Zombie's Apocalypse	150
True Sanctuary	156
The End of the World	160
New Heaven and New Earth	162

CHAPTER FOUR: RESISTANCE — 169

Keep Your Eyes on Z.I.O.N.	169
Z.I.O.N. Unit	173
Training and Equipment	174
Armor of God	176
Speaking to the Dead	177
The Direness of Discipleship	181
Resistance is Fertile	185
Futility in Faith	188

CHAPTER FIVE: THE GOSPEL CURE — 191

The Cure to Death	191
Dispensing the Cure	195
Preserving the Cure	197
Examination	199
Self Examination	202
Regeneration	204
Broken Bread and an Overflowing Cup	207
Baptism	208
Communion	210
Revival	212

About the Author

Preface

In the beginning of my faith, I was eager to learn what the Bible taught about God. I had wasted more than 20 years Walking in the Darkness. Even though I had a cursory awareness of God, I did not truly know Him. There was so much I didn't know and so much to learn. I had a long way to go. But I didn't have to Walk alone.

One of the most influential Christian men in my life urged me in my spiritual infancy to dedicate 90% of my time to reading the Scripture. In hindsight, I realize what he meant was that I would spend 90% of the time reading leisurely. But I took him perhaps too literally and spent 90% of all my time reading the Word of God. I would read and listen to the Bible at every opportunity. This discipline did not disappoint. When I met a subject that confused me, I would search for the answer diligently. If I couldn't find it on my own, I would ask someone who knew the answer. Every time I learned something new, I realized that there was more to learn. Eventually, I was driven to take notes because what I was learning in the scripture was too remarkable to forget. Before bed, I would pour over book after book of the Bible looking to gather as much knowledge and wisdom possible. God never failed to show Himself through His Word.

Then at some point through this process I read a very influential selection of verses. These would be the start of this very book. Ephesians 2:1-3 spoke to me in a new way, even though I had read it before. This time the Holy Spirit made me realize something profound. It said that I was Dead! But of course, I was not dead, like a corpse is in the sense of being biologically lifeless. The grim truth was that previously I did not actually know God. Seeing that I did not know God before I was Born Again, it was reasonable to conclude that I also did not know Life. This is the condition of all humankind. We do not know God, as we ought to know him from the moment we enter the world. In effect, we are born spiritually Dead with no natural knowledge of God.

Christianity conveys this message with outstanding clarity. The concept of a relationship with Yahweh is thematically present from the beginning to the end. But it seems that even still there is a spiritual haze obscuring the minds of those who Walk as enemies of the cross, and occasionally it blurs the understanding of even those who think that they know him. I am not better than any other brother or sister in Christ. My goal is to help people realize their desperate need to know the love of God. With this book, I hope to share that same realization that I had, namely that we do not know God as we should. We don't know Him as He wants us to know Him. Because if we knew God as we ought to, then we would live as new creatures. The difference should be as stark as that of the Living compared to the Dead. Our entire Life is dependent upon God. Without God, we are without Life. Do you believe this? If so, then join me in this mission to share the gospel with everyone everywhere. Know then that you have been brought to Life in order to love as the Lord Jesus Christ loved you. All glory to God!

Talon Schneider

*We know that we have **crossed over from death to life**
because we love our fellow Christians.
The one who does not love remains in death.*

1 John 3:14 (ESV)

    In order to accomplish a more succinct understanding of key points being made within the book, I have used boldface in some Scripture to encourage closer examination. Furthermore, the use of capitalized words is implemented to indicate the difference between Spiritual and physical meaning. The use of italics is meant to create further suspenseful emphasis, whether read internally or aloud. There is a tremendous difference between Living and living. If we are Alive, then this means we are in right relationship with God, but if we are Dead, then we are separated from God. If we are alive, then we move, breath, and are biologically functioning. However, if we are dead, then we have physically and certifiably stopped our vital functions such that our breath stops and heartbeat ceases. The Bible says, "The body without the spirit is dead" in James 2:13. We will explore more of this concept within the book, but for now, the groundwork is laid. This approach is intended to bring clarity to what can seem very confusing upon learning that we are all "Dead in our sins," as it is written in Ephesians 2:1. Hence we must be "Born Again," as is discussed in John 3. Therefore please take notice of the special use of capitalized words to indicate a distinction of great importance.

*And God said, "Let there be light," and there was light.
And God saw that the light was good.
And God separated the light from the darkness.
God called the light Day, and the darkness he called Night.
And there was evening, and there was morning, the first day.*

Genesis 1:3-5 (ESV)

CHAPTER ONE

DAWN OF THE DEAD

Introduction to Zombies

If you're reading this, then it's not too late. But try to be still as you read what follows, no need to attract unnecessary attention to yourself. I'm sure you've already experienced some horrible things, and for that, I am sorry. But what you have in your hands is the best I can do to document the Zombie Apocalypse and how we should Walk knowing that the End is near. Although we are living in a wicked generation, it will not always be this way. We've been given an opportunity to be the Resistance needed to cause change. We've been chosen to carry the Cure to Death, but this mission is not for the faint of heart. This mission will require bravery and faith in No Man's Land, a place where none are righteous, not even one. We can be sure that God will prepare us to Walk in the good works that he prepared in advance. He will never leave us nor forsake us. There is no greater work than what God does in saving a sinful Zombie by sending a once Dead messenger to speak Life to the Lifeless. There is only one hope for the living Dead, and his name is Jesus Christ.

> And there is **salvation in no one else**, for there is no other name under heaven given among men by which we must be saved.
>
> Acts 4:12 (ESV)

Where did all of this evil come from? In the beginning, there was no death, no shame, no crying, and no pain. But when sin came into the world, everything good was twisted. Through the temptation of a deceptive tongue, mankind swallowed a lie that changed their life drastically. Death followed their woeful choice like a shadow to its source, and the purity of humanity was tainted. After that, nothing was as it should've been. Sin reigned in death and enslaved all of humanity into rebellion against God. No one escaped, no, not one. Nevertheless, there was granted a grace to all, an opportunity for mercy to triumph over judgment. For a short time, the conclusion of the matter was stalled. The living Dead were given the incredible gift of true Life if they would only choose to believe.

To this very day, the living Dead wander the world aimlessly. They walk wherever their instinctual desires take them. They can be found to the ends of the earth, lurking in the shadows and even carousing in broad daylight. They have no regard for you or for God. They are lovers of darkness rather than light. They are quick to shed blood. Their hunger is for the Flesh, and they follow its cravings. "Their mind is set on earthly and unspiritual things. Their glory is in their shame. Their god is their stomach. Their destiny is destruction (Philippians 3:19 NIV). They are ungodly and Undead. I know because I was once as they still are. I was a Zombie.

> *O LORD, you pulled me up from Sheol;* **you rescued me from among those descending into the grave.** *Sing to the LORD, you faithful followers of his; give thanks to his holy name.*
> Psalms 30:3-4 (NET)

TESTIMONY: A MATTER OF LIFE AND DEATH

I thought I knew what Life was, but I was Dead wrong. There were many ways that I tried to feel alive, but they all ended up in failure, disappointment, and spiritual Death. To make matters worse, I was a Dead man walking ever closer to my demise. With every self-satisfying decision, I was making my heart more callous and unwilling to change. I was a despicable creature with no means to change what I truly was. I didn't know Life at all, and I was running headfirst into the gates of hell. My man-made religion catered to my own cravings, and through it, I worshiped myself. I had made myself into a god and had turned my sources of temporary gratification into my pagan pantheon. My idle idolatry petrified my ability to see, hear, or understand anything of true value. In turn, I couldn't be healed despite my desperate self-medication. Shrouded in darkness, my sins sedated me from the painful reality of my Lifeless condition. I was without God and without hope in the world. I was Dead to the core.

But God, in His great love and mercy, made His light shine in my heart. He loved me not because of anything that I had done, but because that was His choice. By faith, I turned to Him in repentance and believed in the atonement offered through Christ Jesus. His sacrifice for my sins gave me new life, His Life. I was made into a new creature who had a new nature and a new Living Hope through the resurrection of Jesus Christ from the dead. However, as I arose from baptism, my joy was mixed with sorrow. There were still so many people in the World who were being deceived by the Devil and Living off of the desires of their Flesh. They were heading to hell just as I was, and it terrified me. I had come to know how close I had been to the Second Death—eternal separation from God. I couldn't stand by and watch so many others take the wide path that leads to death and destruction.

The **LIVING DEAD** Revival Guide

Knowing the fear of the Lord, we must no longer Walk according to the Flesh but according to the Spirit. Our calling is to Walk Worthy in love and light even as our Lord Jesus Christ Walked. Indeed, it would be far better to be at home with the Lord and away from our body. Yet we remain in this wicked World to serve a purpose. We are those who were Dead but now Alive because of Jesus. Now we have become an army of dry bones brought back to Life in order to bring the message of Life to those of whom we once were. That is not without reason. We must carry out what we were made to do: love God and our neighbors. It is this undying love that we have from God that must be delivered to the Dead if we truly desire to see Revival.

Indeed, our mission is the revival of the living Dead. It is a Death-defying call to Walk by faith in the risen Lord. The only way the Dead are raised is by the powerful love of God. It is the most excellent way of love that thoroughly changes lives. We cannot force the Dead to change because God has saved by grace and not by works so that no one may boast before Him. Certainly, that is how it was with me. I merely cooperated with the will of God, but it was certainly a Salvation wrought by Yahweh and not by my own effort. Furthermore, I knew as soon as I was Alive that I couldn't waste any more time. There was a high calling upon me and upon all those who call upon the Name of the Lord. Immediately after I was brought to Life, I was equipped with a Bible, the Living Word of God, so that I could understand the newness of Life in Christ. Death still haunted me, though now without fear, because the love of God had defeated Death for me.

Nevertheless, the conflict between Life and Death surrounded me. Many questions needed to be answered, but three remained most vital. What is Death? Where did Death originate? Why does Death *Live*? The fact that Death not only Lives but thrives and spreads relentlessly has become an ordinary nuance to the unscrupulous. But the answers to these questions are truly life-changing. We must return to the beginning to fully understand— the source of sin, the Dawn of Death, and the Catalysts that continue to spread the Zombie plague even to this day.

> *Because experiencing your loyal love is better than life itself,*
> *my lips will praise you.*
>
> Psalms 63:3 (NET)

The Genesis Account

Behold the Genesis Account, and suddenly the index case is made clear. It is as if a secret document has been laid out before you, detailing the mysterious underpinnings of reality, as we know it. But this is no secret because it has been made clearly known to us so that we are without excuse. Undeniably the importance of the Living Word of God has been neglected. We must retain our persistent reliance on the Holy Scriptures if we dare to overcome sin and Death through faith in Christ Jesus. If we are to comprehend the darkness, we must understand that the Dawn of the Dead originated from the Garden of Eden, where human life first began.

Adam and Eve

The Bible teaches that in the beginning, the Lord God created everything, and it was good. He made light shine in darkness. He made the heavens, the earth, and the sea and all that is in them. The Lord God made mankind in His own image, male and female He made them. But their great honor was coupled with great humility. He formed Adam out of the dirt of the earth and breathed life into him. He formed Eve from the bone and flesh of Adam. Together they were perfect complements and were told by the Lord God to be productive, even reproductive so that they could fill the earth and reign in life as good stewards over God's good creation. They were given produce that could reproduce with seeds as food, and along with the other living creatures, they were given the green plants for food as well. The Lord God saw all that He had made, and it was very good. On the seventh day, the Lord God rested. He blessed the day and made it holy. The creation week was complete, but destruction lurked.

The Lord God commanded Adam to work in the Garden of Eden in order to care for it and cultivate it. Adam was called to rule over the creatures from the heavens, the earth, and the sea. Though Adam had the privilege of naming all the creatures, only Eve was competent to complete him. It was not good for man to be alone, and that remains true to this day. All of this was to the glory of God. Adam and Eve were naked, shameless, sinless, free, and alive but not for very long.

The Serpent

Genesis chapter three reveals the answers to our three vital questions. Adam and Eve were in the Garden when a strange creature approached them with a suspicious conversation. The Serpent was considered more clever than any of the other beasts and was even able to communicate with the first humans. His poisonous speech convinced

Eve to eat the fruit that God had forbidden while Adam did nothing to resist the temptation. Adam was intended to represent the future all humanity, and therefore his every choice carried immense responsibility and repercussions. His willing disobedience was such a departure from his purpose that it changed him and all humans that came after him.

Upon eating the forbidden fruit, there were noticeable changes. Immediately, Adam and Eve had their eyes opened, and they felt shame. They covered their bodies with leaves and hid from God. This was relational death, between Adam, Eve, and God! But God soon asked for Adam, knowing all along what had happened. Adam reluctantly answered and directed blame for the sin upon Eve. He even went as far as to blame God for giving her to him. But Eve confessed truly that the serpent had deceived her. The serpent had nothing to say, for he was indeed Satan, the antagonist of all that is loved by God. The punishment for these actions was quickly administered. The serpent was humiliated and cursed; Satan was given the pronouncement of his demise. Eve was punished with increased pain in childbearing. But hope for redemption would come through a child born of a woman. Eve would desire her husband, but he would rule over her. Adam was punished with the increased difficulty of living.

In stark contrast to the paradise of God's Garden, Adam would learn the error of his arrogance through hard work in a harsh world. He was intended to be the representative of all humans, but his failure caused a terrible Fall out of the presence of God. This Fall, the result of sin, was certain death to the first humans and all who followed after them. But this was not as one might expect. Adam and Eve were no longer naked, shameless, sinless, or free, but they were alive. Yes, they were alive physically, but now dead spiritually. They were living as we have become accustomed but not truly living as God intended. They were banished from the Garden of Eden and from the direct presence of God because they were no longer free of sin. This banishment from the presence of God was death to Adam and Eve, for they were separated from the source of Life!

But God provided His life-saving grace in the form of a subtle sacrifice when He covered them with animal skins. They had certainly died spiritually when they were severed from the immediate presence of God. Additionally, their physical death would serve as a perpetual reminder to all humanity after them of this fatal decision to disobey God. Their disobedience was so significant that it has plagued all of life ever since. Our life on earth is filled with spiritual tension. We must choose to Walk by the Flesh toward destruction or by the Spirit towards Life and peace. In this way, the Dawn of the Dead has caused all human life to begin as Zombified beings and disconnected from God. The proof of this was sudden and sorrowful for Adam and Eve.

Talon Schneider

CAIN AND ABEL

The immediate offspring of Adam and Eve were made in their own fallen image. Their names were Cain and Abel. Cain was a farmer, and Abel was a shepherd. One day they both brought an offering before God. God was pleased with what Abel offered but was displeased with the offering of Cain. Cain became angry and jealous of his brother.

> *The Lord said to Cain, 'Why are you angry, and why has your face fallen? If you do well, will you not be accepted? And if you do not do well,* **sin is crouching at the door. Its desire is contrary to you, but you must rule over it.***'*
> Genesis 4:6-7 (ESV)

God had instructed Cain that he still had an opportunity to make better choices and, by faith, bring a better sacrifice. But at the same time, it was clear that sin was waiting to pounce like a ferocious animal on its prey. Like a beast, Cain lured his brother into a field and struck him down in cold blood. His violent actions had actually separated Abel from his body. The separation of the body from the spirit is physical death (James 2:26). But just as Cain had prepared an ambush for Abel, so had sin sprang to life in Cain resulting in spiritual death (Romans 7). When God asked Cain the whereabouts of his brother, he defiantly retorted that he was not responsible for keeping his brother safe. Though this was quite untrue, God was well aware of Cain's defection.

> *And the Lord said, "What have you done?* **The voice of your brother's blood is crying to me from the ground.** *And now you are cursed from the ground, which has opened its mouth to receive your brother's blood from your hand.*
> Genesis 4:10-11 (ESV)

Cain was cursed so that the land would defy him, and he was banished to a desolate land where he would be a restless wanderer; he was a Deadman walking because of his brutal sin. Cain bemoaned his plight, believing that his punishment was too severe and that anyone who found him would kill him just as he had killed his brother. Remarkably God had mercy on him!

> *Then the Lord said to him,* **"Not so! If anyone kills Cain, vengeance shall be taken on him sevenfold."** *And the Lord put a mark on Cain, lest any who found him should attack him. Then Cain went away from the presence of the Lord and settled in the land of Nod, east of Eden.*
> Genesis 4:15-16 (ESV)

The **LIVING DEAD** Revival Guide

The spread of the living Dead had reared its ugly head. Just as Adam and Eve had by their actions separated themselves from the beautiful paradise of Eden, and the accessibility of God, so too had Cain exhibited his Zombified spirit. What shall we make of this mortifying predicament? Mankind seems doomed to be Dead in sins and displeasing to their Creator. There is hope, however, but it must be lived out by faith. We, like Adam and Eve, will be tested for our faithfulness. We, like Cain, have a choice to make.

> *We should not be like Cain, who was of the evil one and murdered his brother. And why did he murder him?* ***Because his own deeds were evil and his brother's righteous****.*
> 1 John 3:12 (ESV)

We, like Abel, will die physically. But just as Abel lived by faith, we can Live spiritually as well. We can have a dynamic relationship with the living God that results in the resurrection of our bodies and the glorification of our Savior.

> *By faith Abel offered to God a more acceptable sacrifice than Cain, through which he was commended as righteous, God commending him by accepting his gifts.* ***And through his faith, though he died, he still speaks****.*
> Hebrews 11:4 (ESV)

The Genesis Account does not end with Adam and Eve nor Cain and Abel. Every human after Adam was subject to death, and Genesis, chapter five, is very clear about their lifetime. Death came to all, apart from the curious case of Enoch.

> ***Enoch walked with God***, *and then he disappeared because God took him away.*
> Genesis 5:24 (NET)

Enoch was an example that evading death was far from ordinary. The reality was that death hungrily swallowed up every life, whether righteous or wicked. This is a harrowing truth that the Genesis Account unveils. Our Dead works do not turn us into Zombies. We are Zombies, and our works are Dead before God. They hang on us like filthy rags. Our own efforts cannot overcome the chasm that separates us from a God that is holy, holy, holy. It is the holiness of God that provokes a reverential awe. However, denying God produces a terrible evil in the hearts of mankind that will end in a true and just judgment.

Talon Schneider

*The LORD saw how great the wickedness of the human race had become on the earth, and that **every inclination of the thoughts of the human heart was only evil all the time**.*

Genesis 6:5 (NIV)

DEATH SENTENCE

Sin results in Death, which is separation, and Death Lives because of the same catalysts our ancestors encountered. As we understand these truths we will be better equipped for our Revival Mission. What difference does it make to the Zombie to tell them that they are Dead? They know that these things they are doing are opposed to God, but they do not care. They are so callous that they not only condone sin, but they approve and encourage those who practice such behavior (Romans 1:32). Therefore, it is of great significance to be able to clearly explain to them who ask us for the reason behind our Living Hope. We not only believe the Gospel; we also Live it. The Gospel Cure is the information that leads to a Living relationship with the God who always Lives. It is not merely a religious practice or a method of keeping rules, but it is a real relationship, the hope of glory, Christ in us (Colossians 1:27). Therefore, we must be completely confident in sharing this message with the utmost clarity because by knowing it ourselves, we may perhaps lead others to know it as well. We may perhaps lead others to the One who can save them from the wrath that is due for sin. Thus, we have our answers from the Genesis Account: What is Death? Where did Death originate? Why does Death Live?

WHAT IS DEATH?

Death is separation in essence and expression. We are born Dead in our sins and have no natural relationship with God who created us. Death can also be that of various other relationships such as marital Death, which would be called divorce. Death can be seen as the opposite of that which is Alive. Christians have Living Hope while Zombies Hopes are Dead. (Genesis 3:7-8, 3:23-24, James 2:26a).

WHERE DID DEATH ORIGINATE?

Sin originated in the Garden and results in Death. The original sin of Adam is attributed to all humans (Genesis 3:3-8, 1 Corinthians 15:45-49, Romans 3:23, 5:12, and 6:23).

The LIVING DEAD Revival Guide

WHY DOES DEATH LIVE?

Death Lives or continues because of the compounded involvement of the Devil, the Flesh, and the World causing sin (Genesis 3-6, Ephesians 2:1-3, Romans 7:9).

These are the factors that caused the original sin and the index case of the Living Dead. But the Dawn of the Dead was only the beginning. The Dead just won't stay dead. They continue to live, at least partially, as a gift of God's universal grace. God did not permit Adam and Eve to reach out and eat of the tree of life in their Zombified spiritual state (Genesis 3:22) lest they live forever in their sinfulness. Truly it is by grace that we are not destroyed and by grace that we are saved. But if there is no repentance from sin, then there is no reconciliation for those who are Dead in their sins. They will weep and gnash their teeth for all eternity completely separated from God.

The Genesis Account illuminates the significance of every choice we make. We have come to learn what death is and where it came from, but failure to recognize the seriousness of sin will result in certain and eternal death. With this in view, we must ready ourselves for war. Not the kind of war that the world fights nor with their weapons but a spiritual battle. The choice has been set before us is not so different from that of Moses to the Israelites before they entered the Promised Land.

> *See, I have set before you today **life and good, death and evil**. If you obey the commandments of the Lord your God that I command you today, by **loving** the Lord your God, by **walking** in his ways, and by **keeping** his commandments and his statutes and his rules, then you shall live and multiply, and the Lord your God will bless you in the land that you are entering to take possession of it.*
>
> Deuteronomy 30:15-16 (ESV)

This, then, is the condition of all humans. All are born spiritually dead. We are living and dying at the same time until the ultimate end, where all are judged (Hebrews 9:27). This separation from God is not eternal until what is called the second death. Between now and then, each human has a choice to make. The choice is divided between believing God or refusing him just as it was with Adam and Eve. This dilemma is truly a matter of life and death. There will be shame on us if we treat it as anything less. And there will be shame on us if we ignore the severity of sin. We must not refuse the Lord God Almighty. Therefore, let us prepare ourselves with the readiness that comes from the gospel of peace, a peace we have with God. However, this peace puts us at war with the Catalysts of sin and Death. The resistance is against the Devil, the Flesh, and the World. We will do well to know how our enemy opposes us so that we do not fall into the same error that our ancestors did all that long while ago in the Garden of Eden.

> *But I am afraid that, even as the serpent beguiled Eve by his cunning, your minds may be corrupted and led away from the simplicity of* [your sincere and] *pure devotion to Christ.*
>
> 2 Corinthians 11:3 (AMP)

THE CATALYSTS

We know what Death is and where it came from, but there are Catalysts that continue to perpetuate Death as though Death Lived and moved and multiplied. The Catalysts of Sin and Death are opposed to us. We have entrusted our souls to our Faithful Creator and will press onward. But we must beware of these enemies of our souls. Ever since the Dawn of the Dead, the world has been a post-apocalyptic wasteland compared to what it once was and should've been. Someday soon, it will be a New Heavens and New Earth, and because we know this, we ought to live Godly and holy lives as we hasten that great Day that the Lord returns. But we do not know at what time He will return, and so we must be vigilant in our cause so as not to be caught unprepared for the return of our Master.

Our research into the Genesis Account has demonstrated that the onset of sin and Death was from the Garden of Eden, but the ordeal did not end there. It has continued to plague human life ever since. The Zombie infestation has spread across the entire earth! A resistance must be made. We cannot stand by as though we did not care for those that are perishing right before our eyes. Who are we to think so highly of ourselves that we could not reach down into the very pit from which we were pulled? If we love as the Lord Jesus has loved us, then we will indeed make the necessary sacrifices to bring many others to the Lord. We make these spiritual sacrifices unto the Lord, knowing that He will cause us to succeed if it is His will. But we know that the end of the matter is drawing near. The time is short. We do not know how long any of us shall live. We do not know how long our opposition, or we shall Walk. Therefore, we must make every effort to dispense the Gospel Cure as a proof of a love that cannot Die.

There are some who rigidly deny that the Dead Walk (often it is the Dead who vehemently deny this fact). Some suggest the source stems from the Haitian legend of a witch doctor wielding voodoo as a way to control hordes of mindless slave laborers. There are others who propose that the Walking Dead are the result of a pernicious primordial virus that plagues all flesh even to this day. And yet others consider the cause to be from a long-forgotten catastrophe of epic proportions. Or perhaps it is of a current and clandestine governmental mishap. What do you say? What does the scripture say? What caused the Zombie Apocalypse? What continues to cause sin and Death even in this present evil age?

Can it be that the Dead Walk because of the manipulation of a powerful prince of darkness who preys on degenerate and depraved nature so long as they remain in the fallen World? According to our research, this is true! The evidence suggests that the Devil, the Flesh, and the World brought about the first case of sin and Death. But that was a bitter foretaste of what has become all too familiar. Zombies are so numerous we could scarcely count them all. They now engulf the whole world. But God is aware of every one of them. And He does not hate them, but rather wants all to come to repentance. He has sent those who were once Dead to bring Zombies to Life with the Gospel Cure. But the Devil, the Flesh, and the World will not stand down because we are at enmity with them. These forces are still a serious threat and pose a cataclysmic problem to all life. The truth about these Catalysts will necessitate the Gospel Cure, which is the only hope for the Living Dead.

> *Who can live and not see **death**, or who can escape the power of the grave?*
> Psalm 89:48 (NIV)

Death terrorizes humanity, and the fear of death grips all. The Zombie is the manifestation of the fear of death without any hope for a cure. But there is hope, even if it is a hope against all hope (Romans 4:18). The Catalysts perpetuated Death, and they must be stopped. We must resist them by holding firm to our faith. We know that if we resist the Devil that he will flee from us (James 4:7). But we cannot think to ourselves that we have the power to accomplish these things. The power to do the will of God comes from the Holy Spirit, who Lives in the Saint. The power comes from God so that the glory would likewise go to God.

The Devil, the Flesh, and the World all contributed to the debacle of the Walking Dead but each in diverse ways. They were all involved with the original sin and the Death that followed. Ephesians 2:1-3 explains how these forces once overruled a person and still perpetuate the (physically) living (spiritually) Dead.

> *And you were **dead in the trespasses and sins in which you once walked**, following the **course of this world**, following the **prince of the power of the air**, the spirit that is now at work in the sons of*

disobedience—among whom we all once **lived in the passions of our flesh, carrying out the desires of the body and the mind**, *and were by* **nature** *children of wrath, like the rest of mankind.*

Ephesians 2:1-3 (ESV)

This verse has clearly outlined the Catalysts. But we know this and will not be caught off guard. Those that are against us are not greater than He that Lives in us (1 John 4:4). We must not let anything restrict us from the mission of revival that our Lord Jesus commanded. We must proclaim the Gospel Cure to the Dead! But there is no doubt that we will face opposition from the Catalysts of sin and Death. Faithful consideration of each Catalyst will equip us with useful strategy as we walk along the Way. Whether we must resist the deception of the Devil, the lust of the Flesh, or the corruption of the World, it is clear that the Zombie Apocalypse is upon us. Without a clear knowledge of these forces, it would be as though we were fighting in the dark. But with the Light emitted by the truth of the Living Word of God, we will see a new day Dawn.

THE DEVIL

... **the prince of the power of the air***, the spirit that is* **now at work** *in the* **sons of disobedience***.*

Ephesians 2:2b ESV

CASE FILE

Perhaps the most opportunistic Catalyst of sin is none other than the ancient serpent we know to be Satan (Revelation 12:9, 20:2). He has been sinning from the beginning, and we know that all who practice sin belong to him (1 John 3:8). He is the Father of All Lies and always speaks lies because that is his native language (John 8:44). Furthermore, all who sin are enslaved to sin, and Satan becomes their tyrannical master (John 8:34). Clearly, this Catalyst cannot be disregarded. But some are in the habit of giving him more power than he has. He is a created being and has no power compared to the Lord Almighty. We must take careful steps in how we address this Catalyst, just as it is written that the Archangel Michael did not rebuke the devil himself but rather called upon the Lord to the rebuke him (Jude 1:9). This Catalyst seeks the place and honor that belong to Yahweh, and therefore he will use deception and despotism to control Zombies.

The **LIVING DEAD** Revival Guide

*They promise them freedom, but they themselves are **slaves of corruption**.*
For whatever overcomes a person, to that he is enslaved.

2 Peter 2:19 (ESV)

If we dare to make our stand against the schemes of this vicious voodoo despot, then we must stand firm in the truth. He twisted the words of Yahweh in the Garden to get what he wanted out of Adam and Eve. But we cannot fall for the same tricks. We must remember that the Lord Jesus was tempted at all points—yet without sin. Because Jesus was tempted, we likewise know how we ought to respond to the wiles of the devil. We must be absolutely reliant upon the Spirit and the Scripture if we are to wage war against this enemy of ours. Without the assistance of the scriptures and the advocation of the Holy Spirit, the toxic lies of the devil could put any unsuspecting soul in grave danger. There are *three* considerations to be made in regard to the Devil as a Catalyst to this Zombie Apocalypse.

- He is <u>*the prince of the power of the air*</u>. He is a despot with significant power and is considered the god of this world (2 Corinthians 4:4). His serpentine scheme in the Garden of Eden usurped some measure of control over the world, which ought to have belonged to humanity. As 1 John 5:19 says, "We know that we are from God, and the whole world lies in the power of the evil one." He came to Adam and Eve disguised as a messenger of enlightenment, but his deception only wreaked havoc for humanity (2 Corinthians 11:14). Now humans have an innate desire to disobey God, and this plays right into Satan's strategy to be hailed as the ruler of the unrighteous. At the heart of his despotism is a fiery arrogance that refuses to be humbled (Isaiah 14, Ezekiel 28, and Revelation 20:7). His tenacity to be worshipped fuels the fire of his pride and seemingly blinds him in a furious rage. He will stop at nothing to have his way (Revelation 20:7-10). *Beware his despotism.*

- He is <u>*now at work*</u> primarily through the means of deception. He is like a necromancer who uses his dark powers to animate the living Dead to do his bidding. He deceives individuals and entire nations in an effort to thwart the sovereign will of the only true God. Strategically, his lies are not so different from the poison of a snake. In both cases, the attacks originate outside of the prey before infiltrating vital systems. Therefore, his lies must be prevented or expelled at all costs. Through means of deception, he has slithered his way into power. Through constriction, he keeps his hold on people. As the living Dead feed on their Fleshly sins, Satan maintains control over them like a slave master or governmental tyrant. He squeezes them into the pattern of disobedience inherited from Adam. Even the righteous feel the asphyxiating pressure of his temptations. He prowls around looking for someone to devour (1 Peter 5:8) and attempts to coil the cords of death around the necks of the unaware. This macabre master of lies will stop at nothing in order to be worshipped as though he was truly god, even if it means that he must beguile his subjects. His ultimate goal is to steal, kill, and destroy all that is loved by God (John 10:10a). *Beware his deception.*

- <u>The sons of disobedience</u> are no less than his Zombie horde. By means of his deception, he urges all the Walking Dead to worship him mindlessly. They do his bidding even though they are unaware of his influence. This is the trap of the devil (2 Timothy 2:26). The wrath of God is coming on the sons of disobedience because of sexual immorality, impurity, shameful passion, evil desire, and idolatrous greed and the like (Colossians 3:5-6). These things are coming in part because of the deception of empty words hissed into the ear of the unbelieving (Ephesians 5:6). Inevitably there will come a man of lawlessness—the son of destruction—who will be empowered by Satan to carry out his desire to be worshipped through the hidden power of sinfulness in people (2 Thessalonians 2:3-10). *Beware his Dead horde of sinners.*

GARDEN CONNECTION

In some ways, the suspicion that the Zombie Apocalypse had its origin in the Haitian myth of a voodoo wielding witch doctor is not so far-fetched. But in every way, it is far worse. Satan is not raising up the dead and reanimating their bodies to carry out thoughtless tasks. He is orchestrating a devious plan to keep everyone Dead to God and eventually attempt to overthrow the Lord of lords and King of kings. His deception is the powerful voodoo that urges the ungodly to live in sin. His deception is the poison that dreadfully incapacitated his prey. His deception is the force that manipulates every nation, tribe, tongue, and person. And yet his deception is only one factor that has brought about the Zombie Apocalypse. There is still the Flesh and the World to contend with in our mission of revival.

> *Is the law then contrary to the promises of God? Certainly not! For if a law had been given that could give **life**, then righteousness would indeed be by the law. But the Scripture imprisoned everything under sin so that*

the promise by faith in Jesus Christ might be given **to those who believe***. Now before faith came, we were held captive under the law, imprisoned until the coming faith would be revealed. So then, the law was our guardian until Christ came, in order that we might be* **justified by faith***. But now that faith has come, we are no longer under a guardian, for in Christ Jesus, you are all sons of God, through faith.*

Galatians 3:21-26 ESV

The Flesh

Among whom **we all** *once lived in the* **passions of our flesh***, carrying out* **the desires of the body and the mind***, and were by nature children of wrath, like the rest of mankind.*

Ephesians 2:3 (ESV)

Case File

Undoubtedly the flesh was a powerful participant in the outbreak of sin and death in humanity. From the very beginning, God gave his crowning creation the right to choose, but not without consequences. As a Catalyst of the Zombie Apocalypse, the Flesh is not only engulfing people with destructive desires, but it is driving people to devour one another like ravaging beasts. The scriptures are clear that there are many different kinds of flesh (1 Corinthians 15:39-41). But our attention is on human nature, understood to be the Flesh because it has been infected by sin. The Flesh is destructive, decaying, and denied access to the kingdom of God. All humans are born sinners (Psalm 51:5) and, by nature, are driven to continually sin. Sin has been inherited by all because of Adam's irresponsibility (Romans 5:12), but sin is also compounded by each individual's actions. The Adamic and pandemic sin problem will plague humanity until God makes all things new (Revelation 20:7-9, 21:1). Therefore, it is incredibly important that we understand how the Flesh revolts against what is spiritual. Understanding the implications of a body that is subject to death is critical for the message concerning true Life. There are three major considerations concerning the Flesh as Catalysts of the Zombie Apocalypse.

I collapse in the dirt. **Revive me with your word!**

Psalms 119:25 (NET)

- <u>*We all*</u> experience the effects of the outbreak of sin because of our infected Flesh. The Flesh constitutes the natural condition of all humans, the image-bearers of God. Although the glory of being image-bearers has been damaged by sin, it can still reflect creativity, emotion, volition, and many other characteristics of the Creator. We all live in a physical body with genetic identification, but the influence of sin has caused various weaknesses in our total being. In the end, we all will be judged for our actions done in the body (2 Corinthians 5:10). We all have been infected with the sin virus, which we inherited because of Adam. It is worth observing that the etymology of the word "virus" has connections with a Latin word that refers to a slimy liquid or poison believed to be from a snake. With our study of the Genesis Account, we know that the sin virus was the result of the satanic serpent's virulent deception and the defiant choice of our ancestor to partake of the forbidden fruit. Sadly, not all will be cured because not all want to be healed from their sinful condition. Rather the vast throng of the world endorses and encourages sinful living even though they know that the outcome of their actions is death (Romans 1:32). Indeed we must not blame God when we are tested by various temptations for God is not tempted and does not tempt anyone but instead, both the righteous and the wicked give way to temptation when their Flesh drags them off to indulge in sinful passions; in this way, desire conceives sin and sin when it is full-grown brings forth death (James 1:13-15). *Beware the infected flesh*.

- <u>*The passions of the Flesh*</u> are evident and obvious (Galatians 5:19-21). They produce Fruit that is diseased and rotten and will be discarded along with the source of the bad Fruit itself (Matthew 7:17-18, 12:33, John 15:2, Romans 7:5). Each person will bear the consequences of their choices, and God will not be deceived (Galatians 6:7-8). The temptations that we face may be various, but they are not permitted to go beyond our ability to endure them (1 Corinthians 10:13). Ultimately our desires must return to their original purpose, which was to love and listen to the Lord our God. The only way to override the passions of the Flesh is to Walk in the Spirit and bear Fruit for Life. The sin that results from the Flesh is like a parasite that feeds on its host so long as there is a source of lawlessness. Adam and Eve premiered the pattern of disobedience that has leeched off of the Flesh ever since the beginning. However, if one is able to put to Death the sin that enervates them, they may have the appearance of righteousness by their own deeds. Though there is no cure for the sin virus except for death itself. *Beware feeding the Flesh with sin only to see sin eat away at your flesh*.

- *The desires of the body and the mind* can be neutral apart from sin but deadly if infected with lawlessness. This can turn what was meant for good (the Law, for example, Romans 7:2-6) into something used to bring about death through utter sinfulness (Romans 7:13). Morally neutral desires of the flesh, such as hunger and thirst, can be degraded into gluttonous sins. Even the pleasure of sex can be distorted and perverted by sin's corruption if outside of the commanded guidelines of God (Romans 1:26-27). The desires of the body and mind were meant to be received with gratitude as a gift of the Creator, but wherever there is law, there is sin also lying in the shadows (Romans 3:20). Just as it was with Cain, sin desires to rule over us, but we must learn to master it. The unregenerate and undead Zombie lusts after the flesh and hungers for the gratification it experiences temporarily from sin. But the desire of the upright is to please not themselves but God. *Beware sin's contamination of what is holy and pure.*

Garden Connection

Just as many have suspected there was something intrinsically wrong with the Flesh from the very beginning. The outbreak from a time long ago is not long forgotten. Sin spreads quickly and contaminates what should've remained pure. The effects of sin on the Flesh are unmistakable. Pride, anger, jealously, deceit, and the like ruin lives and plague the whole world over. The Walking Dead are senseless in their defiance of the commandment of God, but a day of reckoning is fast approaching.

Adam's decision to eat the forbidden fruit from the tree of the knowledge of good and evil has drastically changed the base nature of humankind. Evidently, the impact of sin and Death on the Flesh is comparable to a virus in some ways and a parasite in other ways. What is clear is that the Dead are infested with a contagious and virulent Flesh condition that cannot be resolved by the infected. The interaction of the Devil and the flesh from the Garden has conspired to the drastic levels of infection that are seen today. The tension between the living and the Dead intensifies even further when considering the impact that the Dawn of the Dead had upon the entire World.

The World

In which you once walked, following the course of this world.
Ephesians 2:2 (ESV)

Case File

The ends of the earth have become infested with the living Dead, who are making the World a decrepit wasteland. The Genesis Account detailed the banishment of Adam and Eve from the Garden and the banishment of Cain from the ground that soaked up his brother's righteous blood, but what came after them was climactic on a global scale. The flood that Noah and his family survived was a worldwide cataclysm. Yet even after washing away nearly every form of life from the planet, the terribly evil inclinations of the human heart persisted (Genesis 8:21). Not only did the evil tendencies remain in the Flesh but the impact of the Fallout radiated across the World. As a result, the World, as a spiritual system of thought, has been drastically warped by the Adam Bomb. There was no longer a lush Garden paradise where the Creator and His creations cohabited. Instead what we see is the World being polluted by evil desires. It consists of empty idols, enmity with God, and other spiritually toxic corruptions. The World has *three* factors that demand our immediate attention.

- Adam and Eve <u>once walked</u> in a world free of sin. They were at the heart of *Ground Zero*, being themselves the first case of the Walking Dead. They once Walked with God in the cool of the day, but after their Fallout, they were severed from His refreshing presence. Ground Zero reminds us of two significant implications. First, that mankind was made of dust, and to dust, he shall return (Genesis 2:7, 3:19). We will do well to heed the humility produced by our mortality (Psalm 90:12). Second, Ground Zero reminds us how suddenly the World around us can change. Adam and Eve were meant to cultivate and care for the plants and animals as good stewards, but their actions swiftly resulted in adverse effects on creation. Food was no longer plentiful; instead, it was difficult to acquire; the terrain was tough; the ground did not yield itself to them as it once did. Eventually, the creatures feared mankind, and the dread of Zombies terrified them all (Genesis 9:2). All of creation was subjected to futility, not without reason, but because creation was subjected to corruption, decay, and pollution with the hope of seeing redemption. We all once Walked in the pattern of disobedience inherited from Adam, but a new way has opened by faith to those who Walk not according to the Flesh but according to the Spirit. At the resurrection, the children of God will be brought into their glory, and creation will be set free to experience that glory. Until the time that all things are restored, both the Flesh and the World groan in anticipation of the wonders that are to be revealed (Romans 8:20-23). *Beware the World's temptation to pridefully take what God forbids because of the lust of the eyes.*

- *Following the course* of our ancestors, we are denied access to God with only one way presented to us. The resulting path is one that inevitably leads to death. The course that we all Walk through has become a spiritual wasteland where all are born Dead spiritually. It is known as *No Man's Land,* and there are many environmental hazards to beware. The foremost is that no man comes to the Father except through Christ, who is the way, the truth, and the life (John 14:6). Being Dead on arrival, there is no one righteous, not even one. Because of the intense holiness of God, no man will gain access to Him by their own works. No one will be saved except through Jesus Christ as it is written in Acts 4:12, "And there is salvation in no one else, for there is no other name under heaven given among men by which we must be saved." *Beware the World's temptation to earn salvation because of the lust of the Flesh.*

- *This world* was decimated by the Adam Bomb, that is the magnitude of Adam's sin, which caused all of creation to groan under corruption, pollution, and decay ccording to the will of God (Romans 8:19-23). With their banishment from the Garden, Adam and Eve were forced to live in a harsh environment that would defy them as they had defied God. The World should have relied upon faith, hope, and love. Instead, the World mutated for the worse and is overrun with the lust of the eyes, lust of the flesh, and the pride of life (1 John 2:16). The overwhelming impact of the Adam Bomb has produced *spiritual fallout expressed in physical decay and morally hazardous radiation*. The Flesh has experienced spiritual Fallout, and the World provided the environment for sin to explode with the force of a spiritually epic catastrophe. *Beware the World's temptation to have pride in possessions that pass away like sun-scorched grass.*

GARDEN CONNECTION

When Adam and Eve were placed in the Garden, they were expressly commanded not to eat from the tree of the knowledge of good and evil (Genesis 2:17). This command intensifies when considering God had already provided trees that were good for food and pleasing to the eye (Genesis 2:9). Additionally, the desirability of wisdom that the forbidden fruit teased cannot compare with the endless repository of wisdom of God (Proverbs 2:6) who gives wisdom abundantly to all who ask in faith (James 1:5). Not only did God supply everything needed for life and godliness, but Adam and Eve were fully aware of the commandment before they broke it (Genesis 3:3). These factors show that God wanted his creation to have a choice to obey him or not. The fact that the commandment was broken did not surprise God in any way. He knew it would happen before humanity was even created. For that reason, Jesus Christ is known as the lamb that was slain from before the foundation of the world (2 Timothy 1:9, 1 Peter 1:20, Revelation 13:8). Many have attempted to remedy the condition of Death in the world, but there is only one way to resolve the problem. The answer is to receive the Gospel Cure that administers the truth about the life, death, and resurrection of Jesus Christ. Whoever loves the World is at enmity with God for whoever loves the World does not have the love of the Father in them. The World is passing away along with all its desires, but a new heaven and earth are promised to the one who does the will of God (1 John 2:15,17 and Revelation 21:1). God's will is that we would receive Jesus Christ as Lord and Savior.

Darkest Before the Dawn

Abundantly clear from our research is the complex matrix weaved by the Devil, the Flesh, and the World. These forces affect all humans in numerous ways. The Devil pressures us from the outside, the Flesh writhes from within, and the World decomposes around us. But the Dawn of the Dead is not the only inception that demands attention; there is also the Dawn of the Life.

The incarnation of Jesus Christ is the Dawn of the Life. The Word that was in the beginning, with God, and actually God is the very One who became like flesh (John 1 and Philippians 2) in order to redeem sinners by his Death. The meteoric condescension of God was the first step in the overarching redemptive plan hinted at in the Garden (Genesis 3:15). The Death of Christ on the cross in the place of sinful humanity was an infinitely worthy sacrifice to satisfy the justice of God. The resurrection of Jesus from the dead testifies further to his deity and our own hope for Life to defeat Death. Therefore, we will consider the Dawn of the Life before addressing how His life changes ours.

Dawn of Life

> *In him was life, and the life was the **light** of mankind. And the light shines on in the **darkness**, but the darkness has not mastered it.*
>
> John 1:4-5 (NET)

The LIVING DEAD Revival Guide

CASE FILE

There is an intrinsic fear of death and darkness that belongs to human beings. It was placed there by past events. The Catalysts plunged all life into these fears when the first Zombies lurched out of God's presence. Only God can save them. God is the one who grants repentance and faith to those who hear Him calling. He is the one who saves us, not by works that we have done but by His grace. We have received mercy from the Lord Almighty, and we can rest assured that Jesus Christ came and finished the work set before Him by going to the cross. Jesus paid for our sin debt with His own life and we who have believed this now enter into a Rest that cannot be taken from us. We must make every effort to enter the Rest of Christ because it is for us true salvation. The gift of God is for the Saint, but the gift of the enemy is no gift at all. Satan's "gift" to humanity was actually a curse. We were cursed by the Fall, and the Fallout has left all of us as Zombies from birth. We were cursed into a Dead World, which is an apocalyptic wasteland, instead of the beautiful Garden we were made to enjoy. But God's gift to humanity, his only begotten Son, removed the curse by becoming a curse for us (Galatians 3:13). Will you receive the gift that is Jesus Christ?

> **Light dawns in the darkness for the upright;**
> he is gracious, merciful, and righteous.
>
> Psalms 112:4 (ESV)

After the Fallout, humans tried to appease God with good works, but it was a Dead effort. Their righteousness was as filthy rags compared to the righteousness God requires. Even though God's creation had abandoned His will, He did not abandon them. He is patient with the wicked and generous to the ungrateful. God's remarkable kindness is intended to lead us to repentance (Romans 2:4). But the Dead mistake his kindness and patience as being absence and apathy on the part of God. Their errors will haunt them forever.

> But it will not go well with the wicked, nor will they prolong their days like a shadow, because **they do not stand in fear before God**.
>
> Ecclesiastes 8:13 (NET)

How can we know the light and love of God? We know that He loves us because while we were as good as Dead, He sent Jesus Christ to die for us (Romans 5:8). Knowing this truth illuminates Life and godliness in a person. The Dawn of the Light is vital for our mission of Revival via the Gospel Cure. We must discern how the Dawn of the Life conquers the Dawn of the Dead.

> *But the path of the righteous is like the **light of dawn**,*
> *which shines brighter and brighter until full day.*
> Proverbs 4:18 (ESV)

> *For with you is the fountain of **life; in your light, we see light**.*
> Psalm 36:9 (NIV)

TRUE LIFE DEFEATS THE DEVIL

We know that the Son of God was revealed to destroy the works of the Devil (1 John 3:8b). We have determined that the Devil works iniquity primarily through deception, with the end goal being domination over the sons of disobedience. Though Satan's appearance in the Garden was that of a serpent, he distorts his true identity by presuming to be something that he is not. The Walking Dead innately draw near to his temporary pleasures but, in the end, are ensnared by dark dependencies, entangled in sin, and everything that hinders a holy life.

Satan desires to steal, kill, and destroy while exalting himself above God, but Jesus Christ came to seek and save the lost with meekness and humility. Satan attempts to overthrow God by raising up an army of the Dead while God, through Jesus, raises up an army of those who have Died to sin through Christ. Where Satan deceives, Christ gives discernment. Where Satan enslaves, Christ liberates. There is a palpable tension between these forces, but Satan will certainly be defeated by the power of the Lord's breath and the splendor of his manifestation (2 Thessalonians 2:8). Until that time, we must draw near to God and so resist the Devil until he flees from us.

TRUE LIFE DEFEATS THE FLESH

The Flesh, as we have learned, presents unique challenges to both the Living and the Dead. All are born Dead spiritually and inclined toward sinful tendencies. Like an ancient virus, sin plagues all Flesh, and like a parasite, sin feeds off of the lawlessness of its host. Because of these terrible constraints Jesus Christ, who is the image of the invisible God, was necessary for the salvation of sinful humanity. Through a miraculous conception, Jesus Christ was born of a virgin, and so He was the son of God and the son of Man. He was fully God, fully Man, and fully able to redeem sinners before an infinitely holy God! The Word became flesh (John 1), even though He appeared in the flesh bodily, He himself was without sin (Philippians 2). He walked on earth and lived a perfect and sinless life culminating in a once and for all sacrificial atonement by His blood shed on the cross.

> *Therefore, since the children share in flesh and blood, he likewise **shared in their humanity**, so that through death he could destroy **the one who holds the power of death (that is, the devil)**, and set free those who were held in slavery all their lives by their fear of death.*
> Hebrews 2:14-15 (NET)

Because God the Father meted out the punishment for sin on his perfectly sinless son, the Lamb of God, a new and Living way has been opened up to all who approach God by faith. This new and Living way to God goes inextricably through the body of Christ. Indeed, God made Him who knew no sin to be sin for us, the Dead now made Alive, so that we could become the very righteousness of God (2 Corinthians 5:21). Through faith in the Gospel Cure, all who Walk in step with the Spirit have Died with Christ and have their Life with Him. The Flesh and the Law no longer restrain us as we once were because of the grace of God and his indwelling Holy Spirit.

> *You know that he appeared in order to **take away sins**, and in him, there is no sin.*
> 1 John 3:5 (ESV)

And yet, the Flesh persistently revolts against the Spirit, meaning that even the good we want to do is not always carried out (Galatians 5:7). The evil we don't want to do drags us away in our desires (Romans 7). But these struggles remind us, as they ought, that the grace of God was not without a price. This is very precious reminder that we needed a Savior and still need Him and will always need Him.

> *And **even though you were dead** in your transgressions and in the uncircumcision of your flesh, **he nevertheless made you alive with him**, having forgiven all your transgressions. He has destroyed what was against us, a certificate of indebtedness expressed in decrees opposed to us. He has taken it away by nailing it to the cross. Disarming the rulers and*

authorities, he has made a public disgrace of them, triumphing over them by the cross.

Colossians 2:13-15 (NET)

TRUE LIFE DEFEATS THE WORLD

Jesus Christ suffered in the flesh even as we do and was tempted in like manner so that He is able to help us in our weakness (Hebrews 2:18). He disciplined his body by fasting for 40 days. When He had become very physically exhausted, Satan appeared to him with temptations that are reminiscent of the same that befell Adam and Eve (Genesis 3, Luke 4:1-13, Matthew 4:1-11). Jesus was tempted with the *lust of the flesh* to satiate his hunger by turning a stone into bread (vv. 2-3). Jesus was tempted with the *lust of the eyes* when presented with all the kingdoms of the world in their splendor (vv. 8-9). Jesus was tempted with the *pride of life* when dared to risk his life by jumping off of the Temple and, in so doing, put his Father to the test (vv. 5-6). All of these temptations of Satan were met with an answer from the Living Word of God. Though Satan sought to distract Jesus and deceive him even by misusing scripture, it was no match for God incarnate. Though His flesh was weak, hungry, and tired, Jesus did not surrender even under the pressure of the World's corruption. He emerged victorious, and Satan left him until a more opportune time (Luke 4:13).

Nothing would stop Jesus from Walking according to the will of God, not even a brutal and undeserved death. It was fitting that the pioneer of salvation would bring many sons and daughters to glory through his suffering. A perfect suffering that produced an incomparable glory and joy! If Jesus did not stop to suffer for His people, then He will by no means be stopped from returning to them. His second coming into the World is near, and his people have been empowered by his victory!

I have told you these things so that in me you may have peace.
In the world, you have trouble and suffering but take courage—
I have conquered the world.

John 16:33 (NET)

WHEN CATALYSTS CONCLUDE

Even though the Catalysts of sin and Death persist, they will not last forever. The Devil was served a deadly warning of his impending doom, the Spirit of God has conquered the Flesh, and the World has met its Maker. The irreducible fact is that God, as He did in the Garden, desires those who will worship Him in Spirit and in truth. He requires that a choice be made. Will you receive the Gospel Cure? Will you love the Lord your God with your entire being and love your neighbor as yourself? Will we love the truth and so be saved? Even if your neighbor is a Zombie? Or will you love darkness and resist the light? If you hear the Spirit today, do not harden your heart, for God so loved the world that He gave his only Son so that whoever believes in him should not perish but have everlasting life (John 3:16)!

> *Whoever believes in him is not condemned, but whoever does not believe is condemned already, because he has not believed in the name of the only Son of God. And this is the judgment:* **the light has come into the world, and people loved the darkness rather than the light because their works were evil.** *For everyone who does wicked things hates the light and does not come to the light, lest his works should be exposed.* **But whoever does what is true comes to the light***, so that it may be clearly seen that his works have been carried out in God.*
>
> John 3:18-21 (ESV)

> *At the same time, it is a new commandment that I am writing to you, which is true in him and in you* **because the darkness is passing away and the true light is already shining***.*
>
> 1 John 2:8 (ESV)

CHAPTER TWO

THE WALK

DEAD WALKER

IDENTITY CRISIS

> *Do not merely listen to the word, and so deceive yourselves. Do what it says. Anyone who listens to the word but does not do what it says is like someone **who looks at his face in a mirror and, after looking at himself, goes away and immediately forgets what he looks like**.*
> James 1:22-24 (NIV)

Have we forgotten who we really are? Or have we ignored what we know about ourselves? It seems we prefer to live a lie rather than face the truth. It's easier that way. But that doesn't make it right. We are all born Dead to God and Alive toward sin. We are urged to be much the opposite according to the Gospel Cure, and it's effects upon us (Romans 6:11-13).

Instead, we stray off course because we are prone to wander. It is the nature of all mankind. All have fallen short of the glory of God (Romans 3:23). All have the capacity and proclivity to sin. Despite what can be known about God and what we already know about ourselves, we continue on our way unwilling to change. We refuse to recognize our need for a Savior even though it's painfully obvious. There is no more dangerous path that could be taken than to defy the Living God.

> ***It is a dreadful thing to fall into the hands of the living God.***
> Hebrews 10:31 (NIV)

The Bible says God created mankind in His image. Like God, we have an intellect, emotion, and volition. God made us with incredible honor and dignity. We were made to love Him, represent Him, and to care for His creation according to His rules. We were made to bring Him glory. But sin caused severe damage to the image we bear and fundamentally changed us. As creatures of free will, we made the wrong choice and are now haunted by the ramifications of our choices.

There was a time before God brought me to Life that I, too, was a Restless vagabond. I wandered through the Wasteland with no hope for change. I gratified my Fleshly appetite like the rest of the Dead around me. I craved the Flesh just as they did. I was a Zombie lost in the deep darkness, and my worn and tattered self-righteousness was like a filthy rag upon my body. I remember those horrid days but do my best to leave them behind (Philippians 3:13). My memory of them fades as I cast off the Old Self and put on the New Self-made to be like Christ (Colossians 3:9-10). The calling of all Saints is that which is onward toward the heavenly calling of Christ Jesus. He is our Lord. All the bodies of the Saints will be made like His glorious body by His power. Then will our adoption as sons be made complete. Then we will know true redemption (Romans 8:23).

I'm no longer the same person. I was blind, but now I See. Even though I was Dead, now I am Alive. God has made me new! Although I was once a Zombie, I regrettably admit that I can, at times, look scornfully at Zombies as if wasn't once like them. I see them and become repulsed by their actions and words. They behave like unreasoning animals and only act in accordance with what they understand, which in the end is the very thing that is killing them (2 Peter 2:12 and Jude 1:10). But we have come to know better than to treat them like we don't know what it's like. We shouldn't hate the Dead. This is the wrong attitude because they need mercy just as I did - just as we all do. God showed his perfect patience upon me so that my life would be an example to others who seek to know Jesus (1 Timothy 1:16). We must be mindful of the mercy and grace we have received if we are to give mercy and grace to others.

> *And **have mercy** on those who doubt; **save others** by snatching them out of the fire; to others show mercy with fear, **hating even the garment stained by the flesh**.*
> Jude 1:22-23 (ESV)

But if the Dead don't know that they're Dead, what can be done for them? How can we help those who do not want to be helped? They do not see themselves truly. They stare Lifelessly at their reflection and remain unchanged. If a Zombie looks deeply at a mirror but doesn't recognize their decomposition and depravity, then how can they be helped? They see that their actions lead to death, but they don't change (Romans 1:32). They are unrepentant, disobedient, and defiant. The Dead vilify those who refuse to join them in sin. Worse yet, the Dead condone sin and corrupt others with their sinful contagion.

The LIVING DEAD Revival Guide

> ***Do not be deceived: Bad company ruins good morals. Wake up** from your drunken stupor, as is right, and **do not go on sinning**. For some, have **no knowledge of God**. I say this to your shame.*
>
> 1 Corinthians 15:33-34 (ESV)

We must know who we are *in Christ*. Knowledge of our identity is absolutely vital to the Saint. We are nothing without Christ. In fact, we are most of all people to be pitied if we have believed in a risen Savior if, in fact, He was not raised (1 Corinthians 15:19). But we have the prophetic word that has confirmed furthermore that which we have come to believe. Jesus Christ was fully man and fully God, He took our sins and died for us on the cross, He was buried for three days and on raised again from the dead according to the scriptures (1 Corinthians 15:3-4). Namely that Jesus Christ is Lord to the glory of God the Father, and therefore having believed this, we are now indwelled by the Holy Spirit. We are forgiven sinners with the hope of God's glory! Our work is not in vain, so long as we labor in the Lord. But our effort is not the catalyst that brings salvation to the Dead. Zombies won't be won over by arguments of reason and truth, though they should, their ears are Dead and cannot accept Life. The spiritual words of the Bible are rejected by Zombies because they don't have the mind to conceive of its truth. They have the spirit of the world, not the Spirit of God who reveals truth like a gift to the Living (1 Corinthians 2:12-14). Ultimately it is the Lord himself who regenerates the Dead so that they could respond to the gospel message. We all who have been regenerated remain in the World to participate in God's plan for salvation.

> *For to me **to live is Christ, and to die is gain**. If I am to live in the flesh, that means **fruitful labor** for me. Yet which I shall choose I cannot tell. I am hard-pressed between the two. My desire is to depart and be with Christ, for that is far better. But **to remain in the flesh is more necessary on your account**. Convinced of this, I know that I will remain and continue with you all, for your progress and joy in the faith.*
>
> Philippians 1:21-25 (ESV)

We have prevailed through trial and tribulation, not by might but by His Spirit. We faithfully follow the voice of the Shepherd even though we Walk through the Valley of the Shadow of Death. Though our desire is to see Him as He is and to be like Him in holiness, we do not yet see Him. Yet, not seeing Him, we are still filled with a joy so glorious that we simply cannot fully express it (1 Peter 1:18). We are receiving the result of our faith, which is the salvation of our souls. We remain in the World but not of the

World. Indeed, it is not as though we are to disassociate ourselves so thoroughly from the Dead that we never interact with them. If that were the case, then we would have to leave the world (1 Corinthians 5:10)! There may be a time for that departure, but it is not now. There is a need, however, for us to recognize who Walks the Walk and Talks the Talk. But if Zombies don't even recognize that they're Dead, how can we expect to identify the difference between the Living and the Dead? They may cover their identity with the illusion of good deeds, but inwardly they are ravenous beasts (Matthew 7:15). Again, we turn to the Scriptures and listen closely for the leading of the Spirit, who reminds us of Jesus' words.

> ***You will recognize them by their fruits***. *Are grapes gathered from thorn bushes, or figs from thistles? So, every thornbush bears good fruit, but the diseased tree bears bad fruit. A healthy tree cannot bear bad fruit, nor can a diseased tree bear good fruit.* ***Every tree that does not bear good fruit is cut down and thrown into the fire***. *Thus, you will recognize them by their fruits.*
> Matthew 7:15-20 (ESV)

We must familiarize ourselves with what typifies the behavior of the Dead. The Fruit of these "diseased trees" are their actions and reactions - the cause and effect of their life. These identifiers will help us distinguish between the Living and the Dead. Knowing how they Walk and their determinations will greatly assist us on our mission. It may even unlock a better way to reach them with true Revival. In other words, we must recognize their *Gait* and their *Gate*. Regardless of the Walk of an individual, we know that our calling is to love the Lord our God entirely and to love our neighbor as ourselves. In this way, we represent Christ and are ambassadors of His undying love.

Our motivation to Walk Worthy is not shallow. We deny ourselves, carry our cross, and follow Christ because his love compels us. Many of us who have been raised by Christ's faithfulness know the pain of seeing our family and friends continue on the path that leads to destruction (Matthew 7:13-14). Those who remain Dead in their sins may yet come to Life if we remain faithful to the command of our Lord Jesus Christ to go and make disciples of every nation. Our light and our example must not be concealed. It should be easily determined that we have been changed. The Dead can be recognized by the smell of rotting Flesh. They smell of their diseased Fruit, which are bad results of their actions (Romans 7:4-5). While the Living will be recognized by the fruit that the Holy Spirit produces in them (Galatians 5:22-24). Those who have been brought to Life abide in Christ, and He abides in them.

> *By this my Father is glorified, that you **bear much fruit** and so prove to be my disciples.*
>
> John 15:8 (ESV)

Indeed, we should barely recognize ourselves once we are Born Again because of how thoroughly God changes us. We also begin to see others differently. In some ways, we see them for the better. We may see them with the dignity that image bearers deserve. Or we may begin to see more clearly that the Dead are all around us. It is a heart-crushing sorrow to see people that you love continue to defy God. We have been called by God not to serve ourselves but to serve others above ourselves. It is God's amazing plan and grace to use the previously Dead to be Walking examples of his life-changing love. If we Walk Worthy, we may indeed see God win over the souls of the people dearest to us. The scripture is true; we must not only hear the word of life and yet deceive ourselves. We must do what it says (James 1:22)!

Zombie Myths

> ***Death and life are in the power of the tongue,***
> *and those who love it will eat its fruits.*
>
> Proverbs 18:21 (ESV)

It would help us if we knew what we were actually dealing with rather than relying upon misguided assumptions. There are many myths and rumors that have tried to intercept the excellencies of Him who called us out of Darkness and into the Light (1 Peter 2:9). But it takes time for the truth to set in while compared to a lie that can infect deep into a person before they even become aware of it. The tongue holds the power to change lives for the better or for the worse. On some occasions, it sets people free, and on other occasions, it can enslave. Satan, The Father of Lies, will do anything to deceive itching ears. He knows very well that humans can spread lies like a wildfire, and all it takes is a little spark.

> *And the tongue is a fire, a **world of unrighteousness**. The tongue is set among our members, staining the whole body, **setting on fire the entire course of life**, and set on fire by hell.*
>
> James 3:6 (ESV)

Though there are a myriad of misconceptions regarding the living Dead, the truth can be known if we seek it out (Acts 17:11, Proverbs 25:2). All of the misinformation disrupts what we need to know about Zombies and our Revival Mission. Clarification must be made if we are to make progress on the Way. We can know the truth if we search the Scriptures and trust the Holy Spirit. We will see with our own eyes what the Word of God teaches. But be like those of greater nobility, who search the scriptures intently to understand if these things be true or not (Acts 17:11).

- Zombies are not the reanimated dead, but they are unregenerated and spiritually inanimate because of sin (Ephesians 2:1, Romans 8:5-8).
- Satan blinds the minds of unbelievers, making them slaves of unrighteousness. Satan manipulates the Dead so that they disobey God (2 Corinthians 4:3-4, Ephesians 2:2, 1 John 5:19).
- All people begin life craving the desires of the Flesh and, if left undeterred, will follow their craze unto destruction (Ephesians 2:3, Matthew 7:13-14).
- The Dead can be Revived by receiving the grace of God and having faith in the Savior Jesus Christ (Ephesians 2:4-5, 1 Peter 1:9).
- All have fallen short of God's glorious standard of perfection and are therefore deserving of death (Romans 3:23, 6:23).
- Whatever is not done from faith is sin (Romans 14:23b).
- The sting of death is sin, and the power of sin is the law (1 Corinthians 15:56).
- The body apart from the spirit is dead, so also faith apart from works is Dead (James 2:26).
- Once physically dead, a Zombie cannot come back to Life (Luke 16:26, 40-32). In other words, there is no Life after the second Death because separation from the source of Life would be final.
- After death, all will be judged for what they have done while in the flesh (Hebrews 9:27, Revelation 20:11-15).
- Zombies still carry the image of God but defame it's dignity by their actions and words (James 3:9, Titus 1:16).
- Zombies contaminate others with sinful corruption that is intensified by the Devil, the Flesh, and The World (1 Corinthians 15:33, 1 Peter 1:4).
- All people waste away like a moth, but Zombies are decomposing both outwardly in a physical sense and inwardly in a spiritual sense (Job 13:28, 2 Corinthians 4:16).
- No one brought to Life can revert back to being a Zombie. Salvation is eternally secure (Romans 8:38-39, John 10:28-29).

- No Zombie can become a Christian and revert back to their previous state of Deadness (Hebrews 4:4-6, 2 Peter 2:20-21).
- As much as possible, we must not kill a Zombie. For if we kill that which is Dead, then they will never have a chance for repentance. Matters of war and self-defense must be carefully examined. But the Christian must leave room for the Lord to avenge. We must not be overcome by evil, but we overcome evil with good (Romans 12:21).

ACTS OF THE FLESH

*When evildoers assail me to **eat up my flesh**, my adversaries and foes, it is they who stumble and fall.*

Psalms 27:2 (ESV)

One the most disgusting characteristic of the Dead is their incessant gorging upon the Flesh. Zombies show through the Acts of the Flesh the gruesome truth of their nature. Even if they seek to deny or hide this truth, it will be how their nature is shown. Their identity is inexorably connected to the near parasitic dependence upon sin that is sustained by feeding upon the Flesh. The Flesh is not the body by itself, but rather it is the perversion of what was meant for good. The Flesh is more like the chaotic opposite to the Spirit in that they both produce Fruit or results in a person. But where the Holy Spirit produces Fruit unto Life, the Flesh produces Fruit unto Death.

*For while we were living in the flesh, our sinful passions, aroused by the law, were at work in our members to bear **fruit for death**.*

Romans 7:5 (ESV)

The misuse of the body and its desires constitute the Flesh. For the Apostle James says that we ought to praise Yahweh with our tongue, but if we blaspheme and curse against our fellow image-bearers, we are like a spring of water divided into its inherent identity (James 3:9-11). So, it is with the whole of the Flesh, the desires of the body and mind that are corrupted by sin are the true cause of desecration to what God once made very good. Though the Zombie is still made as image-bearers of God, they clearly are not Walking as they were intended. But so that God would be glorified in all things, the Zombie will either turn in repentance or be judged according to what they have done.

These truths are inexorably connected because it binds all things together. The glory of God will come, and it will be agreed to because His justice, love, and mercy are all true.

Zombies feast upon the horrid desires of their sinful nature with an unstoppable hunger. Like a leech that never has its fill is the appetite of the Dead. The Zombie never has its fill. Even as the grave, a barren womb, dry land, and fire can never have enough (Proverbs 30:15-16). Their consumption of sin is as vain as it is gruesome. No matter how much they feed themselves to appease that feeling of emptiness, they are only ever able to taste for a moment what makes them happy. After that, they again hunger because the fulfillment that they truly need is not that which they are seeking. They are not seeking after Jesus, who is the bread from heaven (John 6:35-38).

> *All the toil of man is for his mouth, **yet his appetite is not satisfied**.*
> Ecclesiastes 6:7 (ESV)

Overwhelmed and possessed by greed, they want more and more. But more is never enough. They compulsively fill themselves up to the brim with their morbid feasting but are never truly filled. In the end, it will be the Zombies who stumble over their own transgressions and into the pits they dug for others. They set out traps to catch others but only end up catching themselves in a problem they cannot handle alone. But why do they do this? Why do the Dead Walk in this way?

> *It is better to be content with what the eyes can see than for one's heart **always to crave more**. This continual longing is futile - like chasing the wind.*
> Ecclesiastes 6:9 (NET)

Seemingly unaware of their motivations, the Dead rely on their basest instincts to *live* at any cost, even if it costs the life of others. One reason they behave this way is because they are enslaved by their fear of Death. They fear that physical death will remove all of their possessions, and in response, they obsessively hoard what they have, but Life does not consist in an abundance of possessions (Luke 12:15). What point is there in gaining the whole world if it costs your soul (Luke 9:25)? Their greed is deeply entrenched in their hearts like a bottomless pit that can never be filled by Worldly possessions. Their hunger for more consumes them - they are entirely self-consumed.

The Dead not only hoard possessions they also compulsively act out their deranged desires. Even if their actions are self-destructive, they continue seeking them out because they have become convinced that they want what they shouldn't want at all. Although the created order can be clearly observed, they have worshipped created things instead of the Creator. Their thinking has become futile because of the darkness in their hearts (Romans 1).

> *But these, **like irrational animals, creatures of instinct, born to be caught and destroyed**, blaspheming about matters of which they are ignorant, will also be **destroyed in their destruction**, suffering wrong as the wage for their wrongdoing. **They count it pleasure to revel in the daytime**. They are blots and blemishes, reveling in their deceptions while they feast with you. They have eyes full of adultery, insatiable for sin. They entice unsteady souls. **They have hearts trained in greed**. Accursed children!*
>
> 2 Peter 2:12-14 (ESV)

If the eyes of the Dead are full of adultery, then they never stop looking elsewhere to satisfy their lusts. Although they should belong to God who created them, they are tempted away by Satan, the Father of All Lies. This insidious relationship contributes to their insatiable appetite for sin. Always hungry for more of what is killing them. The Depravity deepens because the Dead contaminate others with their vile affections. They convince others to join them in their debauchery and will share in the consequences of their polluting influence. Woe unto them! Their hearts are trained in greed. They know full well how to desire more and long for what does not belong to them. They are accursed offspring in need of Revival found only in the true love of God.

> *But God shows his love for us in that **while we were still sinners**, Christ died for us.*
>
> Romans 5:8 (ESV)

We must guard ourselves against hypocrisy, which hides in ambush to pounce upon even Worthy Walkers. We must never forget that God saved us while we were still sinners; otherwise, we run the risk of becoming deluded in how we think about ourselves. Our identity in Christ is more important to us than ever. All of us have the capacity to stumble into sin, but anyone who belongs to Christ will no longer practice sin habitually (1 John 3:8). Believers in Jesus Christ are righteous because of His faithfulness, not because of their own efforts. Christians may fall in sin, but God will always cause them to rise again because His glorious grace is greater than the grave (Proverbs 24:17). The amazing truth is that a Christian's sin no longer results in the same Death that it once did before they were brought to Life. Jesus has defeated Death, and it no longer has power over Him or those who belong to Him (Hebrews 2:14-15).

> *If anyone sees his fellow Christian committing a* **sin not resulting in death**, *he should ask, and God will grant life to the person who commits a sin not resulting in death.* **There is a sin resulting in death**. *I do not say that he should ask about that. All unrighteousness is sin, but there is sin not resulting in death.*
>
> 1 John 5:16-17 (NET)

The unrighteousness that is sin can be detected by recognizing the acts of the Flesh. What are the Deathly acts of the Flesh? They are the result of tainted desires festering within a Depraved nature that are in direct opposition to the will of God. When these desires can be restrained no longer, they are acted upon regardless of consequences.

Indeed, there is a fierce animosity between the Spirit of God and the Fleshly nature of the Dead. These forces are opposed to one another with such distinction that even Born Again believers are assailed to the point of consternation, rendering them unable to always do what is right (Galatians 5:17). Christians are not perfect in that they never fail because we all stumble in many ways. But the difference between the sin of a Saint and the sin of a Zombie is as vast as the East is from the West. The blood of the Lamb of God has already paid for the sin of a believer in Jesus Christ. This means the offering of Jesus Christ has perfected us forever (Hebrews 10:14). Indeed, God is able to present us before himself as though we were blameless (Jude 1:24). Christians have been justified and deemed righteous by the One who perfectly judges both the Living and the Dead. But the Zombies disregard these truths as mere foolishness because they cannot see the splendor of God's redemption.

In addition to the insatiable appetite of the Dead, the works of the Flesh can be diagnosed by recognizing their symptoms. The better we become at detecting these conditions and consequences, the better we will become at spreading the Gospel Cure. Consider these five vice lists and what we can learn from them. They are found within the Living Word of God, our most vital source of truth. These are not lists for us to use to sniff out the sin of others so much as they serve as an example of the kind of sins that all humans are prone to commit before coming to faith in Christ. Therefore, do not think too highly of yourself, lest you too be tempted and fall.

> *All Scripture is God-breathed and is useful for teaching, rebuking, correcting, and training in righteousness,* **so that the servant of God may be thoroughly equipped for every good work**.
>
> 2 Timothy 3:16-17 (NIV)

The LIVING DEAD Revival Guide

UNDENIABLE

The first warning sign about the *Acts of the Flesh* is that they are obvious and overt. Even though most Zombies conceal their deeds by the cover of darkness, they are nonetheless dreadfully apparent. Most deeds of darkness are too indecent to even mention (Ephesians 5:11-12). Worse yet is that some of the Dead engage in their insolent actions in broad daylight! Some sins are obvious, and their destruction goes before them, while other sins remain hidden for a time (1 Timothy 5:24). Ultimately nothing remains hidden forever because all will give an account of their Walk before the Judge of the Living and the Dead (1 Peter 4:5).

It is not difficult to recognize sinful behavior, especially if you have been brought to Life out of the ignorant darkness. For we are all too familiar with the Dead deeds of our former Walk that brought shame and Death (Romans 6:21)! The Acts of the Flesh are saturated in the stench of sin. For all of these reasons, we must see sin as it truly is, as a repulsive and disgusting offense before an intensely holy and perfect God.

> ***You are too just to tolerate evil; you are unable to condone wrongdoing.***
> *So why do you put up with such treacherous people? Why do you say nothing when **the wicked devour** those more righteous than they are?*
> Habakkuk 1:13 (NET)

God has made it abundantly clear that his intense holiness cannot allow for sin to persist in his presence. But his plan for redemption and salvation is already underway! Now is the day of salvation, today is the day to call upon His Name! We must turn away from darkness to light, from Satan to God, and receive forgiveness of our sins by His grace and through faith in Jesus Christ (Acts 26:18).

Those that insatiably indulge in the desires of the Flesh and the shedding of innocent blood will never enter the Kingdom of God (Revelation 22:14-15). Do we believe this? Will we obey the Lord knowing what we now know? Beware the obvious and undeniable betrayal of sin.

> ***Now the works of the flesh are evident****: sexual immorality, impurity, sensuality, idolatry, sorcery, enmity, strife, jealousy, fits of anger, rivalries, dissensions, divisions, envy, drunkenness, orgies, and things like these. I warn you, as I warned you before, that **those who do such things will not inherit the kingdom of God**.*
> Galatians 5:19-21 (ESV)

UNDOING

The second warning sign concerning the *Acts of the Flesh* is that the Law, which was meant to bring about righteousness, instead brought about death because of sin (Romans 7:8-11). The Law and the commandment are holy, good, and righteous. They also serve as a guiding light that reveals the need for God's Life-saving grace (Romans 7:7, 12, and Galatians 3:23-24). But sin rears its ugly head by perverting what was meant for good into something pernicious and insidiously evil. In this way, sin enslaves its host and creates an addiction that ensnares it's prey perpetually.

> *Is the law, therefore, opposed to the promises of God? Absolutely not! For if a law had been given that could impart life, then righteousness would certainly have come by the law.* **But Scripture has locked up everything under the control of sin**, *so that what was promised, being given through faith in Jesus Christ, might be given to those who believe. Before the coming of this faith,* **we were held in custody under the law, locked up until the faith that was to come would be revealed.** *So the law was our guardian until Christ came that we might be justified by faith. Now that this faith has come, we are no longer under a guardian.*
>
> Galatians 3:21-25 (NIV)

Before faith in Christ, the Law was like a guardian that protected its practitioners until the revelation of salvation through Jesus Christ arrived. The scriptures have locked up everything under the power of sin so that faith in God's promises could result in Salvation. For if a law had been given that could impart life, then righteousness would certainly have come by the law. Furthermore, if righteousness could come by the law, then Christ died for nothing (Galatians 3:19-29)!

The Law increases the transgression by bringing awareness to it—bringing it to *Life*. In this way (spiritual), Death lives in us by separating us from the source of Life (Isaiah 59:2). Before becoming aware of the Law that says coveting is a sin, it may as well be Dead to you. But upon realizing that coveting is a sin, it springs to *Life* and kills you (Romans 7).

Therefore, we must rely upon the authority of Scripture to garner the flawless truth found only within the Living Word of God. By doing this, we will Walk in love, light, and Life. We will not succumb to the entombing tendency of sin so long as we trust in our Savior to set us free from our indebtedness before God (Colossians 2:14, Romans 8:3-4).

The LIVING DEAD Revival Guide

> ***Understanding this, that the law is not laid down for the just but for the lawless*** *and disobedient, for the ungodly and sinners, for the unholy and profane, for those who strike their fathers and mothers, for murderers, the sexually immoral, men who practice homosexuality, enslavers, liars, perjurers, and **whatever else is contrary to sound doctrine** ….*
>
> 1 Timothy 1:9-10 ESV

Unwilling

The third warning sign to beware when considering the *Acts of the Flesh* is that *Zombies disregard the truth of their condition and defiantly choose Dead acts instead.* Even though the Dead have physical senses, they remain repugnant toward spiritual truth. Whether they are unaware or undisturbed by their status, it remains clear that their sinful condition has rendered them reckless with their eternal destination.

> *Because the mindset on the flesh is **hostile toward God**; for it does not subject itself to the law of God, for it is not even able to do so, and those **who are in the flesh cannot please God.***
>
> Romans 8:7-8 (NASB)

Remember what is at the core of this apocalypse. The Devil, the Flesh, and the World contribute to an illusion concerning the true identity of mankind. This apocalypse is more than wasteland; it is a revelation. That is what the Dead need, and it is what no man alone can provide. God must reveal himself to the Dead by first regenerating them to respond to him. Truly this mystery is beyond my understanding; it is too high and too lofty for me to attain. But I know that in my own experience as a Zombie, even when I thought I was looking for God and seeking Him, the truth was that He had already known me before I was born. God is raising his elected Saints up from the Dead, but there is a mysterious responsibility of turning to God in order to be healed (Matthew 13:15).

Nevertheless, it is clear to the Living when we observe the Dead that they look into the perfect mirror that is the Scripture and, perhaps for a moment, understand the severity of their situation. But moments later, they abandon their glance at the revealed truth and return to their destructive path. Only the Creator can solve this identity problem. But the Creator has chosen to use a peculiar people to reveal himself to a Dead world - those who were once Dead themselves. We now proclaim the excellencies of Him who called us out of darkness and into His marvelous light (1 Peter 2:9).

> ***And since they did not see fit to acknowledge God, God gave them up to a debased mind to do what ought not to be done.*** *They were filled with all manner of unrighteousness, evil, covetousness, malice. They are full of envy, murder, strife, deceit, maliciousness. They are gossips, slanderers, haters of God, insolent, haughty, boastful, inventors of evil, disobedient to parents, foolish, faithless, heartless, ruthless.* ***Though they know God's righteous decree that those who practice such things deserve to die, they not only do them but give approval to those who practice them****.*
>
> Romans 1:28-32 (ESV)

UNVEILING

The fourth warning sign warranted by the *Acts of the Flesh* is that *every sinful thought and action will be revealed.* When Christ returns, and all are judged, it will be as though a light were shining in all the hidden places of our hearts. We will stand before the Lord God Almighty, who judges impartially and with perfect justice. It has been appointed for all flesh to die and then face judgment for their actions.

> *And just as it **is appointed for man to die once, and after that comes judgment**, so Christ, having been offered once to bear the sins of many, will appear a second time, not to deal with sin but to save those who are eagerly waiting for him.*
>
> Hebrews 9:27-28 (ESV)

Jesus spoke of the light that would be shed. He indicated that everyone would give an account for every empty word that they have spoken and that our words would acquit us or condemn us (Matthew 12:36-37). But Zombies continue to do what is heinous before our Holy God. Although we ourselves once viewed Christ as no more than a normal man or myth, we do so no longer (2 Corinthians 5). Rather as people who were once Zombies that have now experienced new Life, we have committed ourselves to seeing with a new perspective as well. Our aim is not merely an appearance but a representation. If we put away the deeds of the flesh, perhaps it will lead to the revival of those who witness our behavior in Christ.

The **LIVING DEAD** Revival Guide

For the time that is past suffices for doing what the Gentiles want to do, living in sensuality, passions, drunkenness, orgies, drinking parties, and lawless idolatry. **With respect to this, they are surprised when you do not join them in the same flood of debauchery, and they malign you; but they will give account to him who is ready to judge the living and the dead.**

1 Peter 4:3-5 (ESV)

Unloving

The fifth warning sign resulting from the *Acts of the Flesh* is that their origin is from within the heart. Indeed, the heart is the source of the desperately wicked desires that precede every sinful action. Before the great and terrible flood of Noah's day, the Lord saw the wretchedness of humankind had increased terribly. Their hearts had become so horrible that their every thought was only evil all the time (Genesis 6:5)! The corruption of sin and the pollution it produces in the World is driven by the defiled desires of the Dead that originates in their stone-cold hearts. The Dead are dragged away by their desires, and the result is fatal.

But each person is tempted when they are dragged away by their own evil desire and enticed. Then, after desire has conceived, it gives birth to sin; and sin, when it is full-grown, gives birth to death.

James 1:14-15 (NIV)

The succession of desire, sin, and death are a clear picture of the signs and symptoms we must recognize as our labor of love endures. We know all too well what it is to fall down that path. We were Dead in our sins before the Lord saved us from the wrath that is now being revealed. I am convinced that the love of God shown to us in the death and resurrection of our Lord Jesus Christ is the only hope for a cure to Death. We know that God loves us because while we were still sinners, Christ Jesus died on our behalf (Romans 5:8). Our hearts were wicked to the deepest places, but He has given us new hearts of flesh to replace the rocky and callous hearts we had by nature. The heart is desperately wicked and incurable by any human means. Therefore, only God can renew our hearts.

The heart is deceitful above all things, and desperately sick; who can understand it? *"I the LORD search the heart and test the mind, to give every man according to his ways, according to the fruit of his deeds.*

Jeremiah 17:9-10 (ESV)

The Dead have hatred in their heart that goes so deep it is like a bottomless pit. This hatred divides households and destroys friendships. I rip apart relationships for lustful longings. It devours resources with greed and disregard for others. This hatred is so serious that it is tantamount to murder. Such is the depravity of the Dead heart.

> *You have heard that it was said to those of old, 'You shall not murder; and whoever murders will be liable to judgment.' But I say to you that* ***everyone who is angry with his brother will be liable to judgment****; whoever insults his brother will be liable to the council; and whoever says, "You fool!" will be liable to the hell of fire.*
> Matthew 5:21-22 (ESV)

Every evil idea originates from within and is expressed outwardly. It is not what goes into the body that defiles, but what comes out! May God have mercy on our ignorance in such a way that His kindness would lead to our repentance.

> *For* ***out of the heart come*** *evil thoughts, murder, adultery, sexual immorality, theft, false witness, slander. These are what defile a person. But to eat with unwashed hands does not defile anyone.*
> Matthew 15:19-20 (ESV)

Beware the Acts of the Flesh, or else they may be your demise. The evidence is undeniable. The Dead acts of Zombies are as noticeable as the stench of rotten flesh. But if we are not careful, we may find that even our garments of righteousness can become soiled by the hypocrisy of prideful, self-righteous actions. Though we were once unwilling in our hearts to acknowledge our sins and preferred that they remain enrobed in darkness, we have stepped into the Light and found forgiveness. The Light, who is Jesus, is faithful and just to forgive us so long as we acknowledge our sin and seek his grace. But if we refuse to admit that we have sin, we have lied, and the truth is not in us. Let this not be so brothers and sisters! Guard against self-deception rooted in bitterness, fear, and pride.

The desires of the heart precede the demonstrated sins commonly connected to the Flesh. If left unhindered, certain Death must be expected. Becoming aware of the warning signs may help in our Revival mission. Even as we become more cognizant of the signs and symptoms of the acts of the Flesh, there will be those who cannot accept the truth. They will continually Walk in darkness and surround themselves with more and more of the Walking Dead. They gather for themselves those who will tell them what their itching ears want to hear. They condone the sinful behavior and shun those who Walk in the Light. They will stop at nothing to find an alternative to the only Cure for their pitiable condition. But all their searching is a hopeless pursuit because the solution to their situation is not possible by their own means. We are only saved by grace through faith in the finished work of Christ on the Cross.

> *For there will be a time when **people will not tolerate sound teaching**. Instead, following their own desires, they will accumulate teachers for themselves because they have an **insatiable curiosity** to hear new things.*
> 2 Timothy 4:3 (NET)

DEPRAVITY OF THE DEAD

> *There is a way that seems right to a man, but its end is the **way to death**.*
> Proverbs 14:12 (ESV)

The Dead presume their path to lead them somewhere prosperous. They know not where they wander. We know that all who practice sin ramble through their restless life in search of meaning and purpose but cannot find what they seek because only in Christ is it found. They moan and groan with each step. Never satisfied with what they have, they covet what is not theirs and hunger continuously for more of something else. Altogether they have become self-consumed in their laziness and greed (Ecclesiastes 4:5). They feed constantly but are never filled. They struggle ever more into darkness, searching for something to remedy their desperate void but find nothing.

> *In just a little while, **the wicked will be no more**; though you look carefully at his place, he will not be there.*
> Psalms 37:10 (ESV)

Ultimately their searching is in vain if they don't reach out and even grope for God (Acts 17:27). All Zombies have Dead eyes and Dead ears that are severed from spiritual truth. In their Depravity, the Dead are found to be spiritually insensate. Though they have eyes, they do not See, though they have ears they do not Hear, nor do they comprehend with their hearts and minds the absolute glory of God who created all life and has the power to heal them (Isaiah 6:9-12, Matthew 13:14-15). If only the Dead would turn in repentance towards the source of Life! For it is the will of God that all would repent. If all would repent, then all would come to love the truth and so be saved. Faith in the grace of God is what saves all those who call on His name (1 Timothy 2:4, 2 Thessalonians 2:10).

But the Dead are predominantly unresponsive to such a wondrous revelation and calling. There are some who would say it would have been better for them never to have been born (Ecclesiastes 6:1-6, Job 3:16). It is not as though they are able to save their own lives. That is why they are considered Depraved and wicked beyond hope of self-preservation. Truly there is no Life without God our Savior because He is Life (1 John 5:11, John 14:6). It is not as if God needed anything particular from His creation. He gives life and breath and everything to everyone (Acts 17:25). However, there is something truly amazing about the way that God would love such a despicable creature that so relentlessly fights against Him. Nevertheless He loves us because that is who He is. He does this so that He would be ultimately and completely glorified (Colossians 1:16)!

Unfortunately, the Dead stumble further down their path, presuming its outcome to be something other than what they have feasted upon all their lives: more sinful gratification. A Zombie's insatiable desire and sinful gorging are fueled by the fear that death would take away everything they've hoarded in the last days (James 5:3). They have become what they fear. Because they fear that death will remove their precious treasures, they hoard their possessions and never cease accumulating. They even go as far as to forcibly take what belongs to others, often without warning, just as death removes our possessions unexpectedly. But all their possessions will fall into the hands of others, and their efforts become little more than a meaningless grasping at the wind (Ecclesiastes 2:18-26).

It is a false hope that good things await the Dead. The truth is very much the opposite (Luke 16:19-31). The Dead will go to hell unless they are Born Again. They will suffer eternal destruction and be shut out from the glory and power and presence of God forever (2 Thessalonians 1:9)! This horror is the truth that few want to acknowledge. All are born Dead to God and are utterly devoid of any hope that they could save themselves. Even if the Dead seemed to be Alive, it is merely a dream-like illusion if the Spirit of Christ is not in them (Romans 8:9, 1 John 4:13). The Spirit within us enables the Living to truthfully confess that Jesus is Lord (1 Corinthians 12:3).

The Dead cannot be saved by their own effort, nor do they really recognize their need for a Savior (Galatians 2:16). They refuse God and have been given over to a debased mind to do things that should never be done (Romans 1:21-32). The Depravity of the Dead is like a cavernous pit. No Zombie can escape. These truths are illuminated by the Holy Scriptures for our sakes so that we would learn to recognize Depravity and all those who are maligned by it, even ourselves. Consider how the Bible describes the Zombie, there is no other creature like it.

The LIVING DEAD Revival Guide

*As it is written: "**None is righteous**, no, not one; no one understands; no one seeks for God. All have turned aside; together, they have become worthless; no one does good, not even one." "**Their throat is an open grave; they use their tongues to deceive.**" "**The venom of asps is under their lips.**" "**Their mouth is full of curses and bitterness.**" "**Their feet are swift to shed blood; in their paths are ruin and misery, and the way of peace they have not known.**"*
"*There is no fear of God before their eyes.*"

Romans 3:10-18 (ESV)

None are righteous, none understand, and none seek after God because all have fallen short of the glory of God (Romans 3:23). Because of the first sin, all humans are born with a sinful nature, a product of the Fallout (Romans 5:12). This nature is marked by a proclivity for pernicious behavior; the Fallen nature drifts ever closer to destruction. This sinful condition is constantly dealing death blows to the already Dead. Yet, the Zombies persist in their wicked ways, devoid of any relationship with God. Their hard hearts become more callous with every jaded sin. This results in the sorrowful truth concerning the fate of every Zombie: unless the Dead are Born Again, they will certainly Die twice.

*But as for the cowardly, the faithless, the detestable, as for murderers, the sexually immoral, sorcerers, idolaters, and all liars, their portion will be in the lake that burns with fire and sulfur, which is the **second death**.*

Revelation 21:8 (ESV)

The Depravity of the Dead is so deep that it permeates them entirely. The heart of each Zombie is dreadfully wicked, and no human effort can cure it nor fully understand it (Jeremiah 17:9). Every evil desire they concoct brings forth sin. The Dead do not resist their urges and desires and are, therefore, dragged away by their hunger for Flesh (James 1:14). Their own desires are the source of their demise.

*They are darkened in their understanding, **alienated from the life of God** because of the ignorance that is in them, due to their **hardness of heart**.*

Ephesians 4:18 (ESV)

The Dead would prefer to blame others for their wickedness. They will not escape their destruction. Their destruction is not far off. Blood is on their hands. Their Dead deeds are stacked high as heaven, and their destruction is not slumbering as they suppose.

> *Now when they are saying, "There is peace and security,"*
> ***then sudden destruction comes on them***, *like labor pains on a pregnant woman, and they will surely not escape.*
>
> 1 Thessalonians 5:3 (NET)

The Dead arrogantly attempt to blame the Creator for their own chaotic volatility! God cannot be tempted and does not tempt (James 1:13-15)! Sin has seeped into the deepest recesses of their Lifeless existence. The Dead are so depraved that it is impossible for them to please God. Indeed they do not truly seek Him or believe that He exists (Hebrews 11:6).

> ***For the mind that is set on the flesh is hostile to God***,
> *for it does not submit to God's law; indeed, it cannot.*
> ***Those who are in the flesh cannot please God.***
>
> Romans 8:7-8 (ESV)

Zombies do not want to please God; they want to please themselves. They gorge on their Fleshly desires and yet are never satisfied. Each day they waste away as they aimlessly wander in search of the next temporary gratification. But everything they are seeking to consume is itself perishing with use (Colossians 2:22). But every Fleshly indulgence last only for a short time before more is needed. Zombies are cursed to remain perpetually *unsatisfied* because all of their desires result in mere vapor and vanities.

The Dead do nothing from faith. Everything they do is driven by sin. They have no true faith, no true hope, no true love. Even their so-called "good" and "righteous" acts are motivated by sin, not by the desire to glorify God! These acts are done without faith towards the Living God and whatever does not proceed from faith is sin (Romans 14:23b ESV). Beyond that, even the evil that they deem to be minor offenses carry on to their inevitable spiritual extensions! They hate murderously, they covet voraciously, they lust excessively, and in their sin, they ultimately defy the One who made them for greater things.

> *And that we may be delivered from wicked and evil men.*
> *For not all have faith.*
>
> 2 Thessalonians 3:2 (ESV)

The so-called "good" and "righteous" acts of the living Dead are no more than a covering of ragged, bloody, and filthy rags before God Almighty. God does not see as mortals do; those who are dependent on physical sustenance fix their eyes only on what can be seen. But God looks within and judges the heart with its secret motives and intentions. The Living Word of God cuts down to joint and marrow - splitting even soul and spirit - to discern the truth presumed to be hidden in the heart. No creature is hidden from God. All things are evident to Him. To Yahweh, we will render an account of our deeds, be they righteous or wicked (Hebrews 4:12-13).

All Zombies attempt to conceal their insidious insides. But they vainly hide the truth of their condition. For by now, even the stench of Dead can be discerned to our disgust. It is in stark contrast to the pleasing aroma of righteousness produced by the Spirit in the Saints of God.

> *But thanks be to God, who in Christ always leads us in triumphal procession, and through us spreads the fragrance of the knowledge of him everywhere.* **For we are the aroma of Christ to God among those who are being saved and among those, who are perishing, to one a fragrance from death to death, to the other a fragrance from life to life.** *Who is sufficient for these things?*
> 2 Corinthians 2:14-16 (ESV)

These Zombies are whitewashed tombs. On the outside, they may be beautiful, but inwardly they are full of the bones of the dead and everything unclean (Matthew 23:27). Despite what it may seem to them, not even their so-called good deeds can cover them. They deny God by their actions because they are not driven by faith but by their Fleshly desires.

> *We have all become like one who is unclean, and all our righteous deeds are like a* **polluted garment**. *We all fade like a leaf, and our iniquities, like the wind, take us away. There is no one who calls upon your name, who rouses himself to take hold of you; for you have hidden your face from us and have made us melt in the hand of our iniquities.*
> Isaiah 64:6-7 (ESV)

> *Man wastes away* **like a rotten thing, like a garment that is moth-eaten.**
> Job 13:28 (ESV)

The decomposition of the Zombie, in addition to their fear of death, contributes to an increased level of aggression. We who have been brought to Life and who Walk by faith, must arm ourselves with the same mind as Christ, who suffered at the hand of sinners but did not retaliate. We must entrust ourselves to the Lord, our God, who is able to raise us from the dead.

Zombies are quick to shed blood and devour the innocent. They lie in wait to ambush from the darkness. Though it is their own deeds that will destroy them in the end (Philippians 1:27-30). They hate the Truth and the light that it illuminates. The Dead are lovers of darkness rather than light for fear that their Deathly deeds be exposed (John 3:19-20).

As the Dead Walk in the Flesh, they further themselves from the source of Life (Romans 8:5-6). To fixate, follow, and feed on the Flesh is Deadly. The Flesh interferes with the work of the Holy Spirit, but Zombies cannot help but feast on the frivolities of the Flesh because it is their nature. It is their hatred of the light and their love of sin that causes the Dead to be so utterly depraved. They are not lovers of the truth because if they were, then they would be saved. Perhaps, if only by the grace of God, they would be granted repentance, then they could be revived (2 Timothy 2:25). But instead, they continue on their path of morbid disobedience and will certainly eat the rotten Fruit of their labors.

This Deathly reality present itself through the *Acts of the Flesh*. These actions and behaviors are craved for and carried out by the Walking Dead, but ultimately, they are doing harm to themselves. They dig a pit for others but will fall for their own trap (Psalm 57:6). It's one thing to see the actions and know their end. It's another thing entirely too understand why the Acts of the Flesh are not immediately resulting in death! And why would God be so patient with such unworthy subjects? We will seek to understand the answers to the questions for in the answer is a valuable truth and chilling conclusion.

For the LORD knows the way of the righteous, but the way of the wicked will perish.
Psalm 1:6 (ESV)

THE UNDEAD DILEMMA

*Why is light given to him who is in misery, and life to the bitter in soul, who long for **death**, but it comes not, and dig for it more than for hidden treasures, who rejoice exceedingly and are glad when they find the **grave**?*
Job 3:20-22 (ESV)

There are many ways to misunderstand what is going on all around us. But despite what we cannot know, there have been many things made known to us. Those things that we now know have become our responsibility. We now know that although we do not visibly see God, as many would like to see Him, that His power is clearly seen in the creation (Romans 1:19-20). But if we have come to know that by our actions, we are guilty of a crime before God that is so heinous that we could by no means pay for it with our temporal offers and meager "good deeds." These efforts on our behalf to save ourselves are a far cry from what is required. An infinitely heinous crime against an infinitely holy God requires an infinitely worthy sacrifice. That exchange is found only in the Gospel Cure, in that Jesus Christ was the only one worthy to pay that price. He has done so, and now that we know this, we consider ourselves Dead to sin because we are no longer allowing it to *Live* in us. We were once alive in our own estimation because we thought we knew what it was to live. But now that we have been made aware that Jesus has beckoned to us to deny ourselves daily, take up our cross, and follow after Him (Luke 9:23), that is all we can devote ourselves to in this life. We are effectively Dead to sin and Alive to Christ. But the Zombies remain Dead in their sins and have left their sins Alive. They are Undead to their sin and must realize that if they do not kill their sin, then their sin will kill them (John 8:24).

*I was **once alive** apart from the law, but when the commandment came,*
sin came alive, and I died.
Romans 7:9 (ESV)

Undead

Zombies cannot live without sinning. This is what makes the Dead Undead. Not only do Zombies remain unaware of their Dead state, but they also deny the truth of what is bringing them to destruction. They hunger for the satisfaction that sin brings them and are unwilling to separate sin from their Walk. When a Zombie feeds off of the temporary gratification that sin brings, it makes them feel alive. Despite their sin being the root cause of their miserable condition, they continue to seek after it. Their hunger for Flesh will lead to their demise because they crave sin as if they had a Death wish. The sad truth is that Zombies will only cease to sin when they finally die. Their death will not set them free but will reveal their judgment.

Zombies are *Undead* to sin because they continue to live in it (Romans 6:1-3). They not only live in sin; they revel in it. They heap abuse on any who would refuse their sinful ways. The living Dead revile righteousness because they must remain in Darkness. All the deeds of Darkness, collectively the acts of the Flesh, are opposed to the Way of Christ. These evil deeds are why the wrath of God is coming against all the ungodliness and unrighteousness of the Undead who suppress the truth (Romans 1:18).

Talon Schneider

> *On account of these, the **wrath of God** is coming.*
> *In these, you too **once walked**, when you were **living in them**.*
>
> Colossians 3:6-7 (ESV)

By their nature, Zombies are driving themselves to their own end through their depraved decisions. We know that is how it was for us before we were brought to Life. We know how hopeless life was before being found in Christ. It was a dark and despondent existence without any real meaning. It was all vanity and chasing after what you could never catch.

> *I have seen everything that is done under the sun, and behold,*
> ***all is vanity and a striving after wind.***"
>
> Ecclesiastes 1:14 (ESV)

Their Dead spirituality and insensitivity have driven Zombies to lust for the sensuality of the Flesh (Ephesians 4:19). The living Dead feast on the Flesh because they must - they are insatiably driven to consume their own end like a moth to the flame. They behave like unreasoning animals in their pursuit of self-gratification. They greedily seek to satisfy their Fleshly desires regardless of the consequences.

> *But these, **like irrational animals, creatures of instinct, born to be caught and destroyed**, blaspheming about matters of which they are ignorant, will also be destroyed in their destruction, suffering wrong as the wage for their wrongdoing. **They count it pleasure to revel in the daytime**. They are blots and blemishes, reveling in their deceptions while they feast with you. They have eyes full of adultery, insatiable for sin. They entice unsteady souls. **They have hearts trained in greed**. Accursed children!*
>
> 2 Peter 2:12-14 (ESV)

The human heart is desperately wicked and beyond conventional cure (Jeremiah 17:9). Our own effort cannot change the inherent drive to cave in upon ourselves in sinful actions and behavior. But God can change us. Though we should have known God because He created us, we all participate in the Fallout and begin life with a proclivity toward sin.

> *They are darkened in their understanding, **alienated from the life of God** because of the ignorance that is in them, **due to their hardness***

The LIVING DEAD Revival Guide

> *of heart. They have become callous and have given themselves up to sensuality, **greedy to practice every kind of impurity**.*
>
> Ephesians 4:18-19 (ESV)

Who will save us from these bodies that are subject to death? Who will restore what we have destroyed? Who could reconcile the living Dead back to the source of Life? If the dead are not raised, then the Dead have no hope at all. The answer is the Lord Jesus Christ. He is the one who gave his body for the Body. He will restore what was destroyed. He is who the Father is using to reconcile the Dead back to Life. Jesus is the one who has risen from the grave as first fruits unto God.

> *Whoever has the Son **has life**; whoever does not have the Son of God **does not have life**.*
>
> 1 John 5:12 (ESV)

But who has believed this message? Only those who have died with Christ believe this brilliant foolishness. Only those that God has elected and regenerated can respond to the call of Life. Meanwhile, the Dead scoff and mock and revile such an idea. They turn against the hand held out to help them. These remain enemies to the cross of Christ. This is a horrible reality. But it is true. Many would rather die than be associated with the Risen One. This leads to an aspect of the Zombie Plague that results in considerable misunderstanding, disappointment, and fear.

> *But these people blaspheme all that they do not understand, and they are destroyed by all that they, like **unreasoning** animals, understand instinctively.*
>
> Jude 1:10 (ESV)

Unreasonable

The *unreasonableness* of the Dead is one of the most intimidating characteristics of the way they Walk. Though they have the instinct of self-preservation, they neglect the greatest threat to their life. This threat is their compulsive sin driven by their Fleshly appetite. Hordes of Zombies roam the earth and are Walking the wide path that leads to destruction. But it is the unreasonable characteristic of the Dead that makes them seem utterly unapproachable. Let us not forget, however, who we were before Christ.

Talon Schneider

> ***For we ourselves*** *were once foolish, disobedient, led astray, slaves to various passions and pleasures, passing our days in malice and envy,* ***hated by others and hating one another***.
> Titus 3:3 (ESV)

We who have been brought to Life may remember our salvation experience. We were formerly enemies of God, but his incredible love has changed us forever. Now the love of Christ compels us, and likewise, we who Walk Worthy of His calling ought to seek to relay the gospel message.

> *For the word of the cross is folly to those who are **perishing**, but to us who are **being saved**, it is the power of God.*
> 1 Corinthians 1:18 (ESV)

The epitome of a Zombie is characterized by their separation from God. They know not Life and therefore are Dead in their sins. Their very nature is defined by not knowing their creator. The Dead will not simply be reasoned to Life. That is not to say that it doesn't help to supply answers and facts regarding the truth, but more importantly, it is the work of God that transforms the heart from callous stone to responsive flesh (Ezekiel 11:19). It is God who calls and elects us for salvation. But He is using those who once Walked in darkness to proclaim the message of his kingdom and our Savior, Jesus Christ.

> *For everyone who calls on the name of the Lord will be saved. How then will they call on him in whom they have not believed? And how are they to believe in him of whom they have never heard? And how are they to hear without someone preaching? And how are they to preach unless they are sent? As it is written, 'How beautiful are the feet of those who preach the good news!'*
> Romans 10:13-15 (ESV)

This salvation is from God. It does not depend on human effort because it depends upon the grace of God to save a wretched creature that denies it's Creator. The Depravity of the Dead has been made clear.

It is evident that sin seizes opportunities to pervert what was intended for pure righteousness and turn it into obscene wickedness (Romans 7:7-13). The Dead demonstrate their depraved nature most obviously through their despicable thoughts and actions - in their Walk and by their hunger for Flesh. But they do not believe that their Walk is one directed toward a fiery end filled with extreme darkness, sorrowful weeping, and the bitter gnashing of teeth. This is due in part to the Catalysts of sin (Devil, Flesh, World) that continue to hold sway over the minds of the unbelieving to this very day.

DEATH THREAT

The Dead present other threats to the Living, but those threats are not to be overestimated. Too often, it seems that the outreach of Revival is slowed by the perceived threat of the Dead. Let this not be misunderstood: the Dead do pose a threat, but we must not threaten them.. The Saint must evaluate every situation so that in all circumstances, we may Walk wisely and make the most of every opportunity. Even though there are hordes of Zombies, it is not the Dead that should be feared, but rather we should fear God.

> *And do not fear those who kill the body but cannot kill the soul.*
> **Rather fear him who can destroy both soul and body in hell.**
> Matthew 10:28 (ESV)

The Living must make good use of their time because the days are evil. There are those who remain in the World that may yet have the hope of seeing God before they die. At any moment, the Lord may bring salvation to them in a way that they were not expecting. Some have come to faith because of the example laid out before them by other Worthy Walkers. Others have come to saving faith through dreams and visions. However, it is the Lord that brings about their salvation. We must be obedient to the call we have received. For there is laid up in heaven a great hope for us who have believed. Therefore, we do not fear death because Jesus has paid it for us. We know that to be absent from our bodies would mean that our hope is realized, for then we would be with the Lord. Yet we remain in the World to carry out our calling. We must help the helpless such as widows and orphans, and endeavor to keep ourselves from becoming polluted by the World. But most importantly, we must Walk in a way that would help point others to the Lord Jesus Christ and speak the message of Life to them as it was delivered unto us.

Our desires are pure if they are ultimately desires that seek to bring glory to God. But there are ways that seem right to a man that end in Death. Those are the natural desires of all Zombies. The Dead seek to corrupt those that get close to them. Bad company tarnishes good character (1 Corinthians 15). But it is not as though we could escape them entirely. If that were the case, then we would have to leave this world altogether. That is not why we remain. Our purpose is clear. We are to live as Christ lived, giving our lives for others. For if we die, then we gain! But if we remain then, others stand to gain, which is more necessary (Philippians 1). Therefore, let us make the most of our opportunities while in the body and in the world. For the Day of the Lord is nearer now than when we first believed.

We know that no one who has crossed over from Death to Life will continue in perpetual sin. We are no longer slaves of unrighteousness so that we would make a practice out of what was once alienating us from our Lord.

However, it would seem that the Living fear the corruption and contamination of the Dead more than the Dead fear the influence and Light of the Living. It is true that Light and Dark have no true fellowship with one another. Even as idols have no place among the one true God, so too, it could be said that Saints should not have too much intimacy with Zombies. Some closeness to the Dead is required in order to speak the message of Life to them. But far be it from the Living to mingle with the Dead as though there were no great chasm between them.

> *What agreement has the temple of God with idols? For we are the temple of the living God; as God said, "I will make my dwelling among them and walk among them, and I will be their God, and they shall be my people.* **Therefore go out from their midst, and be separate from them***, says the Lord, and touch no unclean thing; then I will welcome you, and I will be a father to you, and you shall be sons and daughters to me, says the Lord Almighty.*
> 2 Corinthians 6:16-18 (ESV)

We must Walk in wisdom if we are to carry out our purpose in God's plan of salvation. We should separate ourselves from all that defiles, whether that be thoughts, actions, and associations. All who have the blessed hope of Lord Jesus Christ return are submitting to sanctification and purifying themselves even as He is pure (1 John 3:1). We do this with the reverential awe and wisdom produced by the Fear of the Lord.

> *Since we have these promises, beloved,* **let us cleanse ourselves from every defilement of body and spirit***, bringing holiness to completion in the fear of God.*
> 2 Corinthians 7:1 (ESV)

The **LIVING DEAD** Revival Guide

*And they shall go out and look on the dead bodies of the men who have rebelled against me. For their **worm shall not die, their fire shall not be quenched, and they shall be an abhorrence to all flesh**.*

Isaiah 66:24 (ESV)

Dead End

*Whatever your hand finds to do, do it with all your might, **for in the realm of the dead**, where you are going, there is neither working nor planning nor knowledge nor wisdom.*

Ecclesiastes 9:10 (NIV)

*They will suffer the punishment of **eternal destruction, away from the presence of the Lord and from the glory of his might**, when he comes on that day to be glorified in his saints and to be marveled at among all who have believed because our testimony to you was believed.*

2 Thessalonians 1:9-10 (ESV)

The great and terrible Day of the Lord will bring with it apocalypse and revelation. For all those who did not love the truth, there will be consequences. But for those who loved the truth concerning the salvation offered through the blood of Christ, it will be cause for celebration. When the Lord Jesus Christ returns, it will not be to bear sin but rather to bring judgment upon sinners and salvation for his people (Hebrews 9:28).

The Dead seem disastrously oblivious to their impending doom. Although they have seen the power of God in creation, they remain obstinate. Although death ought to be a strange and unnatural thing, those who are Dead seem unimpressed by its presence. Even though they have been conscience that should convict of immorality, many of the Dead have hardened their hearts through repeating the same sins that desecrate the beautiful image of God that they bear. We have observed with our own eyes (and at times our own lives) that the Dead are destined to disobey the word.

And "A stone of stumbling, and a rock of offense."
*They stumble because they disobey the word, as they were **destined** to do.*

1 Peter 2:8 (ESV)

Not only are the Living Dead destined to disobey the word of God, but it gets worse. Indeed, we all stumble in many ways (James 3 or 4?). But those who remain unrepentant in their sinful condition will undoubtedly meet a miserable fate. But this should come as no surprise to us who have heeded the words of Life. The Bible is very clear when it describes the nature, conditions, and destination of the Zombie.

> ... *For I tell you, now as before, even with tears that many live as enemies of the cross of Christ.* **Their destiny is destruction, their god is their stomach, and their glory is in their shame**.
> Philippians 3:17b-19

To some, it may seem unfair or unjust for some to be elected for Life and others to be destined for Death, but this blatantly ignores what we have already studied regarding the depravity of the Dead. But perhaps this bothers our soul in an effectual way. If only all people would be disturbed by the impending peril upon the Walking Dead, then we might truly see Revival. The time of God's grace is now, but there will come an end to this time of patient waiting on God's part. If anyone is out there who is bothered by the idea of election, then perhaps it is better to align with what it indicates. That there is an uneasiness, which accompanies the thought of the Second Death, which ought to provoke all souls to faith in the grace of God.

In actuality it is unfair that the Dead are forgiven of their sins at all. For not even the angels who sinned were given an opportunity for redemption. The fact that God made him who knew no sin to become sin so that those who knew only sin could become truly righteous is a matter that angels long to see. How incredible that God would transform such lowly creatures of filthy sin into his own children. Yes, through the incarnation of the God-man, Jesus Christ, salvation is made possible for humanity because He became like them and lived a life worthy of God. His perfect life and death through sacrifice is the only adequate payment for the debt of sin upon humanity.

> **For surely, his concern is not for angels, but he is concerned for Abraham's descendants**. *Therefore, he had to be made like his brothers and sisters in every respect, so that he could become a merciful and faithful high priest in things relating to God, to make atonement for the sins of the people.* **For since he himself suffered when he was tempted, he is able to help those who are tempted**.
> Hebrews 2:16-18 (NET)

The LIVING DEAD Revival Guide

But the angels who sinned and rebelled against God (Genesis 6 and other places) went against their Creator who made them good just as humans were made good, but their rebellion did not entail forgiveness and redemption as it does for the once Dead now made Alive! Indeed, Yahweh has made humans a little lower than the angels, and they are to serve those who are inheriting salvation (1 Peter 1:12, Hebrews 1:14). Remarkably all of us who were once Dead in our sins, walking according to the course of this World, being deceived by the Antagonist, and catering to the shameful desires of the Flesh will be the ones who judges the angels! We are given such great honor from the Living God. It is our responsibility to walk worthy of His calling by discerning the dangerous destiny of those who remain dead in their sins in the hope that some might hear our messages and believe in the One who can save them.

> *Do you not know that we are to judge angels?*
> ***How much more, then, matters pertaining to this life!***
> 1 Corinthians 6:3 (ESV)

Perilous

> *The wicked plots against the righteous and **gnashes his teeth at him.***
> Psalms 37:12 (ESV)

Undoubtedly the Dead recoil at the message of Life, considering it nonsense, foolishness, and even madness. Just as we all are born Dead in our sins, we all express at times a vehement human will. Though we should know God as our Creator, we do not. And though we should simply hear the message and believe some do not believe. Consider the response given to Paul when he made his defense in the court of King Agrippa.

> *"King Agrippa, do you believe the prophets? I know that you believe."*
> *And Agrippa said to Paul,* ***"In a short time would you persuade me to be a Christian?"*** *And Paul said, "Whether short or long, I would to God that not only you but also all who hear me this day might become such as I am--except for these chains."*
> Acts 26:27-29 (ESV)

Again, we are reminded that the Way is narrow that leads to life, and few enter through that one and only way. Jesus Christ is the only escape from No Man's Land. Through Him, there is hope and life. But many, such as King Agrippa, denied the Way and have gone the way that is natural to the Flesh only to find a dead end.

It should sadden us to know that so many would refuse Christ and place their path in their own hands. They are spiritually blind and thus lead themselves into a pit. Many friends, family, and loved ones stubbornly refuse the gracious gift of God. For we had love for them, but if they deny Christ, He will deny them (2 Timothy). This should motivate us in our Revival Mission. We must resist the temptation of the Flesh that leads to doubt, depression, and desperation. We who have been raised to life should no longer perceive our existence as merely vanity under the sun.

> *Again, I saw all the oppressions that are done under the sun. And behold, the tears of the oppressed, and they had no one to comfort them! On the side of their oppressors, there was power, and there was no one to comfort them.* ***And I thought the dead who are already dead more fortunate than the living who are still alive.*** *But better than both is he who has not yet been and has not seen the evil deeds that are done under the sun.*
> Ecclesiastes 4:1-3 (ESV)

The Dead who are already dead are indeed in a perilous situation. The redemptive work of the Savior has advanced the plan that God has in place. Those who have died in the sin of unbelief have no hope to escape their fate. Jesus tells a story about two men who lived very different lives while in this World. One was very rich and could afford to do whatever he wanted, while the other, Lazarus, was very poor in biologically, socially, and monetarily. When they died each man was sent to a different place in the afterlife. Lazarus was taken to a place of comfort, but the rich man was taken to a place of torment. Despite the pleading of the rich man, it was not possible for him to receive any comfort whatsoever, for there was fixed an impassible chasm between his dwelling place and that of Lazarus. In lieu of that fact, the rich man begged that some type of message could be sent back from the land of the dead to the land of the living so that a warning could be issued concerning the place of torment. But the problem is not that the dead are unaware of the message, for it has been divinely preserved and disseminated to them so that they are without excuse. The tormented rich man argued that perhaps someone sent back from the land of the dead could convey adequately the impending danger. But he was told that if the word of God that speaks of Jesus Christ, found in the writings of the law and the prophets, was not believed, then neither would someone be convinced if they should witness the dead rise to life (Luke 16:19-31). We know what the Dead deserve for we were once in the Darkness as they are now. We deserved the full wrath of God against sin. But that is not what we have received.

He does not deal with us according to our sins, nor repay us according to our iniquities. *For as high as the heavens are above the earth, so great is his steadfast love toward those who fear him; as far as the east is from the west, so far does he remove our transgressions from us. As a father shows compassion to his children, so the LORD shows compassion to those who fear him.* ***For he knows our frame; he remembers that we are dust.***

Psalms 103:10-14 (ESV)

Thus, we who know God and are known by Him should put forth our best effort to share the only hope of a cure to the Zombie Apocalypse: Jesus Christ.

Therefore, ***knowing the fear of the Lord, we persuade others.***
But what we are is known to God, and I hope it is known also to your conscience.

2 Corinthians 5:11 (ESV)

SLEEPWALKER

IDENTIFICATION CRISIS

Dreams are mysterious and, at times, difficult to understand. Several biblical characters received dreams that were beyond their ability to understand (Pharaoh and Nebuchadnezzar). Others found themselves interpreting those enigmatic dreams (Joseph and Daniel). We ourselves have dreams that are not always as clear as we would like them to be. Dreams are not trustworthy unless it is Yahweh who gives us more clarity as to their meaning. Mostly, they pass quicker than we can even remember. Like the wind that slips between the fingers are the wispy dreams of most people. Our lives are compared to dreams due to the brevity of their moment and memory in life (Job 20:8).

What then can be gained from them? On the one hand, they can help us work through issues that our waking life encounters. On the other hand, they can be used figuratively to represent a deeper understanding of an issue if God's wisdom is applied to them. We must not deceive ourselves into thinking that our dreams have our best intentions at heart. The elusive nature of them alone confirms that our faith is better placed in the solidity of the Scriptures. Within a dream, what should be easily recognizable may not be what it seems. The allure to accept what we see as what we should believe is denounced by those who Walk by faith and not by sight; nor by any other senses which are inferior to faith. Yahweh does speak through dreams in some instances, but everything before us should be tested through the Scripture. By this precaution, we guard against accepting a different gospel or different "Savior" preached by a man or even an angel who presumes to be of the Light. This is confirmed for us on many occasions. Many notable biblical characters received dreams directed by The Lord. Here is a list of some of them.

Dreamers

Joseph, the son of Jacob (Genesis 37:5-10)
Solomon (1 Kings 3:5-15)
Daniel (Daniel 2:1 and 7:1)
Joseph, the husband of Mary (Matthew 2:12-22)
Several others (Matthew 27:19). There is also a prophecy of Joel (Joel 2:28) that Peter quotes in Acts 2:17, which refers to God using dreams to communicate with people.

Dreams Not As They Seem

A dream does not abide by the rules of reality. It is not a reliable resource for the governance of our lives. But a dream may tempt us to believe such things. How can we rely upon something that changes so unpredictably? Why would we place any dependence on something that so often shows a distorted (and false) reality? Most likely, because dreams can make us *feel* good for a time. We may see ourselves as more attractive or wealthy, but these temporary indulgences vanish so quickly that we scantly remember them.

Have you ever seen yourself while in a dream? Have you ever seen your face in a mirror or perhaps from a different angle or perspective? Rarely is the representation accurate. Whether it is the hairstyle or facial structure that is known to be different or perhaps teeth missing or physical ability is vastly increased or decreased, what is certain is that dreams are uncertain. Unless certifiably discernible with the help of the scripture, they hold little more value than some form of psychological release.

> *Just as there is **futility** in many dreams, so also in many words.*
> *Therefore, **fear God!***
> Ecclesiastes 5:7 (NET)

But as analogies, we can see that dreams actually represent very well the middling reality of all those who Walk precariously between the land of the Living and the land of the Dead. That is to say, that just as dreams can misrepresent reality, so too can a Sleep Walker be misrepresented. The Living may appear to be a Zombie because of questionable behaviors. Or perhaps the Dead may masquerade as being full of Life and good Fruit only for the clock to chime its final note, and the truth of their nightmare be revealed.

Considering this, we must make careful preparations and observations so that our assessment of actions will not be through poor judgment. May we all strive to judge accurately and not with false motives or beguiling emotions. Indeed, the Sleep Walker needs the same that any other needs. We all need the truth of the Gospel mystery revealed to us. And until all have responded to the alarm of our desperate condition before Yahweh, let us strive to make known the message of Life through Christ.

> *"But when anything is exposed by the light, it becomes visible, for anything that becomes visible is light. Therefore, it says,* **"Awake, O sleeper, and arise from the dead, and Christ will shine on you."** *Look carefully then how you walk, not as unwise but as wise, making the best use of the time because the days are evil.*
>
> Ephesians 5:13-16 (ESV)

IDENTITY CRISIS

It's one thing for a Zombie to have an identity crisis and another thing entirely to have a crisis of identification. How can we know the difference between the Living and the Dead if it doesn't always come down to outward appearances? Certainly, the actions and behaviors indicate what kind of Fruit each person produces. For some, it is the Fruit of light, representing all that is good and right and true (Ephesians 5:9). For others, that Fruit is rotten and full of shame and Death.

> *For while we were living in the flesh, our sinful passions, aroused by the law, were at work in our members to bear **fruit for death**.*
>
> Romans 7:5 (ESV)

But who do we think we are? Do we somehow think that we were superior to others? Are we deceiving ourselves by deliberately forgetting our battle with the old self-controlled by the Flesh and the new self-controlled by the Spirit (Galatians 5:17)? Do we think that we have earned our salvation? How wrong we would be to think such things.

> *For **consider your calling**, brothers: not many of you were wise according to worldly standards, not many were powerful, not many were of noble birth.*
> 1 Corinthians 1:26 (ESV)

It's not just the fact that few of us were wise, powerful, or noble. It's the reality of who we were before Christ or even who we are without him. Without Jesus Christ, we are not truly Alive. Without Christ, we remain Dead in our sins (Colossians 2:12-13). Without Christ, we are without hope and the most pitiable of all people.

We must become better at evaluating others and ourselves. Hazy self-perception can lead to self-deception (1 Corinthians 3:18). Inadequate observation and evaluation of others can have similarly disastrous results. It is possible to wrongfully associate with the sinful Walk of others to the point that it would seem we have given our endorsement of such behavior (2 Corinthians 6:14-18). But rather, we are blessed if we "...Do not walk in the counsel of the wicked, nor stand in the way of sinners, nor sit in the seat of scoffers" (Psalm 1:1).

> ***Do not be hasty** in the laying on of hands, nor take part in the sins of others; **keep yourself pure**.*
> 1 Timothy 5:22 (ESV)

> *Therefore go out from their midst, and **be separate from them**, says the Lord, and touch no unclean thing; then I will welcome you, and I will be a father to you, and you shall be sons and daughters to me, says the Lord Almighty.*
> 2 Corinthians 6:17-18 (ESV)

In many ways, we must Die to our old self. We already see how Zombies are Undead to their sin because they continue to feed it and feed off of it. But just as they have determined to feed off of that which is killing them, we Saints must determine to feed off of that which is keeping us alive. We must not create distance with God by thinking we can have true Life apart from Him. He came to give us Life, which was true and abundant Life (John 10:10). We must put on Christ and conform to his example in service, suffering, and sacrifice if necessary (Romans 13:14). The apostle Paul thought of it this way.

The LIVING DEAD Revival Guide

*But far be it from me to boast except in the cross of our Lord Jesus Christ, by which **the world has been crucified to me, and I to the world**.*
Galatians 6:14 (ESV)

Our good intentions are not always what God intends. We don't know everything, and we have not yet been perfected. But all who want to follow Christ must take up their cross, deny themselves, and follow their savior tenaciously (Luke 9:23).

Certainly, we can conceive that it is far greater to gain Christ compared to anything else (Philippians 3:8-9). The apostle Paul illuminates what our focus should be in the following verses. That is if we have turned away from the darkness and stepped into the light of the Lord.

*My aim is to **know him**, to experience the **power of his resurrection**, to share in his sufferings, and to **be like him in his death**, and so, somehow, to attain to the **resurrection from the dead**.*
Philippians 3:10-11 (NET)

Our goal should be to know the One in whom we have believed (2 Timothy 1:12). We do this by drawing near to him through faith with repentance from the dirty works of our hands and impurity of our hearts and minds (James 4:8). He loved us while we were ignorant enemies, and surely, He loves us even more as his faithful children (Romans 5:8-10).

Indeed, we have been made alive in Christ! However, the humility of our physical bodies remains unchanged, for now (1 Corinthians 15). We dwell in the same tattered tent as before. We do not necessarily transform bodily at our conversion, though there seems to be certainty that all will eventually be changed (1 Corinthians 15). Even though we desire this to be the case, not even Paul, the self-proclaimed least of the apostles - who worked harder than the rest (1 Corinthians 15:9-10), didn't yet consider himself to be perfected.

*Not that I have already attained this—that is, **I have not already been perfected**—but I strive to lay hold of that for which Christ Jesus also laid hold of me. Brothers and sisters, I do not consider myself to have attained this. Instead, I am single-minded: **Forgetting the things that are behind and reaching out for the things that are ahead**. With this goal in mind, I strive toward the prize of the upward call of God in Christ Jesus. Therefore, let those of us who are "perfect" embrace this point of view.*

> *If you think otherwise, God will reveal to you the error of your ways. Nevertheless, let us live up to the standard that we have already attained.*
> Philippians 3:12-16 (NET)

Yes, believers are saved and righteous before God Almighty, but if we say we have no sin, then we are deeply deceived (1 John 1:9). Maturity will bring with it the attitude that causes us to go beyond what once held us back and onward to the calling to Walk Worthy. It is undeniable that we who have believed the message about Christ have brought along with us hindrances that slow us down. For we all stumble in many ways, we are hardly able to control our tongues, let alone the rest of our Flesh (James 3:2). Perhaps we have a lingering temptation or proclivity toward anger or something else, but whatever it may be, we are responsible for our actions. But we know that sanctification, the process of becoming more Christ-like, takes time. And God is the one who works in us and through us to accomplish his holy plan for us (Philippians 2:13).

> **Do not be deceived:** *God is not mocked, for whatever one sows, that will he also reap. For the one who sows to his own flesh will from the **flesh reap corruption**, but the one who sows to the **Spirit will from the Spirit reap** eternal life. And let us not grow weary of doing good, for in due season we will reap, if we **do not give up**. So then, as we have opportunity, let us do good to everyone, and especially to those who are of the household of faith.*
> Galatians 6:7-10 (ESV)

Our new Life in Christ has pardoned us from all our sin—such is the extravagant glory and grace of God. This glorious grace is not to be misused as though we could sin without consequence. We should not sin so that grace increases, and we should not give our Flesh an opportunity to indulge because of our freedom in Christ.

Some burdens we carry though they should be dropped, and other burdens are given to us as a sort of gift. A gift meant to bring out the best in us. Our challenges mold us into worthy vessels of God's glorious Gospel Cure. Amazingly the Living may still choose to sin even after dying to the law and sin through Christ. This is the remarkable mystery of Yahweh's sovereignty and our free will. But his undying love cannot be defeated by our errors.

> *All wrongdoing is sin,* **but there is sin that does not lead to death***.*
> 1 John 5:17 (ESV)

The LIVING DEAD Revival Guide

We know the One in whom we have believed. He is faithful and true and is both just, and the justifier of all the Dead brought to Life (Romans 3:26). By the sacrifice of Jesus Christ, a completely worthy exchange has taken place wherein all of the wrath of God against sin is doled out. But because of the righteousness of Christ, all who believe in him have atonement before the Holy One. Undoubtedly this mystery is a beautiful demonstration of the glory of God at work in our lives.

> *For our sake, **he made him to be sin who knew no sin so that in him, we might become the righteousness of God.***
> 2 Corinthians 5:21 (ESV)

In view of this incredible justice, mercy, and grace, the Dead who believe should no longer offer their bodies to what once enslaved them (Romans 6:16-22).

> *But now that you have been set free from sin and have become slaves of God, **the fruit you get leads to sanctification and its end, eternal life**.*
> Romans 6:22 (ESV)

The Devil, the Flesh, and the World are not in control of God's people! All of the passions and desires that dragged us away no longer have hold over us as our master. We have become slaves of righteousness, and it is our newborn desire for righteousness that replaces our old despicable ways. We are no longer running away from our Creator; instead, we are now running for our life —to our Life. This race is marked out for us by the Forerunner, Jesus Christ.

> *Therefore, since we are surrounded by so great a cloud of witnesses, **let us also lay aside every weight, and sin which clings so closely**, and let us run with endurance the race that is set before us, looking to Jesus, the founder and perfecter of our faith, who for the joy that was set before him endured the cross, despising the shame, and is **seated at the right hand of the throne of God**.*
> Hebrews 12:1-2 (ESV)

It remains, however, that the Saint is opposed by the Devil in that he tempts us to defy the Lord Jesus Christ (James 4:7). The Flesh is still opposed to the Spirit, and thus, we are restricted from fulfilling perfection and complete holiness (Galatians 5:17). The World reviles the children of God because we do not belong to it and thus are hated (1 John 3:13). All of these factors help explain why there could be such confusion surrounding the truth of God living in people who remain susceptible to sin. It also serves as a reminder to be humble, knowing that the only reason for our standing in Christ is because of the grace of God.

> *Therefore, since we have been justified by faith, we have **peace with God through our Lord Jesus Christ**. Through him, we have also obtained access by faith into this grace in which we stand, and we rejoice in hope of the glory of God.*
> Romans 5:1-2 (ESV)

Vitally held together is the free will of God's image-bearers. Consider, for example, that the saved are forgiven of all their sins and, in a sense, are already With God but not yet with him. We are spiritually seated in heavenly places in Christ Jesus (Ephesians 2:6). We remain in this world but not of the World, and seek to bring others out of its grip. The apostle Paul knew it was of greater value to remain in the flesh of his body, although his personal desire was to be with Christ completely, it was of greater need that he completed his purpose in bringing many to know the saving power of the Lord (Philippians 1:25-26). Our choices matter tremendously.

One of the greatest choices given to us is to love. We show the confirmation of our transformation from Death to Life in how we love one another. If necessary, we are called to love one another just as Jesus did by giving his life. By this, we show the evidence of our conversion. We must choose to show the love that Christ has shown. This Living Sacrifice is what differentiates us from the Old Self and our Dead ways that were dragging us to hell. We are no longer enemies of Christ but followers of Him, so it stands to reason that we likewise will love even to the point of death if necessary. All this is for the glory of God and not for us. For the one who loves only to suit their own cause will find a swift end to such an effort. Because God provides for us to Walk according to His will.

> *We know that we have **passed out of death into life** because we love the brothers. Whoever does not love **abides in death**.*
> 1 John 3:14 (ESV)

The experience of conversion from Death to Life includes sanctification or a process of continually drawing near to God in such a way that we resemble him more and more. We are set apart, like a special treasure of God's, intended to be holy. We go from glory to glory. We are going from the glory of image-bearing to the glory of image sharing and showing. We were once Dead in sins, but He has made us alive in Christ - the true hope of glory fulfilled by proper identification with Christ!

> *And we all, with unveiled face, beholding the glory of the Lord, are being transformed into the same image **from one degree of glory to another**. For this comes from the Lord, who is the Spirit.*
> 2 Corinthians 3:18 (ESV)

We the Light of the world (Matthew 5:14) that is intended to shine Christ into the dark Wasteland we once wandered. Our Lord Jesus urges us to be righteous influences to the Dead and calls us both Salt and Light. Though now we are not natives to No Man's Land but rather exiles. For our Heavenly Father transferred us from the domain of darkness to his Son's Kingdom of Light (Colossians 1:13-14).

All of this drives the question that shrouds the Sleep Walker in mystery. What shall we do when God's people Walk in a stupor or roll around in idleness but the Dead Walk with an appearance of godliness that denies the truth? How can we discern the Living from the Dead when the line between them becomes nearly indiscernible? How do we pull the Sleep Walker out of their daydreams and nightmares? What do we do if it is ourselves that remain shrouded by self-deception? We must seek the truth.

> *Woe to those who call evil good and good evil, who put darkness for light and light for darkness, who put bitter for sweet and sweet for bitter!*
> Isaiah 5:20 (ESV)

Through A Glass Dimly

> ***For now, we see in a mirror dimly**, but then face to face. Now I know in part; then I shall know fully, even as I have been fully known.*
> 1 Corinthians 13:12 (ESV)

There is still so much we don't know about ourselves. Even though we have had our minds renewed, there is much to be learned. We are being made ever more into the image of our savior, the Lord Jesus Christ. He has the power to subdue all things and to transform our lowly bodies to become like his glorious body. But the fact remains that we are abiding in a tattered old tent that is not fit to enter the kingdom of God. Flesh and blood cannot enter into the Kingdom. Thus, we know that our lowly mortal bodies will be replaced and transformed into glorious spiritual bodies made to dwell with Yahweh forever (1 Corinthians 15:44).

Although we do not see Him now, we believe in Him and have faithful hope that we will see Him face to face (2 Peter 1). We only know a part of the whole, but from the perspective of our Heavenly Father, we are fully known. We are called to be in the world but not of it. We are concurrently in our fleshly bodies and yet, in some sense, seated in Christ in heavenly places (Ephesians 2:6). We are caught up in a great duality of already but not yet. Therefore, we ought to make use of our time. We should Walk wisely and circumspect so that we may know the purpose for which we have been called. We cannot accomplish the calling of God on our own. We have not pulled ourselves out of our perilous predicament on our own. Yahweh saved us in Jesus Christ so that we would spread the message of his Life offering. We do this by offering our own life as an example of what we know Jesus did for us. Therefore, while we are in the World, we must focus our eyes upon Jesus. As we follow the Risen Lord, we will be made more like Him. In effect, we become like what we worship. Some worship idles that cannot talk, hear, or move, and similarly, the Dead are limited, but the Living will Walk with God both now and forever.

Having our faith firmly established on the truth of the scripture is essential to our Life as God's holy people. We know who our Savior is, and He knows us, but there is still much to be learned. There are mysteries yet unveiled, and adventures still to be had. We don't know what we will become but what we can know for certain is that upon seeing our risen Lord, we will be like Him because we will see him as He is (1 John 3:1-3). We will see him clearly without our natural limitations. But as for now, it can be said that even the Christian sees an obscured image of what's to come. It is the glory of God to withhold and conceal a matter, while it is our glory to seek it out, and in doing so, find Him (Proverbs 25:2).

If the Zombie peers at their own reflection but Walks away unchanged undeterred, then a Christian should be ever-changing to become more Christ-like. However, sanctification is a process intended to craft us for the glory of God. In some sense, we have been completed and perfected before the Father already, that is, if we are in Christ (Hebrews 10:14). What does that leave us with? How are we going to understand this dichotomy? Admittedly we might demand more clarity because our uncertainty in these matters leaves us with a reflection from a foggy mirror. This can cause us to have an incomplete picture of who we really are. The issue is with the beholder because we should have known who we were, but we did not before God caused us to see the truth. Our human nature provokes our uncertainty and distrust about what we cannot see. But the scripture tells us that what is seen is temporary and what is unseen is eternal. We are therefore called to fix our eyes on that which is unseen if we are to truly perceive what is to come (2 Corinthians 4:16-18).

> ***If then you have been raised with Christ**, seek the things that are above, where Christ is, seated at the right hand of God. Set your minds on things that are above, not on things that are on earth. **For you have died, and your life is hidden with Christ in God. When Christ, who is your life appears, then you also will appear with him in glory.***
>
> Colossians 3:1-4 (ESV)

Yahweh demonstrated his love for us in that while we were Zombies, hostile to His will. He sent Jesus to die in for us (Romans 5:8). Thus, through his sacrifice and our faith, we have been restored unto Him. We know this truth and still, find ways to stumble. But where sin increases, grace abounds all the more (Romans 5:21). This is not to say that our sin is an encouraged behavior. This is merely another way of understanding the brilliant gospel message. What we didn't earn by what we do will not be taken from us by what we fail to do. Only the fool would think that unrestrained and unrepentant sin is permissible (Romans 6:1). The Father will not allow unrepentant sin. He will correct misconduct. For truly, we are called to be members of a holy family, and so holy conduct is expected. But what will be made of the people who straddle the line and Walk precariously close to the edge? How can we recognize the difference in time to make an impact in the lives of those who Walk in the Darkness?

> *For it is time for judgment to begin at the household of God; and **if it begins with us, what will be the outcome for those who do not obey the gospel of God?** And 'f the righteous is scarcely saved, what will become of the ungodly and the sinner?*
>
> 1 Peter 4:17-18 (ESV)

IDENTIFYING WHO'S WHO

Why does there persist the pestilent capacity for sin among the Living? And why can the Dead dawn the appearance of righteousness in such a way that they even deceive themselves? Why is it so hard to see the difference between the Living and the Dead? One reason for the confusion is that man does not see as God sees.

Consider, for example, how the prophet Samuel was predisposed to look for a king based on external factors like appearance, whereas The Lord had chosen David in part because he had a heart that sought-after God.

> But the LORD said to Samuel, "**Do not look on his appearance or on the height of his stature, because I have rejected him. For the LORD sees not as man sees; man looks on the outward appearance, but the LORD looks on the heart.**"
>
> 1 Samuel 16:7 (ESV)

> *Do not judge by appearances, but judge with right judgment.*
>
> John 7:24 (ESV)

God is not confused about who belongs to him, He chose us, and we follow His voice like sheep follow a good shepherd (John 10:27). He is all-knowing and has known before we were even born what our life would become. But it is not so obvious to us who are at times so limited by our physicality, or rather by our dependence upon physicality. Remember that the Saint Walks not by sight but by faith (2 Corinthians 5:7). The Dead Walk by their base senses and not by faith. Their sensuality misleads them.

> **They have become callous and have given themselves up to sensuality,** *greedy to practice every kind of impurity.*
>
> Ephesians 4:19 (ESV)

The tendency of all humans is to judge by mere appearances. That is the natural response. Thus, the Living are urged not to judge others simply because of what they look like. This is not the appropriate way to make godly discernment. If the Living were to do that, then they would be drifting hazily out of faith minded decision making into the Fleshly process that was provoking sin and Death.

> *My brothers,* **show no partiality as you hold the faith in our Lord Jesus Christ***, the Lord of glory. For if a man wearing a gold ring and fine clothing comes into your assembly, and a* **poor man in shabby clothing** *also comes in, and if you pay attention to the one who wears the fine clothing and say, "You sit here in a good place," while you say to the poor man, "You stand over there," or, "Sit down at my feet," have you not then made distinctions among yourselves and become judges with evil thoughts? Listen, my beloved*

The LIVING DEAD Revival Guide

*brothers, has not God chosen those who are poor in the world to be rich in faith and heirs of the kingdom, which **he has promised to those who love him?** But you have dishonored the poor man. Are not the rich the ones who oppress you, and the ones who drag you into court? Are they not the ones who blaspheme the **honorable name by which you were called?***

James 2:1-7 (ESV)

It will be unfamiliar to evaluate others and ourselves in this new way, but it is recommended and righteous. James describes the perplexity of identity appropriately. Some may imagine the Zombie to be dressed in the shabby clothing and the Lively Saint to be adorned in fine clothing and gold jewelry. But we deliberately make a false judgment if we treat others with favoritism only because of how they look rather than how they act. There will be a time when the Saints rule and reign with Christ, but it is not this time. That time is coming, but it is not yet here in completion. For that reason, Paul calls upon his companions to quicken that day, not for their own gain, rather for the betterment of all the Saints.

Already you have all you want! Already you have become rich! You have begun to reign--and that without us! *How I wish that you really **had begun to reign so that we also might reign with you!***

1 Corinthians 4:8 (NIV)

The Kingdom of Heaven is counter-intuitive to our worldly predisposition. Our Flesh also resists the holy ways of God. But as we become more familiar with the way of faith, we become more conformed to the will He has for us. The rich in the Kingdom are those who were poor on earth, while those who are rich on the earth and accept Christ will rejoice in their humbling (James 1:9-10). Don't trust appearances but rather test all things and retain only what is good (1 Thessalonians 5:21).

The scripture teaches that appearances are not to be quickly trusted. The apostle Paul warned the Corinthian church of such imposters of the faith. He went as far as to draw a connection between false apostles and Satan, who disguises himself as an angel of light, the same Enemy who is somehow the master over the Dead along with the rest of the evil spirits (Psalm 82 and 89).

*And what I am doing I will continue to do, in order to undermine the claim of those who would like to claim that in their boasted mission they work on the same terms as we do. **For such men are false apostles, deceitful workmen, disguising themselves as apostles of Christ. And no***

> ***wonder, for even Satan disguises himself as an angel of light.*** *So, it is no surprise if his servants also disguise themselves as servants of righteousness. Their end will correspond to their deeds.*
>
> 2 Corinthians 11:12-15 (ESV)

WOLVES AND SHEEP

Jesus spoke of a type of person who was like a wolf in sheep's clothing. In some ways, they appeared to be a sheep, a member of the group, but in reality, was a deadly doppelganger. We see this dilemma resurface in far too many areas. Whether the imposters are seeking to share in the experiential benefits of the Christian life such as fidelity and peace or perhaps to partake in the power of God. Some imposters seek to peddle the gospel for a different kind of *false profit* (2 Corinthian 2:17).

The prevalence of this issue is spread by a variety of causes. Most notably among these causes must be the identification crisis, in both directions. There is much difficulty recognizing imposters in the faith that contributes to the overall problem. But the fact that the Dead are unaware of their true condition only worsens the issue. There are the Born Again believers who backslide into sin. Though for many Christians, that is only a matter of time before the Lord eradicates errant behavior and carries out sanctification. In that regard, we must learn to take captive not only the wayward thoughts of others but also those incorrect thoughts that belong to us (2 Corinthians 10:5). Perhaps more disturbing than the Dead are those who refer to themselves as Christians; meanwhile, they strangely continue in willful and habitual sin even after being confronted.

Consider the myriad perspectives in another way. Yahweh knows who belongs to Him. And his sheep follow the voice of the Good Shepherd. So, then we can conclude there are, in essence, two disparate identities: sheep or goat, believer or unbeliever, saved or unsaved, Living or Dead. But there is undeniably confusion between the two groups.

If we were to think about it in terms not so dissimilar to what Jesus used, then it may sound like this. There are wolves in sheep's clothing, and there are sheep in wolves' clothing. That is to say that there are the Dead who have a reputation that they are Alive but, in fact, are not (Revelation 3:1). Similarly, there are the Living who, for a brief time, may seem to be Dead because of their actions. But given time and the grace of God, they will be sanctified through and through to the point that the Flesh will be destroyed (1 Corinthians 5:5, 2 Corinthians 2:1-11, 2 Corinthians 7:8-12).

But what can be said of the clear and unambiguous representations at the extremities of this spectrum? Isn't it obvious to us when we see a sheep in sheep's clothing or a wolf in wolves' clothing? Furthermore, is it possible to see ourselves in these terms? Because at one time, we were ourselves Dead in sin and without hope in the world. We should at least be able to recognize who we were compared to who we are now, right? Well, of course, there are times when our faith couldn't be clearer, and there are times when doubt afflicts even the most fervent follower of Christ (Mark 14:30-31 and John 21:17).

Overall it would seem that it is clearer and more obvious when someone claims Christ and proves their faith by their actions. Even James argued that faith without works is Dead. But faith that works is Alive and well. Simply put, faith works, and its movement proves it's vitality. If you are Alive because of your faith in the grace of God, then He who dwells within you will present proof of His presence in the form of love, joy, peace, patience, kindness, gentleness, and self-control (Galatians 5:22-23).

Conversely, it seems rather conclusive when a Zombie actively and vehemently rebels against God and hates the Saints that they are not pretending to be followers of the Way, the Truth, and the Life of Jesus Christ. This much is sure. The Flesh is hostile to God, and His law, refusing what is good (Romans 8:7). The Dead will not only seek to alleviate sin-guilt through Dead works; they will also do the works that lead to Death and separation.

> ***Now the works of the flesh are evident:*** *sexual immorality, impurity, sensuality, idolatry, sorcery, enmity, strife, jealousy, fits of anger, rivalries, dissensions, divisions, envy, drunkenness, orgies, and things like these. I warn you, as I warned you before, that those who do such things will not inherit the kingdom of God.*
>
> Galatians 5:19-21 (ESV)

The status of our souls is determined solely by our acceptance or denial of Jesus Christ as savior (Ephesians 2:8-9). There is nothing more and nothing less. Only believers will be with Yahweh forever. Unbelievers will be separated from Yahweh forever. The Living will be made fit to dwell in the presence of the intense holiness of their Creator, whereas the Dead will be fitted to dwell in painful darkness forever.

What is gained by unmerited favor cannot be lost by unsavory behavior. But by no means should the debauchery of Darkness be encouraged or accepted. We must battle those desires in ourselves and help others who struggle against the Flesh. We know that we all stumble in many ways, but that doesn't mean that we should surrender to the Flesh willingly. Even though we see the good, we ought to do and don't always do it. We are aware that the problem is with our body that is subject to death. For our spirit has been purified before the Lord, that is if we stand before Him in Christ Jesus, our Lord. The Spirit and the Flesh are opposed to one another, so that we are frustrated in our efforts. The good things we desire to do are not always carried out. But the bad things we continue to fight and resist seem to follow us out of the grave. We buried them in only to continue to disturb us. Never mind the struggle, for it will not be worth comparing with the glory that will be revealed in us. The Dawn has already manifested, for Christ is the Light that shines in the Dark. We must only Walk in the Light as He is in the Light so that we may know the One who has called us. We must know Him, for it is right that we do. The Dead are the way they are because of their damnable identity crisis. If they realized who the Lord is and who they are before Him, then perhaps they would repent from their sinful behavior and receive forgiveness of their sins.

We are justified by grace through faith, not by works, so that no one may boast. Dead works never brought anyone to Life. However, our involvement in God's redemptive plan certainly includes our actions and intentions. He wants us to participate and hopefully cooperate with His will. Which is by no means burdensome (Matthew 11:29-30).

It may help us to think in more practical terms. This subject is already riddled with uncertainty, so it deserves sufficient clarification. Now in order to further distinguish between the Living and the Dead, let us imagine a church filled with people on the inside and Zombies on the outside. The actions and behaviors of the people involved depict their heart in at least as much as the outflow of the heart is produced by what is stored up from within it. A good tree doesn't produce bad fruit, and a bad tree doesn't produce good fruit.

> *A good man brings good things out of the **good stored up** in his heart,*
> *and an evil man brings evil things out of the **evil stored up** in his heart.*
> *For the mouth speaks what the heart is full of.*
>
> Luke 6:45 (NIV)

There will be people on the inside of the church looking in, that is to say, they will be concerned with matters of salvation and the needs of others. These are the Worthy Walkers. But there will be people inside the church looking out. They may be in the church, but they are not members of the body of Christ. They will be looking out for their own needs. I dare not say that I know the salvific status of someone else unless drastic measures are met. But I can say that they must be warned.

Similarly, there will be the Dead on the outside looking to get in. They may not be Living but may have a type of godliness that denies its true power (2 Timothy 3:5). Ostensibly presenting themselves as something they are not, these are likewise a group of people who are to be carefully warned. Those who are inside looking out and outside looking in compose Sleep Walkers in that they are difficult for us to discern. (Though God knows their true identity, whether Dead or Alive). We must carefully observe them because their actions may betray their intentions, and their behavior may belittle their identity.

And yet, who are we to judge others all the while we ourselves may be struggling with sin (Matthew 7:3-5 and James 2:1-13). I know at one time I was on the outside looking out, A dreadful Zombie. I was a Deadman Walking after my own carnal desires. Righteousness was repulsive to me. I didn't want anything God was offering. But He had victorious mercy on me and delivered me from absolute Death. His mercy was greater than the judgment I deserved (James 2:13).

The Zombie Apocalypse is overflowing with enemies of the cross of Christ (Philippians 3:18-19). But suffice it to say that despite the foggy intersection of the Living and the Dead, there will Dawn a Day of radiant clarity. Yahweh knows beyond the shadow of a doubt who is Alive and who is Dead. More than that, He knows who is His.

> *Even the darkness is not dark to you; the night is bright as the day,*
> ***for darkness is as light with you.***
> Psalms 139:12 (ESV)

Jesus is Lord?

We praise God to know him and rightly to be known by him (Galatians 4:9). Indeed, knowing God IS eternal Life (John 17:3). The dynamic relationship He has graciously offered to us is the foundation of our everlasting existence. The fact that we remain in the World is not evidence of his absence or unreliability but rather the truth about our calling and His plan. We are not meant to remove ourselves from the World and, in so doing, remove our righteous influence with it. Though the acts of the Dead can be repulsive at times, we must not think that we could completely remove ourselves; otherwise, we would have to leave the world entirely (1 Corinthians 5:10)! But God has placed his Spirit in us that we would not only have a promise to propel us through the World but also so that we might do his work in a worthy manner.

> *Therefore, I want you to understand that no one speaking in the Spirit*
> *of God ever says, "Jesus is accursed!" and no one can say,*
> *"Jesus is Lord" except in the Holy Spirit.*
> 1 Corinthians 12:3 (ESV)

The Scripture says that only by the incredible indwelling of the Holy Spirit, may we say that Jesus is Lord. But as we just considered the confusion that is produced by Sleep Walkers, it is clear to see a similar problem emerging. Some may say Jesus is Lord but in a lying confession. Others may say (God forbid) that Jesus is cursed. In their blasphemy, they speak wrongly about God only later to regret their error. And to be sure, the only unforgivable sin is the sin of unbelief. The Holy Spirit is the one who has come to convict the world about sin, righteousness, and judgment (John 16:8). These things point to our blessed Savior, Jesus Christ.

Now obviously, the Worthy Walker will gladly and repeatedly proclaim that Jesus is Lord. They will do so with worshipful hearts by the Spirit and in truth. And clearly, the Dead Walker will waste no time denouncing Jesus as a fraud or fairy tale.

But there is an inevitable event fast approaching wherein all will look upon the one whom we pierced. At that time, all will correctly acknowledge him as the Lord Jesus Christ, who suffered as the servant of Yahweh and is now given a name above all names. This will come because of what He suffered upon the cross when He laid his life down for us.

> *Therefore God has highly exalted him and bestowed on him the name that is above every name, so that at the name of Jesus every knee should bow, in heaven and on earth and under the earth, and every tongue confess that* **Jesus Christ is Lord, to the glory of God the Father**.
>
> Philippians 2:9-11 ESV

The only question is whether we will choose to bow now and confess truthfully that Jesus Christ is Lord to the glory of God the Father. If we do so, we affirm our eternal association with him. Or will we do the antithesis? Hurtling insults at the Son of God just as they did when He was Lifted Up. The Dead will continue to do so until the Day He returns. But even these adversaries and all the evil forces in the spiritual realm will be required to acquiesce to the truth of His Lordship when He appears. Far be it from me to wait until it is too late. I will welcome the glory of God and hasten that Day. Even now, I say, come quickly, Lord Jesus.

THE THIN GRAY LINE

The wise person has his eyes in his head, but the fool walks in darkness.
And yet I perceived that the same event happens to all of them.

Ecclesiastes 2:14 (ESV)

What kind of a creature is it that has eyes but cannot See, has ears but cannot Hear, and a heart but cannot will itself to turn away from the path that is an inevitable Dead end. Invariably the Zombie Walks through No Man's Land perceiving no way, no truth, and no life. In this aimless existence, their minds are darkened and unchanged. They feed on what they think is adding to their life, but in reality, those choices are only Death.

For the Zombie, there is no resistance toward the insatiable appetite for sin. They feed on the Flesh because their Undead existence depends upon it. They long to taste something that makes them feel alive even if only for a fleeting moment. There are others who do not appear to be feasting so boldly and openly upon the Flesh as so many Zombies do. This is little more than an illusion, as we shall soon see.

A Sleep Walker depends upon falsities, fantasies, dreams, and illusions to motivate their own Dead works. Undeniably there is crossover between the truly Living and the truly Dead in this dichotomy. But our vigilance must remain steadfast if we consider ourselves to be fully Awake, sober, and alert so that we can carry out our calling.

We who are children of the Light and of the Day must no longer Walk in Darkness. Many of us remember our old ways. But we must cast off those dying memories and forge ahead. When necessary, we expose the evil deeds of Darkness for we know better now. We see how it alienated us from the Source of Life. May all of God's people walk according to Yahweh's will for their life with more cognizance and clarity.

LIBERTY OR DEATH?

We have been given an incredible gift of grace that frees us from the enslavement to sin and Death. But shame belongs to those who misuse their freedom to indulge in the Flesh. Undoubtedly there are activities that cannot be easily divided into categories. But the Bible has not left this issue unaddressed. There is no sin that becomes a liberty, but there certainly are some liberties that can become sin. The maturity of an individual can often be determined by the way that they react to their liberties being challenged. Some things remain off-limits both before and after revival, such as sexual immorality, idolatry, lying, stealing, and the like. But as we can observe in the Corinthian church, the issue of eating food sacrificed to idols was considered a sin to some and a liberty to others. Jesus himself said that it was not what entered into a person that defiled them but specifically that which comes out of their heart. Are we too attached to our liberties? Perhaps we are, and if so, then we run the risk of holding on to our liberties to the point of Death.

The blurry area between the Living and the Dead makes it very difficult to distinguish between those who are inside looking out and outside looking in. What do we make of the wolves in sheep's clothing and the sheep in wolves' clothing? How should we address the incoherence of such a position? Blind tolerance and acceptance are not recommended (1 Corinthians 5). There will, in fact, be only one reasonable stance. Because all have the same need for salvation, therefore all will be given the urgent message of watchfulness. Truly the Sleep Walker, who is nothing more than the illusion between the Living and the Dead, must be woken up. Their condition is not favorable; in fact, it would seem that Jesus would rather have us hot or cold because the lukewarm are those whom He spits out of his mouth (Revelation 3:16). The groups that are being deciphered are between the goats and the sheep. The parable of the wheat and the tares also illustrates the concept of the Dead intermixed with the Living even until the end. Clearly, there is no third grouping before the Lord. But many are they who enter into the wide path that leads to destruction, thinking that they have chosen the path to life. This is a grave error on their part. The converse is also true. There will be some who enter into heaven who outwardly are not those that we would expect, but before the Lord, they have been deemed righteous (Lot, Samson, and the thief on the cross). Therefore, we must apply our attention to this matter with seriousness because we never know who may need to be roused from their Deadly Slumber.

There are two ways to address the issue. One way is for the Sleep Walker to be made aware by alarming them of their precarious standing (2 Corinthians 5:11). The blind cannot lead the blind, or both will fall into a pit, so it is crucial that we examine ourselves as well. But the second way to resolve the problem of Sleep Walkers is to disassociate from them (2 Thessalonians 3:6-15). Removing them from the Church or, if necessary, removing yourself from their fellowship. All of this must be done with gentleness but seriousness. We are not to treat Sleep Walkers as enemies but as brothers who need to be alarmed by their precarious situation (2 Thessalonians 3:15). If they truly belong to Christ, then they will exhibit a response that is in keeping with the Way we have been taught (Ephesians 4:20-24).

> *For **godly grief** produces a repentance that leads to **salvation without regret**, whereas worldly grief produces **death**.*
> 2 Corinthians 7:10 (ESV)

The Sleep Walker can avoid this if only they would awaken from their slumber in sin and respond spiritually. But it is all too easy to neglect such a great salvation (Hebrews or Peter?). Many are they that do not heed the call to be prepared and watchful. It is a fearful thing to fall into the hands of the living God.

God told Cain that sin, personified as a vicious beast, was crouching at the door seeking to overthrow him but that he had the power to master it. Regrettably, he failed and was mastered by the sin crouching at his door. Cain became a beast himself in murdering his brother. He was not able to defeat the Zombie within. By the Spirit, we must put to death the deeds of the Flesh or suffer the consequences.

We know that no one, except for Jesus, walked in sinless perfection (Philippians 3). We are called to a holy life, not by our own works necessarily, but rather by faith in the awesome life of Christ. We all know what it is to stumble and fail, but hopefully, we also know what it is to rise up and overcome our setbacks. Therefore, we can all sympathize with the struggling believer and perhaps even the restless Zombie because we all experience different struggles throughout our lives. For that reason, we must learn to utilize our various challenges in ways that may even encourage others who have the same struggles (1 Corinthians 10:13, 2 Corinthians 1:3-7).

> *And we urge you, brothers, admonish the idle, encourage the fainthearted, help the weak, **be patient with them all**.*
> 1 Thessalonians 5:14 (ESV)

Ripe or Ruin?

We must Walk wisely as we deal with the ungodly. Our every action is under greater scrutiny because we have aligned ourselves with Jesus Christ. When we address the crooked ways of our generation, we must do so in gentleness and respect or run the risk of doing more harm than good. No one likes to be roused from a deep sleep in a disturbing manner. The same can be said of the way we ought to interact with the Sleeper.

It is acceptable to correct a divisive person a few times before disbanding from their fellowship. When dealing with a brother or sister in Christ, it is worth the hassle if they turn from their sin. Peacemakers sow peace and reap a harvest of righteousness. Every response should be administered with meekness and respect; otherwise, the intended outcome may not surface.

What activities and behaviors are most commonly surrounded by uncertainty? From what we can infer through the Scriptures, it would seem that matters of liberty pertained very often to personal pleasure and convenience. For instance, some of the people that Paul addressed in the Corinthian church were struggling with their newfound freedom, while others were struggling with the lack of maturity from their peers. This issue was most obvious in the eating of meat sacrificed to idols. For those who came from a background teeming with idol worship, this may have been a boundary that they could not easily cross. However, Paul made the case that an idol is really nothing (1 Corinthians 8:4) unless, of course, someone gives it power by their own perception. For indeed, there are evil and vile forces in the World, but they do not compare in any sense to the Most High God. Therefore, it was possible for the mature in faith to eat meat sacrificed to idols so long as they maintained in their hearts the truth about Yahweh and did not do this in such a way as to contaminate a feeble believer with the false perceptions. If our liberties cause our brothers and sisters in Christ to stumble into sin, then it is our responsibility to correct the misunderstanding and remove the offense if necessary.

> *If anyone, then, knows the good they ought to do and doesn't do it,*
> ***it is sin for them.***
> James 4:17 (NIV)

Why would we cause a beloved brother or sister in Christ to stagger due to our mere comfort and pleasure? That is not what we have learned about The Way. Surely not all of us deal with meat sacrificed to idols. At least as far as we know. But there are other seemingly neutral choices that can have negative effects if placed in the wrong context. Perhaps most notably would be that of enjoying alcohol. There is nothing inherently wrong with alcohol. But the error arises from the heart within. Again, Jesus taught that it was not that which entered a person that defiled them but rather that which came out of them. Paul also echoes this idea when he teaches that food will not bring us any closer to God because, like fleshly works, it cannot earn righteousness (1 Corinthians 8:8). But we must guard against self-deception even here because of the significance of our decisions. The ramifications of our actions not only effect our lives but also those around us. So, if we call ourselves people of God, then let us produce the ripe fruit that is appropriate with our profession of faith in Christ.

> ***To the pure, all things are pure, but to the defiled and unbelieving,***
> ***nothing is pure****; but both their minds and their consciences are defiled.*
> ***They profess to know God, but they deny him by their works****. They*
> *are detestable, disobedient, unfit for any good work."*
> Titus 1:15-16 (NIV)

The **LIVING DEAD** Revival Guide

DRIFTING OFF TO DEATH

We must pay the most careful attention, therefore, to what we have heard,
so that we do not drift away.

Hebrews 2:1 (NIV)

We have already concluded that the Dead are notoriously depraved. Their behavior is hostile toward Yahweh and his people. They, both in the daylight and in the darkness, practice things that should not be done. Their way is destructive to themselves and others. Woe unto them who so carelessly sow their destruction and reap their death.

But not all sin is easily detected. Some sin goes on ahead of a person while other sins may linger behind only to be revealed at a later time (1 Timothy 4). The unseen sins of some may lead us to think that there are no sins to be counted or corrected. But that is not the case. For we know that all have sinned (Romans 3:23), and whoever claims to be without sin makes God out to be a liar, thus showing the void of truth (1 John 1:8-10).

It is not always an active resistance to the prompting of the Holy Spirit that we witness. Occasionally it is sluggish lethargy that indicates an area of concern. Again, we ask ourselves how we may know who belongs to the Living and who belongs to the Dead? God is not demanding our perfection in action as if we could possible achieve such a standard. No, rather, He is requiring faith in the truth concerning His son Jesus Christ. To disregard such a great salvation would certainly come back to haunt us. Jesus warned that every idle word would be judged. He is the God who judges the heart and intentions of us all. He knows the secrets whispered in the ear and the deed done in darkness. Others hide themselves from Him, thinking that He does not see, hear, care, or even exist. But in the end, their delusions will run dry, and they will face the Lord with horrible fear.

Busybodies and meddlers delve into matters not pertaining to them in search of something juicy to sink their teeth into, if only for a moment. They devote themselves to the bustling of gossip instead of devotion to the Gospel. Perhaps it is our family and loved ones who seem unconcerned about the evil days we are facing. At other times it may be people we have never actually met. But regardless of our association to them, we have an obligation to all people, particularly to those who belong to the family of the Faith. We must live out the Gospel with our every effort, in the hope that some may turn from their sins and follow us as we follow Christ.

Worthy Walkers are those who adhere to the Way and are, in effect, Ambassadors of Christ. We are compelled by the love of Christ to communicate the seriousness of sin. We remember the kindness and severity of God in our lives that brought us to our knees.

Therefore, we should treat the Sleep Walker with a similar approach to how we would with a Zombie. Make no mistake; all Sleep Walkers align with one group or the other. A Sleep Walker, in truth, is either Dead or Alive, and there is no obfuscation before the Lord God who judges all. Similarly, our purpose remains the same regardless of our own incomplete assessment. Our responsibility is to convey the Gospel, and if necessary, we will use words. But if we are to use words, then let it be in truth and with action (1 John 3:18) and speaking when possible the very words of God found in the Scriptures (1 Peter 4:11). All have a need to hear the gospel truth; even those who have already heard and believed stand to gain by hearing again the reason for their salvation. It is wise to be reminded of what we have already been taught, even though we may already be firmly established in the truth (2 Peter 1:12). May all of the Saints of God put their full effort into reaching the lost, warning the idle, and speaking Life to the Dead.

IDENTIFYING DRIFTERS

Take care, brothers, lest there be in any of you an evil, unbelieving heart,
leading you to fall away from the living God.
Hebrews 3:12 (ESV)

The evidence of spiritual fruit is most discernible from up close. It is not easy to determine how healthy a tree is from afar. How could we expect to know whether or not another person is living in alignment with The Way of Life without actually being involved in their life? Of course, there is the obvious repulsion that comes with the Walking Dead, but our fear belongs not to those who can destroy the body but rather to God, who has the power to destroy body and soul in hell. And that is our fear for the Dead, that they will experience the Second Death, which is the lake of fire and eternal separation from Yahweh. Despite the seriousness of the situation, there is an alarming lack of desperation by those who are perishing. The natural tendency is to drift away from righteousness into the murky waters of sin. This backsliding behavior is of great concern to us who have escaped the corruption of the World through knowing our Lord and Savior Jesus Christ. We cannot afford to become entangled again in the old ways of our now-dead self because that would be worse off than we were at the beginning (2 Peter 2:20). How could we bare to continue in sin once we have experienced the goodness of the Lord? The Scriptures are abundantly clear that the kingdom of heaven will have no place for those who make a habitual practice out of sin. The struggle between the Spirit and the Flesh is very real. Sometimes the struggle is too real, eliciting failure. But our mighty God did not abandon us to the pit while we were his Undead enemies, and He will not fail us now that we have committed our faith to Him.

> *A heart at **peace gives life to the body**, but **envy rots the bones**.*
> Proverbs 14:30 (NIV)

The value of fellowship cannot be overstated. In times of trouble, insufferable temptation, and calamity, we can unite together with our brothers and sisters to find hope and peace. Surely a great cloud of witnesses who have experienced the same trials that we have faced and hear how they are still facing them surrounds us. We can even rally around the example of those brothers and sisters who have Spiritually fallen asleep and still gain incredible insight. The apostle Paul describes a time in his life when all seemed lost, and his life was on the line. He despaired to the point of exhaustion, for a moment, believing all hope was lost. However, his account of this terrible time came with great wisdom.

> *Indeed, we felt that we had received the **sentence of death**. But that was to make us rely not on ourselves but on **God who raises the dead**. He delivered us from such a **deadly peril**, and he will deliver us. On him, we have set our hope that he will deliver us again.*
> 2 Corinthians 2:9-10 (ESV)

This may be the place where the backslider and, in effect, the Sleep Walker find their biggest problem. The combination of plights derived from the unfruitful soils in the Parable of the Sower seem to be breathing down our collective necks. The hard path is given no time. The rocky ground faces tribulation and persecution. The thorny ground chokes out life by the cares of the word and deceitfulness of riches. However, we are promised that God's people will not be burdened beyond what we can withstand. No matter how hopeless, crushing, and tempting, God will always provide a way for his people (1 Corinthians 10:13). We will overcome through Him who gives us the victory.

> *Here is a trustworthy saying: **if we died with him, we will also live with him**; if we endure, we will also reign with him. If we disown him, he will also disown us; if we are faithless, he will remain faithful, for he cannot disown himself.*
> 2 Timothy 2:11-13 (ESV)

Talon Schneider

Unalarmed

What rest is there to be had then for all of the restless vagabonds? We all toil day and night, and at some level, we know that what we gain in this life will just pass to the next person, and we will be forgotten (Ecclesiastes). There is a drastic difference between physical rest and the kind of Rest that God gives. Certainly, He provides rest to those He loves; He also provides for the needs of those who rest (Psalm 127:2). But all others who do not find the Rest of God can be sure that everything they touch as fading away with every use. Therefore, it matters not if we do not touch, do not handle, and do not taste the things that are hoarded in these last days. Knowing that all these things will come to an end, a fiery end, we ought to make every effort to live holy lives in the Fear of the Lord. Those who observe such a Fear know true wisdom and true Rest.

> The **fear of the LORD** is the beginning of wisdom, and knowledge of the Holy One is understanding.
>
> Proverbs 9:10 (NIV)

The Living Dead have a throat gripping fear of death, whether they know it or not. There are many reasons to fear death. The uncertainty of what lays beyond the grave, unpredictability of demise, and the multifaceted pain it represents all contribute to the enslavement the Dead experience. They should fear it. But their fear is incomplete because they disregard the wrath of God against sin. So much time is wasted wandering in No Man's Land looking for something of value. Perhaps one day, something valuable is found by an eager seeker, but what does it gain them? A few brief moments of satisfaction and gratification are quickly brought to an end. Even if someone could exchange their soul for all the world, that would be the ultimate vanity. Nothing temporal can compare with the eternal. The soul is eternal, and its destination is everlasting. Why, then, is there such a lack of concern when death and looms at every moment? The hardness of heart and insensitivity of the Dead are condemning them to perpetual dissatisfaction. Emptiness is clearly at the core of their obsessive gathering and collecting and hoarding. But more will never be enough. Their restless ways will follow them to the grave and dwell with them forever. Consider the call to heed the words of Wisdom.

> For **those who find me find life** and receive favor from the Lord. But those who fail to find me harm themselves; **all who hate me love death**.
>
> Proverbs 8:35-36 (ESV)

The LIVING DEAD Revival Guide

Zombies fear death more than God; they hate wisdom and find death unavoidable. In all of its forms, death is taking away, all of creation groans in decay and destitution (Romans 8:22-25). But the wise find Life because the Fear of the Lord is the wisdom of the Way. A time is coming and indeed has arrived when the Dead will hear the voice of the Son of God, and those who hear will Live (John 5:25). But woe unto those who hear the word concerning the Son of God and ignorantly oppose the gracious gift of God. True Revival of the Living Dead requires that they awaken from their sin induced slumber and rise with the Son of God.

> *This is why it is said:* ***"Wake up, sleeper, rise from the dead, and Christ will shine on you."***
>
> Ephesians 5:14 (ESV)

We were those who were Dead in our sins but are not so any longer. At times it may be difficult to be conscious of our past failures, but we must not forget that we no longer stand condemned (Romans 8:1). We have an obligation then, not to the Flesh, but to the Spirit of Christ in us to shine like the Light that He said we are. If a Light, then it must be a bright one, worthy of waking the Sleeping Dead. And if we are called Salt as well then, we will preserve Life and present the message as carriers of a most holy hope. We are not called Salt and Light without reason (Matthew 5:13-14). Salt preserves Dead Meat, and Light rouses those in Deep Sleep. But God forbid that we lose our flavor or that we hide ourselves from our true purpose. Imagine where you would be if the chain of faithful followers that lead to your believing the Word preached to you had not Walked Worthy. Would you be where you are now if they had refused the call of Wisdom? Would you still fear death if they had not held tightly to the Fear of the Lord?

> *The people **living in darkness** have seen a great light; on those living in the land of the shadow of death, a **light has dawned.***
>
> Matthew 4:16 (NIV)

NIGHT TERRORS

> ***For they cannot rest until they do evil; they are robbed of sleep till they make someone stumble.*** *They eat the bread of wickedness and drink the wine of violence.*
>
> Proverbs 4:16-17 (NIV)

Sleep is not easily found for the Walking Dead. Rest is even more elusive. For only in Christ is our Restlessness taken away. God grants sleep to those He loves, and He provides for them even while they do not toil (Psalm 127:2). But Zombies search and grope about as in darkness without finding what they need. Instead, they settle upon a ration of vice, and they quench their endless thirst with violence. Even the mere thoughts of the Dead are tantamount to physical assault. Hatred becomes murder, and lust becomes molestation. Peace will not be found in such spiritual crimes; there will only be consequences.

> *He makes a pit, digging it out, and falls into the hole that he has made. His mischief returns upon his own head, and* **on his own skull his violence descends**.
>
> Psalms 7:15-16 (ESV)

Many during the days of Moses could not see clearly what was coming. Not even those who read of him afterward understand completely. Some look only with their physical sight, but we can see through faith. This is because we can only see once the veil is removed from our eyes (2 Corinthians 3:12-16). Joshua likewise was not able to grant the Rest that Yahweh alone provides (4:8). This is the Rest we must strive to attain! Christ beckons us to trust him in this way. For He alone can relieve the soul and his yoke is the one that produces true peace for those who carry alongside him.

> *Come to me, all you who are weary and burdened, and* ***I will give you rest***. *Take my yoke upon you and learn from me, for I am gentle and humble in heart, and* ***you will find rest for your souls***. *For my yoke is easy, and my burden is light.*
>
> Matthew 11:28-30 (NIV)

Our participation in God's plan of salvation is vital to the full experience of Life. Cooperation with God is so vital that the first disobedience brought upon all of us a blight of intrinsic defiance toward Him (Romans 5:12). Adam and Eve surely Died on that day that they ate of the forbidden fruit, but God had greater grace prepared for them and all of us if we trust Him. From the Beginning, the Sovereign Lord has commanded our cooperation in the midst of our volition. The Creator graciously welcomes his creation to partake of his divine nature and escape the corruption in the World caused by evil desires, if we would only hold fast to His promises.

The LIVING DEAD Revival Guide

> ***His divine power*** *has given us everything we need for a godly life through our knowledge of him who called us by his own glory and goodness. Through these, he has given us his very **great and precious promises**, so that through them you may participate in the **divine nature, having escaped the corruption in the world caused by evil desires**.*
>
> 2 Peter 1:3-4 (NIV)

The undeniable reality of our true nature stands before us. We will not simply "drift" into the Rest that comes through Christ. We will not stumble our way into his fellowship and Kingdom. The Kingdom of God must be sought earnestly and vigorously (Matthew 11:12 and Luke 16:16). We must work out our salvation with fear and trembling while God works in us to will and act according to his sovereign plan (Philippians 2:12-13).

Of course, we cannot earn entrance to such a holy place but may only enter this Heavenly Rest by faith in the finished work of Jesus Christ upon the cross. We must turn away from evil, and zealously seek peace (Psalm 34:14). We cannot let the Rest offered to us be rescinded by rebellion.

> *Let us, therefore, **strive to enter that rest**, so that no one may fall by the same sort of disobedience.*
>
> Hebrews 4:11 (ESV)

BEYOND THE BASICS

Clearly, the Rest being discussed is more than physical rest. The concept involves the basic essence of the Christian experience. The very foundation of our faith being based not on who we are or what we have done but rather upon who the Lord Jesus Christ is in his holiness and righteousness and what He accomplished on the cross. Who we are must be inexorably connected to who He is! But we must continue to grow and mature in our faith by not becoming idle or continually backsliding. We must advance because movement, growth, and breath, among many other things, exemplify Life.

> *Therefore, we must progress beyond the **elementary instructions about Christ** and move on to maturity, not laying this foundation again: **repentance from dead works and faith in God, teaching about baptisms, laying on of hands, resurrection of the dead, and eternal judgment**.*
>
> Hebrews 6:1-2 (NET)

To be saved from sin, we must cease our lawless behavior that rendered all of us Dead on arrival, no better than aimless Zombies. Now we have repented from our *Dead works*, which alone were not enough to gain God's favor. For just as faith without works is Dead (James 2:26), so too it could be said that works without faith are Dead (Romans 14:23b). They must combine to be effectual. But neither obsessive works nor ostensible faith alone is sufficient evidence of being born anew. Thus, the Fruit of the Spirit comes through faith that works with God and for God.

> **For by him, all things were created**, *in heaven and on earth, visible and invisible, whether thrones or dominions or rulers or authorities—**all things were created through him and for him**.*
> Colossians 1:16 (ESV)

Without *faith in God*, it is impossible to be saved from our sin. For it is the one who confesses that Jesus is Lord, believing in the heart that God raised him from the dead, who will be saved. Righteousness comes from the believing heart and salvation from this gospel affirmation.

> *And you, who once were **alienated and hostile in mind, doing evil deeds**, he has now **reconciled in his body of flesh by his death**, in order to present you holy and blameless and above reproach before him, **if indeed you continue in the faith, stable and steadfast, not shifting from the hope of the gospel that you heard**, which has been proclaimed in all creation under heaven, and of which I, Paul, became a minister.*
> Colossians 1:21-23 (ESV)

Now this confession is made surer by our *baptism*, which in itself is a symbol of our association with the death, burial, and resurrection of Christ. We believe that in our baptism is not only a public declaration of new Life in Christ but the death of our old self!

> *Baptism, which corresponds to this, now saves you, **not as a removal of dirt from the body but as an appeal to God for a good conscience**, through the resurrection of Jesus Christ.*
> 1 Peter 3:21 (ESV)

With this in mind, we are called to Walk in newness of Life, to be Worthy Walkers. The *traditions* that we have received have been handed down to us via the authority of those who first saw the risen Christ and have since then offered us an example to follow. For we maintain that the message we have received is not only the message of men, but the message of God dispersed by men (1 Thessalonians 2:13). Therefore, we are a long line of Christ-followers. Some of us having heard the message with a saving faith in remarkably lonely moments and others of us having received the laying on of hands authorizing leadership and servitude and gospel reception. All of this brought to completion not only by what we have learned, or received, or heard, or seen but by that which was practiced before us (Philippians 4:9).

> *Now we command you, brothers, in the name of our Lord Jesus Christ, that you keep away from any brother who is **walking in idleness and not in accord with the tradition that you received from us**.*
> 2 Thessalonians 3:6 (ESV)

The resurrection of Jesus Christ is more than tradition, however. It is not a cunningly devised story (2 Peter 1:16). Rather many who lived during the events and lived afterwards in persecution witnessed it. But not only did they witness these events; they also understood what the scriptures had been speaking in regard to the glory and suffering of the Messiah! Indeed, if Jesus has not been raised from the dead, then we Christians are the most pitiable of all people (1 Corinthians 15:19). But if Jesus has been raised from the dead, then we too will be raised with him, if His Spirit is in us. Even the Dead will be raised again. But for them, it will be as a nightmare made all too real.

> *And **many of those who sleep in the dust of the earth shall awake, some to everlasting life, and some to shame and everlasting contempt**. And those who are wise shall shine like the brightness of the sky above; and those who turn many to righteousness, like the stars forever and ever.*
> Daniel 12:2-3 (ESV)

There is a resurrection for both the righteous and the wicked. The righteous will not be condemned because they stand in Christ, but the wicked will face judgment and torment. They will have to give an account for every idle word and every evil deed. Their *judgment will be eternal*, and its pain will cause much weeping and gnashing of teeth. All must give an answer for the way that they have lived.

> *And just as it is appointed for man to **die once, and after that comes judgment**, so Christ, having been offered once to bear the sins of many,*

> *will appear a second time,* **not to deal with sin but to save those who are eagerly waiting for him.**
>
> Hebrews 9:27-28 (ESV)

Our temporary life provides the grounds by which we must choose our eternal existence. We must not harden our hearts to the voice of the Holy Spirit. He convicts the World of sin, righteousness, and judgment. But the World and the Zombies infesting it have altogether become callous to the One who can heal them. They do not want God and have no place for him in their deadness of heart. But our obstinance could not stop the magnificent grace and love of Christ. Some disillusioned Sleep Walkers believe they can be saved on their final day, but the only day we know that we have is today. We do not know when we will die, and therefore, we cannot risk living one more day without true Life.

> *As it is said,* "***Today****, if you hear his voice, do not harden your hearts as in the rebellion.*"
>
> Hebrews 3:15 (ESV)

There is no middle ground; there is no blurry line. There is no ambivalence. The proverbial line in the sand has been drawn. That line divides the Living and the Dead, and before God, the book of Life will be opened. If any name is not found written in the book of Life, then they will be permanently cast out of the glory and presence of God. We know all of us begin devastatingly depraved and that none of us is without sin (Romans 3:23). None of us is righteous. None of us deserve to be spared. But the righteous requirement of the law has been met by the perfect life of Jesus Christ. Indeed, He was cursed on behalf of us, the truly accursed.

> **Christ redeemed us from the curse of the law by becoming a curse for us**—*for it is written, "Cursed is everyone who is hanged on a tree."*
>
> Galatians 3:13 (ESV)

The divine transaction of Christ's indestructible life for the ever-corrupted Walking Dead has already been accomplished; it is completely finished (Hebrews 7:16). Now the choice between Life and Death hangs between faith and doubt. Those who Live will walk by faith, and those who die will die by their own hand. There will be no favoritism, only truth. God will judge with flawless determination. He will separate the goats from the sheep, the tares from the wheat, and the Dead from the Living.

The **LIVING DEAD** Revival Guide

For we know him who said, "Vengeance is mine; I will repay."
*And again, "The Lord will judge his people. **It is a fearful thing to fall**
into the hands of the living God."*

Hebrews 10:30-31 (ESV)

Sadly, many are caught up in the sinful snares that continually plague No Man's Land. They are acting as captives who appear to love their captor despite the pain and suffering inflicted upon them. They are in need of much help. There is a Helper who knows what we need in those deep pains we have experienced. Terror strikes them down, but few turn from sin to the One who can heal them. They are corrupted by their evil desires that permeate the fallen World (2 Peter 1:3-4).

They drift in and out of danger as if to sense for a moment the thrill and value of life only to see it fade away once more. But be sure of this; their end will be destruction if they do not repent of their sins and turn in faith toward Jesus Christ. Even the thief on the cross, whom many perceived as a Deadman, had the sense to turn to the one whose wounds can heal others.

Their refusal of Him only leads to soul gripping grief. Restlessness overtakes them day and night. There is no escape from what they fear. Death haunts them, and in a way, they become death as they live only to see everything around them die before their own inevitable demise. Such horror can scarcely be compared. What more will it take before changes are made?

In spite of all this, they still sinned; despite his wonders, they did not believe.
So he made their days vanish like a breath and their years in terror.

Psalms 78:32-33 (ESV)

Nothing can satiate their desires because nothing that they desire is righteous. Though they may appear to desire a form of righteousness and Godliness, it is nullified by their motivations. The Lord will not be mocked; He knows the hearts and minds of men. If good is done, but not for God's sake, will God ultimately be pleased? Will the good that is done in order to make one appear more righteous be received as holy and true? I thank God that I am not the judge of such matters. But we can gather some measure of clarity as we rely upon the Word, He has given us. It is unbiased and without error in its evaluation of our condition before the one to whom we must give an account of our lives.

For the word of God is living and active, *sharper than any two-edged sword, piercing to the division of soul and of spirit, of joints and of marrow, and **discerning the thoughts and intentions of the heart**.*

Hebrews 4:12 (ESV)

The Holy Spirit will guide what we can learn about the Holy Scripture. It is not as though we cannot see the obviously devious actions of the Dead. But we will render patience toward that which we cannot know for sure. What we can see, however, is unbearably flaunted before us in broad daylight. For some, it is the desires of the Flesh; for others, it is the desires of the Eyes, and for others still, it may be the pride of this fleeting life (1 John 2:16). But one thing is certain; the Dead are not Living as they ought to be.

> *See, this alone I found, that God made man upright,*
> *but **they have sought out many schemes**.*
> Ecclesiastes 7:29 (ESV)

Some would say that there is nothing new under the sun. Some would suggest that everything that can be done has already been done. That may be correct in part, but it is not the whole truth. A dark reality persists. The living Dead crave sin so desperately that they invent *new forms of evil* (Romans 1:30). The evil that is being popularized by them can quite literally captivate. The slavery of sin and wickedness is a terrible bane upon the tormented souls of mankind. The machinations of many evil minds will continue to defile many until the very end.

> ***The evildoer must continue to do evil**, and the one who is morally filthy must continue to be filthy. **The one who is righteous must continue to act righteously,** and the one who is holy must continue to be holy.*
> Revelation 22:11 (NET)

The Worthy Walker surely has been set free from many addictions brought on by the Catalysts of sin and Death. But those who are Undead toward sin will not inherit the Kingdom of God. Such a glorious Kingdom is no place for the despicable deeds of darkness. Those who practice evil deeds will be cast into the deep darkness where there are weeping and gnashing of teeth.

Rather the Kingdom belongs to those who now consider themselves Dead to sin and Alive toward God (Romans 6:11). We are akin to an army once Dead brought back to serve our Ruler with a Life debt (Ezekiel 37). He has spoken life to our dry bones and reassembled us into the body of Christ. From here, we can envision the essence of the problem that the Dead cannot overcome own their own. They are severed from the Head, who is Christ.

The **LIVING DEAD** Revival Guide

> ***They have lost connection with the head****, from whom the whole body, supported and held together by its ligaments and sinews, grows as God causes it to grow.*
>
> Colossians 2:19 (NIV)

With God, there will be no immorality, idolatry, stealing, lying, abusing, deceiving, or anything of the sort. We cannot remain enemies of God now that he has given us new Life (1 Peter 1:3). He has called us to Walk Worthy, and that is what we will do. We will be made more so into the image of Christ because the Spirit of Christ abides in us. What a remarkable transformation He has caused in us. We who were once Dead in our sins and Walking about as Zombies have become children of God and co-heirs with Christ.

> ***And that is what some of you were****. But you were washed, you were sanctified, you were justified in the name of the Lord Jesus Christ and by the Spirit of our God.*
>
> 1 Corinthians 6:11 (NIV)

The Dead, however, find themselves in that very situation. They feed on the sin that is killing them. Their paradox abounds as they cater to their own hypostasis. They are stuck between a life Dead toward God and yet Undead toward sin. Their dreadful actions and intentions bring *sin to life* because of their reckless anarchy (Romans 7:7-12)! They are utterly trapped and will not escape their doom if they continue in their rebellious ways. They drift in and out of what they desire and what they detest. Perhaps they do this because deep within what they desire and detest above all else is actually themselves. They hate others, and in return are hated, and somewhere within harbor a hatred for their own being (Titus 3:3). They don't even know that this detriment is deep within them. But we must seek to understand their plight more fully in order to administer to them the very grace that we received in the Gospel Cure. We must warn those who Sleep in spiritual ignorance by alerting them of the coming wrath and also revealing to them the undying love of the Risen Lord Jesus Christ. This is the only way to Wake those who now Walk in a Deathly Sleep.

> *For you are all children of light, children of the day. We are not of the night or of the darkness. So then let us not sleep, as others do, but let us keep awake and be sober.*
>
> 1 Thessalonians 5:5-6 (ESV)

Talon Schneider

AWAKENING

So then, let us not be like others, **who are asleep, but let us be awake and sober.**
1 Thessalonians 5:6 (NIV)

How will we who are Alive withstand the creeping shadow that seeks to pull us under its sway? The flesh of our bodies has its own desires. Without restraint, the old nature will try to make us drift towards the dark embrace of sin and Death. This is not the Way we have learned. We know now that all those who Walk according to the Flesh and have their minds fixated on the things of the Flesh will only find Death. The mindset of the Zombie cannot please God because it cannot submit to him, nor does it want to submit. Zombies cannot please God (Romans 8:5-8). But our Walk is in the Light with Christ, for even when we stumble, we confess our sins to the One who is faithful and true. He is both the One who is just and the One who justifies through His own means. Therefore, through the power of God, we are able to stand, for indeed He will make us stand before Himself as if we had never sinned (Jude 1:24-25). This is because of the faithfulness of Christ, not because of anything we have done for ourselves. We must not be like those who Walk in spiritual darkness. That path is a Dead end. Few or perhaps none who take it ever return from its deep abyss. Despite this somber reality, many still choose to go this way.

If you faint in the day of adversity, your strength is small. Rescue those who are being taken away to death; hold back those who are stumbling to the slaughter
Proverbs 24:10-11 (ESV)

Even those who are ambiguous in their allegiance nevertheless will be divided in the end. God knows the sheep from the goats. Nothing in all creation can hide from the Creator. He is able to divide between the indiscernible things because He alone is God. Clearly, this is an issue for us who, despite many years of training in righteousness, can still be deceived by the deceitfulness of the wicked. The Spirit, however, knows the things that are unknown to us personally. He grants insight to those who listen intently to Him. Perhaps if the Saints can share the Light we have received, then those who heed it will be granted repentance unto Life.

The thief comes only to **steal and kill and destroy.**
I came that they may have **life** *and have it abundantly.*
John 10:10 (ESV)

The LIVING DEAD Revival Guide

Restlessness overtakes the Zombie because they are driven by a desire to be filled, but they can never know the fullness of God by gorging upon the Flesh. Instead, their "god" is their stomach with its greedy appetites and hunger for sensual pleasure. Glory for them is found in that which is shameful even to mention. They carouse around in broad daylight boasting arrogantly about their freedom, which in reality is enslavement to sin. Their minds are bent toward the lowly and based things of this World. There is no Light in their eyes. There is no meaning to their drudgery. With callous hearts, they attack from the shadows. Others display their destitution by how they turn away from those in need of help.

Woe unto those who Sleep in Death and denial. They cannot see nor accept this ghastly truth. This is the plight of all who remain in the Fleshly body and away from the Lord. Aimless and Restless, wandering and wanting, they cannot save themselves. But they will try. Their efforts will fail, because only through the Blood of the Spotless Lamb of God can sin be atoned for ultimately and completely. What is utterly shocking in view of the Gospel made known to us is that some could demonstrate such an indifference to its revelation. We know that we all stumble in many ways. But there are some who continually stumble and that with disregard and disdain for the Lord's teachings. But herein is the hope for those who wander and stumble; God's grace is greater than our sin (Romans 6). And for those whose faith is meager, they may yet still learn to Walk through the valley of the shadow of Death. We must strengthen the weak arms and make sturdy the legs of those who shake in shambles (Hebrews 12:12). The Lord God will strengthen, confirm, and establish us so that we can Walk Worthy of His calling.

> *God is our strong refuge;* ***he is truly our helper in times of trouble****.*
> Psalms 46:1 (NET)

For these reasons, we must become all the more vigilant in how we Walk with our risen Lord Jesus Christ. He is our Light in the Darkness. We are responsible for our own actions, and God will adjudicate their penalty or reward. But as for us, we must warn those who stand idly by as wrath and destruction draws near. Even though many have no Ears to hear these words, we must admonish them with sincerity and love. Perhaps the Dead will be turned toward Life, or the lethargic Living may be compelled to righteousness.

> *Him we proclaim,* ***warning everyone, and teaching everyone*** *with all wisdom, that we may present everyone mature in Christ.*
> Colossians 1:28 (ESV)

An alarm is sounding, and it rings clear and true. In one sense, the alarm is the message of the gospel. Indeed, all have sinned and, therefore, all deserve death, but because of the sacrifice of Jesus Christ, we can all have true life if only we would believe. In the other sense, we who have believed the Gospel become the alarm. Though we carry this treasurable message in lowly vessels, it all points to the greatness of our God. We proclaim with all the saints before us and all those who follow afterward that Jesus Christ is Lord to the glory of God the Father. Apart from this knowledge, there is no Life.

> And **this is eternal life**, that they know you the only true God, and Jesus Christ whom you have sent.
>
> John 17:3 (ESV)

The time to spiritually slumber is coming to an end because the day of Salvation is ever "*today*." There would be nothing more terrifying than to meet our Maker with a presumption of salvation only to be turned away because He never knew us (Matthew 7:22-23). Again, we are confronted with the divisive truth. True Life is a relationship with God, and therefore true Death is the absence of this right relationship. The hell that awaits all unrepentant Zombies is a realization of this truth, along with the permanent separation from any common grace or goodness or glory of God.

> *Therefore,* **knowing the fear of the Lord, we persuade others**. *But what we are is known to God, and I hope it is known also to your conscience.*
>
> 2 Corinthians 5:11 (ESV)

That fear should grip every soul and be so palpable as to leave a very real and bitter taste in the mouth. The Fear of the Lord ought to shake everything out of us that can be shaken. That is to say, whatever does not belong to the heavenly dwelling of the Saints must be removed. For we have been called to a place where there is no decay, no corruption, no decomposition, and no Death. Entropy and chaos have no place in heaven. And yet the thought of standing before Christ and being turned away should elicit such devastating fear that none would dare Walk willfully into the Darkness. But this is the case. Many claim to Walk in the Light, and yet they *are Darkness*.

> *For at one time* ***you were darkness***, *but now you are light in the Lord. Walk as children of light.*
>
> Ephesians 5:8 (ESV)

The LIVING DEAD Revival Guide

The call is clear, and we are not left in the Dark as though we had no knowledge of where we are going. Part of our conversion out of Death and into Life necessitates that we grasp firmly our salvation. We hold fast to our Savior not only because we must but also because we know how sweet this gift truly is. Our heart and our flesh may fail, but we know our God never will. It is a matter of knowledge more than it is a matter of feelings. Feelings of the heart can be led astray by various means. But knowledge of the truth remains solid throughout the ages. What has been made known to us about Jesus, like the truth, will never change. Not by one measure or mark or by any other means will it change!

We must warn the unwary and teach the unknowing. In the scripture, we have both a light for our feet and a lamp for our path (Psalm 119:105). We would do well to pay attention to it as we would to a light radiating in the deep darkness.

> *Moreover, we possess the prophetic word as an altogether reliable thing.* ***You do well if you pay attention to this as you would to a light shining in a murky place until the day dawns and the morning star rises in your hearts.***
>
> 2 Peter 1:19 (NET)

Is it not this very concept that persists as a problem? On one side, there are unscrupulous Saints, if that is really what they are. On the other side are the Dead disguised as the Living by the auspices of self-righteous deeds. The imperceptibly of the situation is what casts this nightmarish problem upon us. What will we do to save our family and neighbors from the wrath that is to come? To what lengths will we go to love as Jesus loved? There is only one answer: to the death.

> *We know that we have **passed out of death into life** because we love the brothers. **Whoever does not love abides in death**. Everyone who hates his brother is a murderer, and you know that no murderer has eternal life abiding in him.*
>
> 1 John 3:14-15 (ESV)

Our motivation is derived from Jesus Christ. It is the power of God working in us to will and to act in line with His plan of salvation (Philippians 2:13). Regardless of the side of the blurry line our neighbors may straddle, our call strides ubiquitously. Neither one should be abandoned in their current state. Both sides need help. All wakeful Worthy Walkers should achieve this realization. We are those who have awoken to the truth and cannot turn back now.

There is fixed a wide chasm of difference between the lazy but saved and the vigorous but unsaved. However, despite their differences, what remains the same is the need to warn, alarm, and awaken both sides of the thin gray line they straddle. Death and destruction are at hand!

> *While people are saying, **"There is peace and security," then sudden destruction will come upon them as labor pains come upon a pregnant woman**, and they will not escape.*
> 1 Thessalonians 5:3 (ESV)

One side may be brought to Life by the thinnest of margins, much like the thief on the cross while the other may be saved from the fire of judgment without much reward to show for it (1 Corinthians 3:15). But sadly, many will not turn from their Dead ways. They will ignorantly pursue the pleasure that is, in fact, killing them.

> *Enter by the narrow gate. For the gate is wide and the way is easy that leads to destruction, and **those who enter by it are many.***
> Matthew 7:13 (ESV)

Salvation by faith through grace is nothing to scoff at; it is the essential precursor for all Saints. Let us, therefore, not neglect this great Salvation by becoming complacent. We must work out our salvation with fear and trembling. If we do so, we will be like lights that shine in the darkness. Perhaps by the light God shines through us, some that see it may believe in its source! We must maintain reverence and purity while awaiting the return of our King and Savior (2 Corinthians 7:1). To this end, we will strive that all may be presented to Christ in maturity and unity (Ephesians 4:13).

> *Rather, **speaking the truth in love, we are to grow up in every way into him who is the head, into Christ**, from whom the whole body, joined and held together by every joint with which it is equipped, when each part is working properly, makes the body grow so that it builds itself up in love.*
> Ephesians 4:15-16 (ESV)

The **LIVING DEAD** Revival Guide

ALARM!

There is no time to wait! Now is the time of salvation, and today is the day to be saved. God did not spare those who, in the wilderness, rebelled against him. And we know judgment begins with the household of God. But even harsher judgment awaits the enemies of God. If we are caught unalarmed by the circumstances and seriousness of our sin, we will surely perish. What terror awaits the Sleep Walker, who realizes they have slept through their call? What must we know in order to help those who may not realize the danger of their condition?

> *But you, beloved, building yourselves up in your most holy faith and praying in the Holy Spirit, keep yourselves in the love of God, **waiting for the mercy of our Lord Jesus Christ that leads to eternal life. And have mercy on those who doubt; save others by snatching them out of the fire; to others show mercy with fear, hating even the garment stained by the flesh**.*
>
> Jude 1:20-23 (ESV)

I was once a doubter hell-bent on denying Christ by my actions. I was heading for the Fire that eternally consumes both the Dying and even Death itself (Revelation 20:14). I was snatched out of the Fire by those who had mercy on me and fear of the Lord. They showed me kindness, even though I looked like a Zombie in ragged and bloody clothes.

If we have been saved, then we ought to know how to reach others in need of salvation. How could we forget the means by which we were redeemed? There must be more willingness to reach the lost; otherwise, we will run the risk of seeing the good that we ought to do and not doing it. Perhaps it is a type of spiritual drowsiness that causes the believer to resist the call to evangelize. We must not be like those that Sleep in their Walk, but we must remain vigilant because the End is near. We must make every effort to enter the Rest of Christ, not the rest of our Flesh. For in the Rest that Christ offers, we can finally find peace with God, but if we seek rest in our Flesh, we will be sorely disappointed.

There is no need to fear the Dead. They are the ones that are filled with fear. The Dead fear death because they know not what it will bring. They prefer rather to believe in the fantasy of their desires and so have gathered around themselves many deceptions. It is as if they have created a dream to Walk about so that they may sedate themselves from the pain of their terrible reality. They have lost sensitivity to that which truly matters and so have given themselves over to sensuality. But this longing and groping after the Flesh will surely be their demise unless they can be reached with the Gospel Cure. The only hope for the living Dead is that they would be brought back to Life by the power of the love of God. Yahweh knew before the beginning of time how these events would play out. And in His wisdom, He sent His son to die for the sins of the world. Those that have been drawn to Christ will by no means be put to shame. Therefore, let us not grow weary in doing good, for the Zombies tire themselves over their vain efforts to do good - a good that perishes and gains no ground on the path to Life. But we who have Died to sin through faith in Christ will be given the assurance that comes from knowing the truth. We will be presented before the Lord our God as those who have been made blameless and innocent of all our sins because He has loved us with such a great love. All our sins have been removed from the record so that we could stand in a righteousness not our own. Knowing these things then, we persuade the Dead, with the hope that they would hear the voice of the Son of Man and leave their whitewashed tombs. No matter how one looks outwardly, the Lord knows the secrets of the heart, and when the time comes, He will bring them to Light. Our responsibility is to be faithful to the ministry we have received. The ministry is one of reconciliation, for the Creator has been redeeming His creation so that we could be presented to Him in a way that would bring Him glory. Why would we shy away from such a great honor? The only reasonable choice is to cooperate with the Lord in His great plan of salvation by offering ourselves to the uttermost so that by any means necessary, the Gospel Cure could be spread among many. God will give us the wisdom and the words we need at the time they are needed. All that we must do is Walk in faith, knowing that our God will never leave us, and He will never fail us.

> *For I am convinced that neither death, nor life, nor angels, nor heavenly rulers, nor things that are present, nor things to come, nor powers, nor height, nor depth,* **nor anything else in creation will be able to separate us from the love of God in Christ Jesus our Lord.**
>
> Romans 8:38-39 (NET)

WORTHY WALKER

IDENTITY IN CHRIST

> **For now, we see in a mirror dimly, but then face to face.** Now I know in part; then I shall know fully, even as I have been fully known.
>
> 1 Corinthians 13:12 (ESV)

The LIVING DEAD Revival Guide

Praise the Lord! We are no longer the Walking Dead. Instead, it would seem that we have become a walking paradox. We are in the world but not of the World. We are in the flesh but not of the Flesh. We have the Spirit dwelling within but are not yet made perfect. And yet by One sacrifice, we who are at this moment being sanctified, have been made perfect forever in Christ (Hebrews 10:14). It is our identity in Christ that has truly changed us.

> *So, you too consider yourselves **dead to sin, but alive to God in Christ Jesus**.*
> Romans 6:11 (NET)

But now that we have been changed, we must turn ourselves over to our God and be used for His glory like a fine mirror that accurately reflects what is shone to it. We must imitate Christ in his sacrifice and obedience. We cannot afford to risk running behind those who meander on the path but must press onward toward our Heavenly calling in Christ (Hebrews 6:12). If we do this rightly, then we will be carrying on the long-standing tradition of all those Worthy Walkers who came before us and are now awaiting our grand entrance into the kingdom of heaven.

> *Therefore, brothers, be all the more diligent to **confirm your calling and election**, for if you practice these qualities, you will never fall. For in this way there will be richly provided for you an entrance into the eternal kingdom of our Lord and Savior Jesus Christ.*
> 2 Peter 1:10-11 (ESV)

Taste Death

> *Truly, truly, I say to you, if anyone keeps my word, he will never see death." The Jews said to him, "Now we know that you have a demon! Abraham died, as did the prophets, yet you say, 'If anyone keeps my word, he will never taste death.'*
> John 8:51-52 (ESV)

Jesus said that anyone who believes in him would never *see* Death. But those who thought of Death as more of a physical certainty rather than a spiritual repercussion opposed Him. This distinction is important because it is by the Death of Jesus Christ that the path to Yahweh was made possible for all of us who were once Dead in our sins. It is the death of Messiah that crowned him with glory (Hebrews 2:9). But the difference between *seeing* death and *tasting* or experiencing death must be made explicit. The difference between being Alive and being Dead can only be truly realized when we Die to our old selves and find our Life in Christ. Physical death will come to all people. But only spiritual Life comes to those who have Died with Christ by faith in the grace of God. Physical life is a gift of God to all, but unless we repent from sin and turn to the Lord of Life, there will be a certain and permanent separation from Yahweh.

Jesus told some of his disciples that they would not *taste death* until they saw the son of man coming in his kingdom. Immediately after this, Peter, James, and John witnessed the transfiguration of Jesus. They saw him more truly than before and yet were still prone to the distraction of the Flesh. Then Peter thought it would be good to stay where they were and install the Kingdom. That peculiar Kingdom that is here and yet still coming in the same moment. Peculiar people inhabit this peculiar Kingdom. Despite the curiosity and mystery of our current condition and future status, what can be known is our calling. We are called to Walk in a manner worthy of Christ Jesus, who gave His life as a ransom for many. The strangeness of our spiritual Life can be seen when we consider who Peter was at the transfiguration and who he was after the resurrection. After Jesus had risen from the dead, Peter understood more clearly what it was that he was seeing (2 Peter 1:16-18).

> *But if Christ is in you, although* **the body is dead because of sin, the Spirit is life because of righteousness***.*
> Romans 8:10 (ESV)

Before the Lord Jesus Christ raised Lazarus from the dead, He proclaimed that He was *the resurrection and the life* and that all who believed in him would Live even though they die (John 11:25). The only question that remains is this: do we believe that? If we say we believe, but in reality, our actions deny him, then we are liars. We will be known by our faithful actions. We must participate in the production of Spiritual fruit with the help of the Holy Spirit; otherwise, we risk being cut off from the True Vine and cast into the fire!

> *You make known to me* **the path of life***; in your presence, there is fullness of joy; at your right hand are pleasures forevermore.*
> Psalms 16:11 (ESV)

What do we see now when we peer into the perfect mirror of scripture? As we consider who we were before Christ, we are able to perceive our wretched condition more clearly. We were sunk in depravity because of our sins. We were Zombies. We were the living Dead. Half alive and half dead but in all the wrong ways. But now we have been made Alive with Christ. We have been made into new creations. We have been made into children of the Living God. We are nearer now to our ultimate reality than when we first believed and although we do not yet know what we will be, what we do know is that we will be conformed into the image of Jesus Christ. We will be made more suitable to reflect the radiant glory of our great God and Savior. That's our true identity.

> *And we all, with **unveiled face**, beholding the glory of the Lord, are being **transformed into the same image from one degree of glory to another**. For this comes from the Lord, who is the Spirit.*
> 2 Corinthians 3:18 (ESV)

WALK IN THE LIGHT

Surely God desires that we would Walk in the Light with him. If we have renounced and repented from our sins, then we are in the Light. If we claim that we have no sin or that we do not sin, we lie and slander the Holy One (1 John 1:9-10). God is patient and kind and does not treat us as our sins deserve. He knows our weakness and frailty.

> *For he knows our frame; he remembers that we are dust. As for man, his days are like grass; he flourishes like a flower of the field; for the wind passes over it, and it is gone, and its place knows it no more.*
> Psalms 103:14-16 (ESV)

It is no surprise that we fail. We all stumble in many ways. But the righteous will not remain in sin because they have been set free from sin and become slaves of righteousness. We can no longer endure the old ways that were alienating us from God.

> *And you, **who once were alienated and hostile in mind, doing evil deeds**, he has now reconciled in his body of flesh by his death, in order to present you holy and blameless and above reproach before him, if indeed you continue in the faith, stable and steadfast, not shifting from the hope of the gospel that you heard, which has been proclaimed in all creation under heaven, and of which I, Paul, became a minister.*
> Colossians 1:21-23 (ESV)

What more could a Worthy Walker truly desire? For if we have been found in him, then all that we seek will also be found in him! A mere moment in His presence is better than a lifetime without Him. If we delight ourselves in Him, then He will surely give us the desires of our hearts (Psalm 37:4). Furthermore, if we Walk in the Light, perhaps those who reside in the domain of Darkness will take notice and be urged by the Holy Spirit to pay heed to such a sign. Even if all they do is acknowledge in the end before the Father that his Light shined in us, it will be enough.

> *In the same way,* **let your light shine before others**, *so that they may see your good works and give glory to your Father who is in heaven.*
> Matthew 5:16 (ESV)

We know the Way. The Way is Jesus Christ. There is no other path. None of us is without sin, but all of us have been given the message concerning Salvation in Christ. We all have this hope extended to us if only we would receive the implanted word, which is able to save our souls. This true Gospel Cure that points all attention to our glorious God and Savior, Jesus Christ.

For we have not followed after strategically devised stories and mythical fables in regard to the Gospel. It has been proven true time and time again. Nevertheless, we know it is not God nor his Word which err, but it is we that remain capable of failure. Our mind and operation cannot be directed by the Flesh, for if it is, we will surely be led off to the place of the Dead (Romans 6:6). No, our bodily urges cannot have control over us any longer. We must fight them and resist them with all that we can muster. We must Walk like those who have been regenerated, born anew to Walk in Light and Life!

> **For you are still influenced by the flesh**. *For since there is still jealousy and dissension among you, are you not influenced by the flesh and behaving like* **unregenerate people**?
> 1 Corinthians 3:3 (NET)

Clearly, the entrapment of sin may cause the Worthy Walker to doze off into dangerous areas. But the Saint will never stay down. God will raise them up if not in this life, then in the life to come! Yes, even if we fail, we will be made blameless and pure by Him and for His glory. Jesus is not unaware of our dire plight. He knows all too well the treachery of this Wasteland of a World.

Woe to the world for temptations to sin! *For it is necessary that temptations come,* ***but woe to the one by whom the temptation comes!***
Matthew 18:7 (ESV)

May God's children Walk in a manner worthy to which we have been called. Let us never willfully wrong others or lead them into sin. But if we do, we know we have an advocate with the Father.

My dear children, ***I write this to you so that you will not sin.*** *But if anybody does sin, we have an* ***advocate*** *with the Father— Jesus Christ, the* ***Righteous One.***
1 John 2:1 (NIV)

We can be outrageously confident before the presence of our almighty God. Before we were saved, our standing would have been so terrifying as to strike one dead in the intense holiness of His presence. What honor we have in being called His own precious possession! And we are His, and for this reason, the World does not know us. Good riddance! We have Died to the World and it to us. Rather now, we find our value and identity in the One who made us. May He eternally shine in all His Saints.

Now to the one who is able to ***keep you from falling****, and to cause you to stand, rejoicing,* ***without blemish before his glorious presence****, to the only God our Savior through Jesus Christ our Lord, be glory, majesty, power, and authority, before all time, and now, and for all eternity. Amen.*
Jude 1:24-25 (NET)

FRUIT OF THE SPIRIT

I am the vine; you are the branches. ***The one who remains in me—and I in him—bears much fruit, because apart from me you can accomplish nothing.***
John 15:5 (NET)

It is far too easy for our Watch to become weary as the Night lingers ever into the Darkness. We remain somewhat susceptible to the influence of sin in its various forms.

This is not to say we are helpless or weak but rather to understand that we are still in the process of perfecting obedience. We are justified, sanctified, and glorified in Christ before the Father. But we must participate in our salvation. We must work it out with fear and trembling. We know with absolute assurance that He who began the good work of salvation in us will carry it out to completion. He will do this if we continue in our faith steadfast and sure. He will present us before Himself as pure, blameless, and innocent in a way that we could never attain in our own strength. We are utterly dependent upon Yahweh. He is our Life.

> *And you were **at one time strangers and enemies** in your minds as expressed through your evil deeds, but now he has reconciled you by his physical body through death to present you holy, without blemish, and blameless before him—**if indeed you remain in the faith**, established and firm, without shifting from the hope of the gospel that you heard. This gospel has also been preached in all creation under heaven, and I, Paul, have become its servant.*
>
> Colossians 1:21-23 (NET)

Enough time has passed for the repulsive ways of the old self. Although we may still feel the pull of our previous sins, we will resist them. Though they pull us like that of a Zombie grasping out for our leg, we will not give in to the lure. How can we?! We are those who have been brought back to Life from the Dead! Therefore, we owe our lives to the One who saved us.

> ***Therefore do not let sin reign in your mortal body so that you obey its desire**s, and do not present your members to sin as instruments to be used for unrighteousness, but present yourselves to God as **those who are alive from the dead** and your members to God as instruments to be used for righteousness. For sin will have no mastery over you, because you are not under law but under grace.*
>
> Romans 6:12-14 (NET)

Clearly, our freedom is meant to give us Life and Life more abundant (John 10:10)! We have been called to Walk Worthy of our new master. He desires that we seek Him and His righteousness first. We know that He will add all of our other needs in due time. He exalts those who are after his own heart, and He provides for their needs.

The **LIVING DEAD** Revival Guide

Delight yourself in the LORD*, and he will give you the desires of your heart.*
Psalm 37:4 (ESV)

Our old master sought to steal, kill, and destroy. We likewise followed those orders. As Zombies, we roamed about looking to capitalize on the suffering of others. Exploitation was very natural to our sin riddled state. We waited in ambush, and when the time was right, would strike to satisfy our own desires. We would hate with such fervor that if given the chance, we would kill. The desire itself testified against us.

*For **we too** were once foolish, disobedient, misled, enslaved to various passions and desires, spending our lives in evil and envy,*
hateful and hating one another*.*
Titus 3:3 (NET)

We have been raised from the Dead. And have deeply identified with the death of Jesus Christ. For this reason, we are buried in baptism to symbolize our Death. But we rise up out of the water to symbolize our resurrection with Christ. Now that we have been raised to Walk in newness of Life, we who live always carry with us the message of the Gospel. God which is the power to save our souls from the grave (Romans 6).

Always carrying around in our body the death of Jesus, so that the life of Jesus may also be made visible in our body*. For we who are alive are constantly being **handed over to death for Jesus' sake**, so that the life of Jesus may also be made visible in our mortal body. As a result, death is at work in us, but life is at work in you.*
2 Corinthians 4:10-12 (NET)

Even if it is death that threatens the Worthy Walker, it is not in vain. For all the martyrs will be forever known by God and his Saints. The Second Death will no longer have any hold over us because Jesus has defeated Death for us. Such marvelous mysteries have been revealed to us. Our hearts and minds can no longer appease the Flesh as they once did. We know that the mind controlled by the Flesh is Death. It alienates and separates, but it is meant to be harmonized and unified with the will of God. Therefore, we have nothing to fear, not even death. Because our God is greater than Death!

Talon Schneider

*And do not fear those who kill the body but cannot kill the soul.
Rather fear him who can destroy both soul and body in hell.*
Matthew 10:28 (ESV)

Recognizing Results

*Thus, you will recognize them **by their fruits**.*
Matthew 7:20 (ESV)

If Jesus said that we would know false prophets by their Fruits, then it follows that his Saints ought to be known by their Fruit as well. Fruit clearly draws our mind to the idea of results. So, we could refer to this as a test of the presence or absence of the Holy Spirit in a person's life. Without the Holy Spirit and without faith in God, how can one possibly expect to produce a bounty of righteousness? It is not possible!

*And **without faith, it is impossible to please him**, for whoever would draw near to God must believe that he exists and that he rewards those who seek him.*
Hebrews 11:6 (ESV)

We are sure that we are saved because we find in ourselves the Deadening of our old self with its self-destructive behavior and the Dawn of a new self. We have been brought to Life, and He is our God because God alone Lives independent of any necessities. He sustains all things and has no need for the fleeting desires of the Flesh as we do. Nevertheless, we make every effort to confirm our calling and election by testing ourselves to be sure if Christ is in us.

***Examine yourselves** to see whether you are in the faith. **Test yourselves**.
Or do you not realize this about yourselves, that Jesus Christ is in you?
—unless indeed you fail to meet the test!*
2 Corinthians 13:5 (ESV)

When we were Zombies, Dead in our sins, we were the broken image of God. We were corrupted to the very bone by our sinful nature and behavior. This was the regrettable reality for all humans, even though we are all image-bearers of God. We are not image bearers because of what we do necessarily but rather because that is simply what we are. We are made in the likeness of God, but because of the Fall, we have a nature that carries the Name of the Lord in vain. By nature, all Zombies are opposed to God even though we were made to know God and to love Him.

> *... **people who are made in the likeness of God.***
> James 3:9 (ESV)

It is remarkable that God would love us. We are creatures by nature that are deeply flawed and sinful. We are hostile towards God and do not do as He desires. Only His grace could reach down to our lowly position. Despite how completely depraved we were, He did not lack in his love for us. He saw an utterly pitiful and despicable creature and loved it to the very End (Romans 8:5). This is a further demonstration of the immense love He has displayed because only God would love something that was so diametrically opposed to Him. Only God could have done this wonderful work in creating us anew.

The Scripture is clear that all humans are made in the image of God. We are imagers of God by his very creation of us. It is not a simple concept to understand but rather a truth to accept. Yet it is undeniable that by our nature, we do not carry the name of the Lord in glory, but rather we have Walked in vain. We break that holy commandment that demands we do not take the Name of the Lord in vain, not merely by the words we utter but by what we do. We cannot do enough to earn His favor, neither can we, by our actions, change what we are before Him. He is the one who must regenerate us. We must be made new, we must be Born Again, and we must be brought back to Life from the Dead.

> *They profess to know God,* ***but they deny him by their works.***
> *They are detestable, disobedient,* ***unfit for any good work.***
> Titus 1:16 (ESV)

But now, by the power of the Holy Spirit Living in us, we can bear righteous Fruit. Before we were brought to Life, we were bearing fruit for Death. We were ruined. We were sickly trees unable to bear good Fruit because it simply was not in us to will and to act according to God's desires (Matthew 7:17-19). We had to die in order to be made Alive as we ought to be. Our standing in Christ makes all the difference. Paul expands this idea in the book of Romans.

> *So, my brothers and sisters, you also died to the law through the body of Christ, so that you could be joined to another, to the one who was raised from the dead,* ***to bear fruit to God.*** *For when we were in the flesh, the*

> *sinful desires, aroused by the law, were active in the members of our body to **bear fruit for death**. But now we have been released from the law because we have died to what controlled us, so that we may serve in the new life of the Spirit and not under the old written code.*
>
> Romans 7:4-6 (NET)

Contrary to the acts of the Flesh, we are now producing Fruit of the Spirit who lives in us. We are no longer capitulating to the desires that drag us to a fiery End. The Fruit we bear is for the sake of Life, and thusly it draws us close to the Creator. Galatians 5 gives us an idea of what kind of fruitful results in the presence of God's Spirit in us will look like.

> ***But the fruit of the Spirit*** *is love, joy, peace, patience, kindness, goodness, faithfulness, gentleness, and self-control. Against such things, there is no law.*
>
> Galatians 5:22-23 (NET)

All of these fruits come from God and go to God as an eternal glory. That which is done for the glory of God will never fade. We are tending to a fruit and treasure that will never fade, mold, rust, or decay! But we can't force these fruits to be brought forth; rather, it is through faithful obedience and cooperation with God that these holy results are presented.

Love like that of Jesus is willing to die. But it will not *stay dead*. The *Joy* that strengthens us is that which endures suffering with an undying hope. The *Peace* of God protects our hearts and minds and elicits peace in those near us despite the most calamitous situations. The *Patience* of a Saint can wait with eyes that see beyond the temporary pleasures of this world and into the eternal promises of God. *Kindness* for a friend is unspectacular, but Worthy Walkers make a practice out of going the extra mile. They know full well that it may lead precisely where they are meant to go. *Goodness* is added to faith in a succession that won't leave good enough alone. They are as diametrically opposite to the depraved cravings of the Dead as possible. Now the hunger for flesh and thirst for blood is replaced with a hungering and thirsting after righteousness. *Faithfulness* from the Spirit helps us Walk not by sight in a World that seeks to draw our focus away from Christ Jesus. It instead pulls us into His holiness as He finishes what He started in us. The *Gentleness* produced by the Holy Spirit is not to be misunderstood as fragility. Rather it should be understood as meekness like that of a wild horse trained to be useful for its master. The gentleness that is fruitful is power held under control. *Self-control* is a Fruit of the Spirit that wraps all the others together into a useful package. God has not removed our volition. We still have free will, but our freedom is not to be used as an excuse to gratify the Flesh. Instead, under the governance of the Spirit, we will lead a life that leads to Heaven, which means we will never again be separated in any sense from our God.

> *And so, from the day we heard, we have not ceased to pray for you, asking that you may be filled with the knowledge of his will in all spiritual wisdom and understanding, so as to **walk in a manner worthy of the Lord**, fully pleasing to him: **bearing fruit** in every good work and increasing in the knowledge of God; being strengthened with all power, according to his glorious might, for all endurance and patience with joy, **giving thanks to the Father, who has qualified you to share in the inheritance of the saints in light**.*
>
> Colossians 1:9-12 (ESV)

FRUITFUL RESISTANCE

> *Submit yourselves therefore to God. **Resist** the devil, and he will flee from you.*
>
> James 4:7 (ESV)

Much transformation has taken place in the people of God as we consider what we were before. He has taken those who were once opposed to him as dire enemies and turned them into his beloved children. Certainly, the spiritual forces of darkness are not pleased with this transference. But they stand no chance against the Lord God Almighty. Nevertheless, they will seek to limit and intimidate the Saints. They think that their opposition will cause futility, but God is able to cause us to conquer against all odds. Their animosity will only strengthen our faith. We will not stop serving our God because we know that resistance is fertile.

> *He has **delivered us from the domain of darkness and transferred us to the kingdom of his beloved Son**, in whom we have redemption, the forgiveness of sins.*
>
> Colossians 1:13-14 (ESV)

We must learn to resist the Devil, the Flesh, and the World, but cumulatively we will find that it is ourselves we are resisting. Because if we can deny ourselves by fixing our eyes upon Jesus, we will be walking more in the purpose for which we were created. The enemy cannot stand the thought of us, reflecting the light of Jesus Christ into this dark world. But that is what we were called to be. We are made to love like Jesus did, even if it cost us our lives. And we are not alone in this calling!

> **Resist him**, *strong in your faith, because you know that your brothers and sisters **throughout the world** are enduring the same kinds of suffering.*
>
> 1 Peter 5:9 (NET)

God will allow us to be challenged beyond what we think we can handle because He knows that is how we grow our faith. When we go through trials of various kinds, we can rejoice, knowing that the testing of our faith will produce perseverance (James 1:2-3). The better we become at persevering, the more clearly, we will see that our Heavenly Father prunes the branches so that they would bear even more fruit. This process may come through the removal of our comfort but what is gained is of much greater value! Therefore, let us all receive with willingness the wise guidance of the Master Gardener.

> *By this, my Father is glorified, that you bear much fruit and so prove to be my disciples.*
>
> John 15:8 (ESV)

TENACITY OF LIFE

> *It is better to go to a house of mourning than to go to a house of feasting,*
> ***for death is the destiny of everyone; the living should take this to heart.***
>
> Ecclesiastes 7:2 (NIV)

What could be better than to be with the Lord? There is nothing greater, for even a single day with the Lord is better than a multitude elsewhere. The Christian embraces this as a source of hope, but the Zombie has no regard for such an idea. The apostle Paul considered it better to be absent from the body and present with the Lord. And like him, we also concur that to Live is Christ and to die is gain (Philippians 1).

Nevertheless, death is the end for all people (save perhaps for the unexpected transference of God's people in the Last Days as described by Paul in 1 Corinthians 15). All of us will depart from our physical bodies, and that much will be true of all regardless if we are Saints or Zombies. We all will meet our end one way or another. We are vividly aware of our mortality. How could we not be? For day after day, we see death all around us. Sometimes we lose those we love, and other times we scarcely know who it is that has departed. Regardless of our acquaintance with them, the fact is undeniable that death is the destiny of mankind. It has been appointed for us to die and then to face the judgment (Hebrews 9:27). But it would seem that the Walking Dead prefer instead to gather unto themselves a great horde of those that celebrate saying, "Eat and drink for tomorrow we die!" It seems that the Dead have chosen to rejoice in their dying state or perhaps that they have obscured the truth so as not to be utterly defeated by it. Either way, they continue to enjoy their fleeting pleasures and continually stack up their sins. But the Christian has become aware of their mortality in an entirely different sense. They have instead recognized their infinite and offensive debt before the Only God, who is intensely holy, loving, and just. We have realized that it is only through the death and resurrection of our Lord and Savior, Jesus Christ, that we may have Life and have it more abundantly. Without Jesus, we are nothing. We are, most of all, to be pitied. But we have ardently believed that this Jesus is both Lord and Savior. We have come to know without a doubt the One in which we have believed. There is no turning back for those of us who have tasted that the Lord is Good. We can no longer go to the house that feasts upon the Flesh. We cannot abide the habitual abuse of the body and soul through devious activities. Rather we are constricted in our hearts and minds to turn those who practice such things away from the doom that haunts them. Some will be saved through the Spirit working in us, and others will hate us for our ministry to them. But what does it matter so long as Christ is preached? Indeed, we will become the enemy of many for speaking the truth to them. But that is our burden to bear, and it is our responsibility to uphold those burdens as a fulfillment of the Law of Christ. We will offer ourselves as Living Sacrifices. Again, and again we will put ourselves below the needs of others if, by any means, it would lead to the salvation of the Lost.

> *So, teach us to consider our **mortality** so that we might **live** wisely.*
> Psalms 90:12 (NET)

Hungering and thirsting without end, it would seem that nothing could appease the appetite of the living Dead. In fact, it can be said of them that their god is their stomach, and the sensualities that accompany it feed their desire for sin. Indeed, they revel in their defiance and rebellion, considering their shame to be glorious. They cannot lift their eyes up from the Dead worldly things (Philippians 3). They are perpetually feeding into a cycle of death, but they do nothing to change it. How can they? They have no ability to save themselves. They Walk as enemies of the cross and enemies of Christ. Sad but true, there is no hope for them to be found within themselves. We know this is true because it was true of us who have been saved out of that terminal cycle. But God has made a new and Living way for the Dead to be redeemed (Hebrews). The power of Life is too extraordinary for Death to contend. The Light came into the World, and the World in its dire Darkness could not overtake it. Do we believe this? We shall see. The test of those who believe is often answered in the laying down of our life. Jesus gave us the ultimate example in laying His life down for our sake, but because He is God, He took it back up. Now the charge is upon us to surrender our lives for His sake and the benefit of others. We will lay our lives down and have complete confidence that our Mighty God will lift us up in due time.

> *And I, when I am lifted up from the earth, will **draw all people to myself**.*
> John 12:32 (ESV)

If we have endured long enough in this World to know that the End is near, then we may also be aware that the Lord is still at work to this day. His grace and character are truly irresistible, for who could withstand such a magnanimous quality? The drawing of all unto Himself is constantly taking place. It would take more time than we have been afforded in order to recount every story of those who have come to Life. But what we can say is that the eternal Life that has been offered to us who have believed in the grace of God is available even now. That is to say that the relationship made possible through the death of Christ can be experienced right now. That relationship and its continual growth is the everlasting Life that all Christians participate in with God, our Creator. Through Jesus, the intended relationship between Creator and created has been restored, and in some ways, it is even better than what Adam and Eve experienced. For now, the Holy Spirit has been poured out into our hearts through the love of our God. The Holy Spirit will be with us forever. What a remarkable joy this is for us who believe. There are many who are Dead in their sins and have no knowledge of eternal Life. Regrettably, there are even those who claim to believe who have no knowledge of God (1 Corinthians 15:34). Eternal Life necessitates that we know the only true God and the means by which we have this restored relationship.

> And **this is eternal life, that they know you** the only true God,
> and Jesus Christ whom you have sent.
> John 17:3 (ESV)

To know God is to know Life. The idea of knowing is more than mere facts and information. It is an intimate relationship created by a shared experience and mutual understanding. If we know God, then we will act like it. If God's Spirit lives in us, then we will bear the fruitful evidence of his presence in us. If we are new creations, then the old has indeed passed away (2 Corinthians 5:17). We know that our old self has been done away with so that we could have a new life marked by a right relationship with God. There are inexpressible emotions that accompany this experience. But what unites all those who truly believe, adhere, and abide in the Lord is an unflinching knowledge of the truth of the Gospel. Without knowledge of the true Gospel that surmises our salvation, how could we be truly saved? How can someone say that they know a person but actually know nothing about them?

Furthermore, are we known by God? There are some who will think that they have been serving God but all along have been serving themselves. To these, it may be said by the Lord Jesus Christ, "Depart from me, you workers of iniquity, for I never knew you."

> *But now that you know God—or **rather are known by God**—how is it that you are turning back to those weak and miserable forces?*
> **Do you wish to be enslaved by them all over again?**
> Galatians 4:9 (NIV)

We have sought to establish the significance of Life and Death in a Biblical context. The reason is because many deceivers have gone out to compromise the faith of some who are not yet resolute. It is our task to solidify the faith of the feeble and bring all to maturity of faith. As we do this, we gain hope that the Day is drawing ever closer. Indeed, the Day is nearer now than when we first believed, and it is only approaching all the more. Even so, come quickly, Lord Jesus. We will not rely upon our own understanding, but in all our ways, we will acknowledge the Lord. We do this knowing that no matter what, He will make the path straight before us (Proverbs 3:5-6). What will it take for the entire Living Army of God to be activated and mobilized to endeavor in the Great Commission? Only the bonding together of the Body of Christ and the empowering presence of the Holy Spirit who leads us into all truth. We will anticipate and cooperate with the sanctification that comes from the truth, which is found in the Word of God. This Living Word of God draws us ever closer to our Lord. The World would have us remain in our naive ignorance. But God has caused us to be Born Again, into a Living Hope, through the resurrection of Jesus Christ from the dead (1 Peter 1:3). Consider, therefore, all that which is bringing us closer to the Living God. But let us do so in reference to the Holy Scripture as we continue to work of our salvation with fear and trembling (Philippians 2:12).

Talon Schneider

*It is a fearful thing to fall into the hands of the **living God**.*
Hebrews 10:31 (ESV)

THE MEANING OF LIFE

*Whoever has the Son has **life**; whoever does not have the Son of God does not have **life**.*
1 John 5:12 (NIV)

Do we believe this? Do we believe that only those who have the Son have Life? Do we believe that those who do not have the Son are Zombies? This is the dividing line between those who aggressively resist the advance of the Gospel and those who relentlessly abide by it. Yes, we believe that without Christ, we are without Life and, therefore, Dead in our sins. That horrid condition is what we once lived in, but we do so no longer. Furthermore, even though we once saw others only through a perspective that was perishing, we now make it our aim to see others as Christ saw them. We make it our effort to see how truly loved the Dead are despite how terrible their Walk may be.

There is a great number of ways that a Saint is drawn to the Lord. We certainly cannot claim to be the Judge, but rather we echo the sentiment of so many other Worthy Walkers. We are merely slaves of righteousness seeking to serve those around us. We are making it our primary way of being because this is the example that Jesus left us.

We do believe in the Son, and therefore we are certainly Alive! We can see that a great many things have come together in order that we may know Life. If something is Life-giving, then it will indeed draw us ever closer to the source of Life, namely Yahweh. Do we truly desire to Live? Do we truly desire to know and love God?

*What man is there who **desires life** and loves many days, that he may see good?*
Psalm 34:12 (ESV)

If all that which separates us from God is sin and Death, then that which connects us and draws us closer to Him is Life. The peculiar way of thinking should not be taken for granted or out of context. But many excellent examples are provided to us in the Holy Scripture. If the Word of God concurs on the concept, then we can rest assured that it is reliable. But let us be as the Bereans who sought earnestly to see if these claims are true. May our discretion and discernment be enlightened by the guidance of the Holy Spirit, who dwells within those who have believed upon the Risen Lord Jesus Christ.

Living Word (Hebrews 4:12, 1 John 2:14),

Living and enduring word of God (1 Peter 1:23),

Living Hope (1 Peter 1:3),

Living Sacrifice (Romans 12:1),

New and Living Way (Hebrews 10:20),

Living Stone (1 Peter 2:4-5),

Living being/life-giving spirit (1 Corinthians 15:45),

Living Bread (John 6:51),

Living Water (John 4:10),

Living Tablets (2 Corinthians 3:3),
Living Truth (2 John 1:2),

Living Faith (James 2:26, 2 Timothy 1:5),

Living Love (Romans 8:38-39, Ephesians 6:24),

Living God (Acts 17:25, 1 Thessalonians 1:9)

As a servant of the Lord Jesus Christ, it has been my aim to make known to a Dead World the Living Hope offered to us. I will give my life to this cause as many who came before me have. The list of those who have done so is full of many zealous believers, but it doesn't always take the most zealous believer to accomplish the will of God. At times it simply requires the modest obedience of the Saint at the proper time. If we consider ourselves to be Alive, then it will naturally follow that we know why we are Alive and no longer Dead. We will also be compelled by the love of Christ to no longer perceive the Zombie as something to be hated but rather in dire need of help. We were once those who hated others and were ourselves hated. We know that a murderous heart that hurls threats both inwardly and externally. We were those who, by our actions, denied the Living God (Titus 1:16). But He had mercy on us that we would serve as vital examples and willing participants in His plan of redemption for the believing and retribution on the unbelieving.

> *For it is time for **judgment to begin at the household of God;**
> **and if it begins with us, what will be the outcome for those**
> **who do not obey the gospel of God?***
>
> 1 Peter 4:17 (ESV)

    For the sake of the chosen and elect, will we not also suffer that they may come to believe? Was not Stephen the martyr willing to testify to the truth even to the very point of death? Were not all those who immediately witnessed the Lord Jesus Christ as crucified and risen willing to lay their lives down? Yes, and even more than are mentionable. The Christian faces opposition to the truth because the World cannot accept it. Neither can the inhabitants of the World abide by the truth, for it is contrary to their nature.

    Furthermore, the evil spiritual forces that resist the Saints know that there is only One God but to this truth, they shudder and shriek because they are aware of their doom and destruction. They are more aware of their fate than the Zombie. Who is it that will reach out to the lost and the damned? If not, those who were themselves both lost and damned before being saved and redeemed? We are charged with such a great opportunity to partake of the same kind of sufferings as the Lord Jesus Christ and, in that way, know Him more intimately. This was the heart behind Paul's counterintuitive boasting in Philippians chapter 3. Wherein he details all that of the Flesh that was cause for him to be boastful and arrogant. That which made him seem to be more than he actually was. Indeed, he was considered extremely zealous, even to the point of persecuting the Body of Christ. He was undoubtedly a witness of the Stoning of Stephen, the martyr, because Stephen's cloak was laid at his feet.

    Yes, Zombies lie in ambush and are quick to shed blood. But none of the Fleshly boasting was able to bring Paul any closer to the Living God. Only faith in the grace of God unto the undeserving Dead is able to bring about salvation. From that vantage point, we, too, consider everything a loss for the surpassing worth of gaining Christ Jesus. He is for us the wisdom and power of God. He is Life in the fullest and most abundant sense. He is absolutely worth the sacrifice of this current and temporary existence if it would mean that somehow, we would partake of the resurrection of the Dead. He experienced the resurrection of the Dead even now as those who have heard the voice of the Son of Man and are therefore brought to a Living relationship with God (John 5:25). But we also know that these bodies that are subject to physical death will also be transformed and redeemed (Romans 8:11). We agree with Paul and all those who have followed after the Risen Savior with steadfast faith. We will face Death daily, but we will know Life forever.

> ***I face death every day***, *brothers, as surely as*
> *I boast about you in Christ Jesus, our Lord.*
> 1 Corinthians 15:31 (NIV)

PREPARE TO DIE

> *So, you also must **consider yourselves dead to sin and alive to God***
> ***in Christ Jesus.***
> Romans 6:11 (ESV)

Vigilance was needed on the night Jesus was betrayed. But on three occasions, Jesus returned to find his friends fast asleep instead of fervent in prayer. Although these three followers would later become unstoppably committed to the Gospel Cure, at that time, they were being washed back and forth by their shortcomings. There is a spiritual apathy that hinders all people. For the sinful nature trends in the direction of lawlessness and disobedience. The Worthy Walker, on the contrary, has trained himself how to respond in various situations through the continual study of the Word of God and through much prayer and fellowship. The Sleep Walker is in the habit of departing from fellowship. Their heart is absent from the quiet places of prayer and study that solidifies our faith. Indeed, this is a constant battle that we will contend with for the duration of our physical lives.

The Spirit and the Flesh are opposed to one another so that we are inhibited and limited from doing that, which we know is righteous (Galatians 5:17). But our weaknesses are more than the cause of our wandering; they are also an opportunity for righteousness to reign through grace (Romans 5:21). If we would submit ourselves completely to the will of God, we would find that even that which we hate about ourselves would, in the end, bring glory to God. He knows that we cannot keep all of the Law in our sinful Flesh, for if the Law could do away with sin, then there would have been no need for Christ Jesus to die on the cross! But when the time was right, Jesus came down to us, so that in His death we would have Life. It is a far too wonderful and lofty for me to even fully comprehend. Did the Father turn away from the Son upon the cross, before the physical death of the Messiah? Perhaps Jesus experienced the separation that was due a sinner, and in return, we have been granted to relationship that Jesus rightfully had with the Father. Certainly, the Scripture speaks to the fact that a divine transaction has taken place. For the Father made Jesus, who knew no sin, to become a sacrifice for sin so that we who that naturally give Life to sin would become the righteousness of Christ Jesus! This marvel and mystery are the hope of glory, Christ in us (Colossians 1:27). But the question we must answer is this: are we willing to die for it?

> *Consequently, when Christ came into the world, he said, "Sacrifices and offerings you have not desired, **but a body have you prepared for me**.*
> Hebrews 10:5 (ESV)

We know that the spirit is willing, but the Flesh is weak. Despite the good we want to do; we remain hindered by so many things. There are some things that merely hinder without crossing the line into sin, while others are clearly not condoned. But regardless of whether the action hinders or condemns, we have been charged to run this race with perseverance (Hebrews 12:1-3). We might even say that we should run for our Lives, that is to say, that we should strive to be ever closer to the Lord our God. There are Zombies that run after their next insatiable delight. They hunger and thirst for a great many sins. But what they desire will only bring Death and destruction. The sad reality is that even some of the believing may be led astray. This should not be, and yet it is. But the judgment has already begun. The Zombie Apocalypse is already upon us, and if we are so lackadaisical as to disregard the warnings at hand, then we too may be caught up in the oncoming devastation. Let us only strive to enter the Rest of Christ so that we may not be found Asleep in a sinful state at the great Day of the Lord. We can prevent ourselves from falling into the Sleepy predicament by staying Wakeful and sober-minded for the sake of making many prayers.

> *And what I say to you I say to all:* **Stay awake**.
> Mark 13:37 (ESV)

Wakefulness is likened to keeping in step with the Spirit (Galatians 5:25). We should no longer be deceived as we were before. There is no time for self-deception that tries to convince us of things that we know are not true. For there is no one who would act carelessly as stewards of the Lord's house if they knew at which time, He was coming to us. That Day remains hidden. Perhaps it is held in tension so that the masses of Sleep

The **LIVING DEAD** Revival Guide

Walkers may be given ample time to confirm their allegiance. This age of the Nations will not go on forever. The time of grace is now, but may the Lord's patience be upheld so that those who Wander in their Walk may enter in unharmed. If it is the Lord's will, we could have yet another thousand years or perhaps ten thousand years before He returns.

Just the same, it could be a matter of only a few days and a few critical events unfolding to bring about the completion of the great and terrible Day of the Lord. What we do know is what we are responsible for. We are tasked with Walking in accordance with the knowledge that we have been given. Therefore, if we say that we have seen the Light and yet continue to Walk in Darkness, we have made ourselves out to be liars (1 John 1:6). Just as there is gain to be had by physical training, let us continue in our spiritual training and hastening of the Day of the Lord. We train ourselves to respond in a righteous way in all circumstances. For we cannot deny the Lord, we cannot refuse the knowledge we have of our Creator. He has liberated us from slavery to sin and the corruption of our Flesh with such great effect that we now consider ourselves to be slaves of righteousness. We are unable to resist the pull of the Spirit onto the path of everlasting Life.

> *Do not present your members to sin as instruments for unrighteousness but **present yourselves to God as those who have been brought from death to life**, and your members to God as instruments for righteousness.*
>
> Romans 6:13 (ESV)

Indeed, we ought to consider ourselves Dead to sin and Alive to God because we were as good as dead when sin was Living in us. We did nothing to resist that cold grip of Death that coiled around our necks. While sin was Alive, righteousness was not found in us. But God had greater things planned. He did not intend for us to remain forever in a state of Death. He even made a covering for Adam and Eve after they had directly defied His command (Genesis 3:21). But He would not permit them to live forever in their fallen state, which is partly why He barred them from returning to the Garden by placing a flaming sword around it (Genesis 3:24). Yes, thank God for His grace to humankind. One can only imagine and then try to forget what has been imagined when we consider what it would be like to live forever in a state of sin and decay. But on the contrary, our Father did not let The Seed see decay, and therefore through Jesus, we too will escape the fate of the Walking Dead.

> *So that just as **sin reigned in death**, so also **grace will reign through righteousness to eternal life** through Jesus Christ our Lord.*
>
> Romans 5:21 (NET)

We were totally depraved and without a hope to save ourselves. As Zombies, we knew nothing about our Creator and his love for us. We were bound to sin and could not resist its influence. But God would not leave us this way. Because His plan was for us to Walk with Him once again. Although we do not yet know what we will be, what we do know is that upon seeing our risen savior face to face, we shall be made like him (1 John 3:1-3). What could that mean? Well, at the very least, it will mean that finally, our sinful nature has been fully removed so that we could be not only practically innocent before our Maker but finally and totally and completely perfected before him. We are assured that He has indeed accomplished this for us by one sacrifice. Through one sacrifice, He has perfected forever, those who are being sanctified (Hebrews 10:14).

> ... And, having been **set free from sin**, have become **slaves of righteousness**. I am speaking in human terms because of your natural limitations. For just as you once presented your members as slaves to impurity and to lawlessness leading to more lawlessness, so now present your members as slaves to righteousness leading to sanctification.
>
> Romans 6:18-19 (ESV)

Clearly, our new Lives in Christ can be understood as the Death of our Old Self. The old self was a miserable creature made of unholy actions and hopeless groping after perishing things. But this new creature has new desires and a new purpose. Despite how often the old self may try to rise up from that watery grave and clutch onto our leg as we match onward unto Life, it will not stop us from being brought unto completion. The reason for this indomitable succession is because it is the Lord who is at work in us (Philippians 2:13). He will not cease to sanctify us to the very end.

> And I am sure of this, that he who began a **good work** in you will bring it to **completion** at the day of Jesus Christ.
>
> Philippians 1:6 (ESV)

We should not fear this process because from the perspective of heaven; it may as well be finished already. Where before we were considered Deadmen Walking, we can now be considered as those Walking in newness of Life. The work of Christ upon the cross on behalf of those who have believed him is so sufficient and perfect that we indeed have been justified, sanctified, and glorified in Him! If He thus intends that we be made perfect and holy - even as He is - then we must press forward steadfastly on the Narrow and Difficult Path. Because of this great certainty, we can be even more bold in trusting God for salvation. We have trusted our lives to the only faithful and true God.

> *Now to him who is **able to keep you from stumbling and to present you blameless before the presence of his glory with great joy**, to the only God, our Savior, through Jesus Christ our Lord, be glory, majesty, dominion, and authority, before all time and now and forever. Amen.*
>
> Jude 1:24-25 (ESV)

PARTICIPATION OF THE SAINTS

We must make every effort to enter the Rest of Christ. As we strive in our faith to Walk worthy and holy in a wicked and crooked generation, we will inevitably be faced with the end of our self. We must prepare to die. Not to take our own lives, no, but rather to submit our lives to the one to whom we belong. Worthy Walkers echo the mindset of Paul in Philippians 1:21, wherein he said, "For me to live is Christ and to die is gain." He was torn between his own desire to depart from this world and be with God or the greater need of remaining in the World to serve those who had faith in Christ. It was the denial of his own desires that God had intended for him. And Paul was faithful in this calling. We, too, must deny ourselves because, in so doing, we will be made more like our Savior Jesus.

> *I appeal to you, therefore, brothers, by the mercies of God, to present your bodies as a **living sacrifice**, holy and acceptable to God, which is your spiritual worship.*
>
> Romans 12:1 (ESV)

We owe our lives to God, and a life of service is the least we could offer. Indeed, in view of his mercy, we ought to offer ourselves as Living Sacrifices. The denial of self and association with Christ is the pivotal element to our Walk with the Lord. This transformation from the living Dead into Living Sacrifices becomes so vital to our existence that we seem incapable of going on without serving God and our neighbors in love. For who is it that has tasted that the Lord is good and does not thereafter become entirely consumed by His legendary love? How can we say that we know Him and not do what He says? Contrary to our old nature that was being led to death and destruction, we have turned from that path to follow after the Risen Lord Jesus Christ. Therefore, it is said among the Living that Christ is our Life and to die is gain (Philippians 1:21).

*And he said to all, "If anyone would come after me, let him **deny himself and take up his cross daily and follow me.***

Luke 9:23 (ESV)

Undeniably this will push us past our comfort zones. But it is good for us to become comfortable with being uncomfortable. Even as Paul himself understood that there is great gain for the godly that have contentedness (1 Timothy 6:6). And furthermore, he knew the secret to contentment was a simple dependence upon Christ no matter the circumstance.

*I know how to be brought low, and I know how to abound. In any and every circumstance, I have learned the secret of facing plenty and hunger, abundance, and need. I can do all things **through him** who strengthens me.*

Philippians 4:12-13 (ESV)

What could stop us? Only disobedience and faithlessness could stop us. Whom shall we fear? No one, except for God Himself! We shall only fear the thought of missing our opportunity to serve the Holy One with reverent adoration and sacrifice. For the sacrifices, God desires spring forth from the spirit and from truth. He desires that we would offer the praise of our lips (Hebrews 13:15) and that we would willingly lay our lives down. We know that we can do all these things because His perfect love has been poured out upon us. We know this is true because of His word and His Spirit Living in us.

*There is no fear in love, but **perfect love casts out fear**. For fear has to do with punishment, and whoever fears has not been perfected in love.*

1 John 4:17-18

Indeed, the love of God is perfect, and it has the power to perfect those who adhere to it. Only in the love and justice of God will we find the cure to Death. But let us meet this resolution to our sinful condition with deep respect and willingness to know something that can never be made unknown. We shall not fear man, but rather we shall fear God. For if we were seeking to serve men, then we would not be hated any longer but rather loved by the world and its Dead inhabitants. What they have deemed foolishness is what we know to be the true wisdom of God. Wisdom follows after the fear of the Lord. But foolishness falls down the path to death. Despite what it may seem to the World, God is gracious to His people even in bringing about their physical death.

> *The righteous perish, and no one takes it to heart; the devout are taken away, and no one understands that the righteous are taken away to be spared from evil. **Those who walk uprightly enter into peace; they find rest as they lie in death**.*
>
> Isaiah 57:1-2 (ESV)

But we must recall that our God is the Living God. Indeed, it is a fearful thing to fall into his hands. He is the one who holds the power to destroy both the body and the soul in hell. At that time, the disobedient will, be faced with the Second Death. But that Death and destruction will never end. The torment will be continuous. It will be a place of weeping and gnashing of teeth. But those who entrust their souls to the faithful Creator and continue in doing good can rest assured that their God lives, and they will live with Him. For all who call on the name of the Lord shall be saved!

> *Now he is not God of the dead, but of the living, for **all live before him**.*
>
> Luke 20:38 (NET)

Fear, not brothers and sisters! Self-denial and the mortification of the Flesh (putting to Death the things in us that separate us from God) have been prepared in advance for us that we should Walk in them (Ephesians 2:10). Because the putting to Death of that which was trying to kill us cannot overcome the one who has conquered the grave. Death could not contain Him, and darkness could not overcome Him. He is Life, and he is Light. And we shall see him face to face.

> *Since we have these promises, beloved, let us cleanse ourselves from every defilement of body and spirit, **bringing holiness to completion in the fear of God**.*
>
> 2 Corinthians 7:1 (ESV)

HOPE OF GLORY

Mysteries abound in the manifold wisdom of God. Not everything has been revealed. Despite the desire of the Dead to ignore the undeniable, they cannot refute His powerful truth forever. Indeed God's, "Invisible attributes have been clearly seen so that we are without excuse" (Romans 1:20). Although they should have known better because of the abundant evidence God supplies, the Dead committed acts of terrible consequence. We all, along with them, sinned in despicable ways and encouraged others to do the same.

> *Though they know God's righteous decree that those who practice s uch things* **deserve to die,** *they not only do them but give approval to those who practice them.*
>
> Romans 1:32 (ESV)

The mystery of God and the majesty of his will had been known only in part. But in these last days, it has been made even more clear that his plan of redemption and salvation cannot be stopped. For even the people of which were "Not his people" have become those that He dearly loves. And why is this? Because anyone who believes, just as Abraham did, has become a partaker of the same faith by which Abraham was counted righteous. This marvelous mystery is revealed in all that trust him. For the hope of glory will not be overshadowed by the despair of our sinfulness. God is for us, with us, and He abides in us. Nothing formed against us shall prevail so long as we Walk Worthy in his will. And if God is for us, nothing can be against us.

Even if, in this life, we experience pain and loss, and suffering, it will not be in vain. It will be rectified and restored to us in immeasurable ways! In this World, we will have trouble, but our hearts are uplifted, knowing that Christ Jesus has overcome the World for us (John 16:33). Furthermore, we participate in the likeness of Christ in how we suffer lovingly and patiently during this earthly dwelling.

> *For it has been granted to you that for the sake of Christ you should not only* **believe** *in him but also* **suffer** *for his sake ….*
>
> Philippians 1:29 (ESV)

It would seem, however, that a great many Christians have had the wool pulled over their eyes. It is as if they cannot see this brightly shining light of hope. This Living Hope that gives us strength in times of weakness and courage in times of trouble. Through this great hope, we can truly consider our sufferings in this life to be so temporary as to be unworthy to distract from the focus upon the glory and grace to be given to us.

> *So, we do not lose heart.* ***Though our outer self is wasting away, our inner self is being renewed day by day****. For this light momentary affliction is preparing for us an eternal weight of glory beyond all comparison, as we look not to the things that are seen but to the things*

The LIVING DEAD Revival Guide

that are unseen. For the things that are seen are transient, but the things that are unseen are eternal.

2 Corinthians 4:16-18 (ESV)

Indeed, the living Dead are in a terrifying condition. We know that the Lord God sees the ridiculous efforts of the Zombie that presents its idea of "righteousness" before the Lord. But in truth, the Lord sees these offerings as ragged and bloody clothes. The Zombie aspires to be presented as righteous by their own deeds, but it is these very actions that have doomed them (Isaiah 64:6). Just as their filthy garments suggest outwardly, so it is inwardly. They are wasting away both inside and outside. Physically decomposing before our eyes in a process we can see. The Zombie can hardly last longer than 70 years or even 80 years of by strength. But their spiritual decomposition is even more immediate. They do not even realize that they are Dead on arrival. And therefore, they accept a lie rather than believe the truth. Because what resides in them is fear and Death covered over by the cold and callous heart.

It would seem too good to be true that this destitute condition could be so incredibly reversed. And yet, that is exactly what the Gospel Cure confirms. We are quite truly the Dead who have been brought to Life. This has been done by no accident. This is the plan that God had from the foundation of the earth. It was in the mind of God to send His Son into the World as a sin offering. For the infinite debt of sin against the infinitely holy Lord can only be appeased by the infinitely worthy sacrifice of Jesus Christ. He is the Lamb of God who takes away the sin of the world, and He is the Light that overcomes the Darkness. He is the One who has the power of Life over Death, and all things were made by Him, and through Him, that glory would resound unto Yahweh. Who are we, that the Creator would be mindful of us? We were made lower than the angels, and we made ourselves even lower through the Fallout of our sins. But God was willing to condescend unto us and take up the form of Man so that through the offering of His body, the sins of many could be forgiven. Just who do we think we are? If we do not agree with God, we will be corrected in due time. But if we have come to know salvation and the truth, then there is only one reasonable response left for us.

But you are a chosen race, a royal priesthood, a holy nation, a people for his own possession, ***that you may proclaim the excellencies of him who called you out of darkness into his marvelous light.***

1 Peter 2:9 (ESV)

So now God has taken the army of the Dead and transformed them into the army of the Living! We have a great responsibility to Walk by faith and serve as we have been served. There will be some that doubt, and we will have mercy and grace on them with the hope that they are led by the Spirit of God through our example. There will be others who perch dangerously on the edge of the Fire. These we will secure even at great cost. And still, others will Walk in shameful garments stained by the Flesh. We will show these both mercy and fear in the hopes that they will understand the graveness of their decisions (Jude 1:22-23). All of these, like we ourselves know, have been Walking in near-death even if they were unaware and remain so. But we will do what is required to bring glory to God through our lives and, if necessary, our deaths. Love covers over a multitude of sins (1 John), and there is great rejoicing at the repentance of even one Zombie (Luke 15:7).

THE HOPELESS

Remember that **at that time, you were separate from Christ**, *excluded from citizenship in Israel and foreigners to the covenants of the promise,* **without hope and without God in the world.**"

Ephesians 2:12 (NIV)

There is no hope for the Dead that remain thus upon their physical death. No amount of prayer can change the choices they made. There is no purgatory for their sins to be burned away. The fire of Hell is an eternal fire, and it torments those being punished forever (Luke 16). Nothing can change the fact that the Dead who die in their sins did not receive Christ as Lord and Savior. The morbidity of this condition ought to motivate all the Worthy Walkers to a fervent dispensation of the Gospel Cure. For we know what we have been saved from and cannot bear to think that those around us may be heading for that fate. The Zombie may not realize what they are currently, but they will be made to know their true nature in the afterlife. The place where they are banished is full of weeping and gnashing of teeth. It is shut out from the glory and the grace of God. They will have no Light, and they will have no hope. Their light has been extinguished, and their hope is Dead. We can be very sure of our salvation, and we can be very sure of their damnation. Does this not motivate the Saint? Does this not cause our hearts to burn in agony over the disregarded Zombie?

The **LIVING DEAD** Revival Guide

*I have labored and toiled and have often gone **without sleep**; I have known **hunger** and **thirst** and have often gone without food; I have been cold and naked. Besides everything else, I face daily the pressure of my concern for all the churches. Who is weak, and I do not feel weak? Who is led into sin, and I do not **inwardly burn**?*

2 Corinthians 11:27-29 (ESV)

Do we not fear the outcome that faces the Dead? Surely, we feared the fate that was before us when we saw the Light. The Light itself revealed our true condition that we were Dead in our sins. When we looked intently into the mirror of Scripture, and it confirmed what we feared, we were compelled to believe. The Holy Spirit prompted us to believe and to do so with the quickest response possible. For how could we know at what time we would be required before the Lord God who judges the Living and the Dead? We do not know when we will die, and we do not know when anyone else will die. In the magnificent grace of God, we even pray that God would spare those who are on the verge of death. But how many of us are willing to do our part in sharing the Gospel Cure. That is if we really have it in us. The Gospel Cure is like a great treasure contained in a modest and feeble vessel. But miraculously, it never runs out so long as we share it. But perhaps we do not venture to share the immensely valuable treasure with the hopelessly Dead? What could be said of a servant such as this? I dare not seek to know for myself. Rather, in the fear of God, I will make the most of the opportunities that the Lord has afforded me. We know that the days are evil, and the generation is wicked. But the Lord is faithful and true. He has saved us, and the least we could do is cooperate with Him in reaching out to those who do not yet know Him. There will be a day when we can no longer say to one another, "Know the Lord," for all will know Him! Is this a joy and a relief to us? One can only know. But those who seek a rich entrance into the presence of the Lord will be devoted to abiding in Christ. Those who abide will do His bidding. Those are the ones of which it will be said, "Well done good and faithful servant, enter into the joy of your Lord" (Matthew 25:21).

Let godly fear work in you as we fight the hopelessness of the Dead. The Zombie cannot have more confidence in their depravity than the Saint has in the Lord's ability to save. The Dead revel in their defiance and disobedience, how much more should the Saint revel in their faithfulness and obedience. Our God shows no partiality, and therefore we must be willing to associate with the great and the small and any in-between. Unless for some reason, we think more of ourselves than we ought to. Then if that is the case, we should be warned, just as the Sleep Walker is alarmed with their precarious standing. For if we are not careful in how we Walk, it may just be that we are destined to Fall. Thank God that He lifts all those who stumble and causes them to stand before Himself in blameless innocence. Our innocence before the Father is not because we have never done wrong but instead because we have accepted the Gospel Cure and, therefore, the Life of Christ as our own. I fear that there are a great many who do not understand what has been done for them. But I am not hopeless in this matter. Rather I am aware that God is working out all things for those who love Him and are called according to his purpose (Romans 8:28). Perhaps it is right that the Saint foster a fear of the doom that hovers over the head of the Zombie. For it is right that the Saint work out their salvation with fear and trembling (Philippians 2:12). We must realize as fully as possible what cost was paid in order to purchase us. It was a high cost. It was a divine payment. It is a finished transaction. It was not made with perishable things like gold and silver. But it was purchased through the blood of Jesus Christ. If we believe this, than truly, we have a Hope that will never Die!

> **Anyone who is among the living has hope**—*even a live dog is better off than a dead lion! For the living know that they will die, but the dead know nothing; they have no further reward, and even their name is forgotten. Their love, their hate, and their jealousy have long since vanished; never again will they have a part in anything that happens under the sun.*
> Ecclesiastes 9:4-6 (NIV)

CHAPTER THREE

ZOMBIE APOCALYPSE

LIVING IN THE ZOMBIE APOCALYPSE

*Then **the end will come**, when he hands over the kingdom to God the Father after he has destroyed all dominion, authority and power.*
1 Corinthians 15:24 (ESV)

There are a great number of Biblical characters that have solidified their stories in our hearts. Some of these characters have done so to great renown. While others have a more infamous standing in the halls of Biblical history. We have been told these stories so that we might remember them and learn from their example. In the case of those who have Walked Worthy, we are called to follow after Christ Jesus just as they have done. While in the other case, we are urged to beware, the mistakes made by those who Walk in their Sleep, or even those who Walk as Zombies upon the earth. We must not set our hearts on the evil things that were done in ignorance of the truth. Those that practice evil deeds can only expect judgment to follow. Those that were in the wilderness were put to death for their disobedience. We must not test Christ as some of them did and therefore be destroyed by the various forces set against us (1 Corinthians 10:1-10). We should not expect to push the limits of what the Lord is willing to endure with our behavior. The Worthy Walker would not willingly continue to sin and make it a habitual practice. But those that Walk with Christ and continue to revert to sin should take heed from these stories. For it was the people that witnessed the miraculous events that saved them out of the clutches of Egypt who were later falling down dead in the wilderness for their disobedience. What will be said of us, who remain even at the end of the ages? These Last Days must be regarded with seriousness because we know that the End will come upon us like labor pains upon a pregnant woman, and those who disregard the signs will be in even greater danger.

*Now these things happened to them as an example, but they were written down for our instruction, **on whom the end of the ages has come**.*
1 Corinthians 10:11

If anything can be said about the Zombie Apocalypse, it is this: all Zombies are Dead before the Holy and Living God. But this is unknown to those whom it is most severe. Perhaps of even greater revelation is the truth that these are the very same that God has decided to graciously call forth into Life. It now rests on us to respond to His call unto Life. Will we harden our hearts as those did that were Walking in the wilderness? Will we neglect to praise our God when he provides food for us? Will we groan against Him when He gives us clothing? We should be well pleased if we have food and clothing. The Sleep Walker finds themselves in search of the things that will please them; perhaps these things please them more than the Lord Himself does. They must be made aware that only the Lord can resolve the tireless seeking after things can never truly satisfy us. Consider what will be said of us at the end of our lives. Will we be counted among those who Walk in Death or spiritual Sleep? Or will we be among those who were wise and turned many towards righteousness so that their Walk could be Worthy?

> *And many of those who **sleep** in the dust of the earth shall **awake**, some to **everlasting life**, and some to **shame and everlasting contempt**. And those who are wise shall shine like the brightness of the sky above; and those who turn many to righteousness, like the stars forever and ever.*
> Daniel 12:2-3 (ESV)

The Zombie and the Saint will both partake of an apocalyptic revelation. Although this term, apocalypse, has been obscured by sensationalism and various misinterpretations. Apocalypse may include destruction, demise, and destitution but more than that, it refers to the uncovering or revealing of truth. But this Zombie Apocalypse is indeed upon us. Not because of any insight of our own but rather because of what the Scripture has revealed to us. The Word of God has made it abundantly clear that the sinful behavior of mankind will not go unpunished. But the mockers reject the truth and instead prefer to believe a lie. They neglect to understand that God has been faithful and discernible to us in ways that have left us with full culpability. The whole world is full of the glory of God, and we can clearly observe His divine nature and power if only we would look. Indeed, creation testifies to a Creator. For the creation groans and we groan as the Saints anticipate the redemption of their bodies (Romans 8)! But who are we to say we know anything? Let us always verify the truth through the help of the Holy Spirit and the Holy Scripture!

The LIVING DEAD Revival Guide

Have the gates of death been revealed to you, *or have you seen the gates of deep darkness? Have you comprehended the expanse of the earth?* ***Declare, if you know all this***.

Job 38:17-18 (ESV)

We hardly know what we have gotten ourselves into, for we are born into a type of spiritual ignorance that plagues all people. When the Fallout of sin came down upon Adam and Eve, we all partook of its repercussions. We cannot save ourselves nor anyone else by the means of our own efforts. But we will undeniably be responsible for our actions before the Holy One who Lives forever. God will not be mocked by our actions as though we could get away with our behavior (Galatians 6:7). We cannot hide our actions in the Dark because even the Darkness is as clear to Him as the Light. Nothing can deceive the One who knows all things. Our old self may have tried to hide from Him, but now we have stepped out into the Light and have come to realize that only faith and repentance are required to have a relationship with the Living God. He is able to sympathize with our weaknesses, seeing that He himself also bore the same kind of frame as we have and yet without sin. Knowing what we know now, how is it that we could return to those Dead works? It is practically impossible! For we are those, who have Died to sin and have been made Alive in Christ (Colossians 2-3). God continually calls us to focus our attention not on the earthly things that are passing away, even as they are used and abused, but rather on the heavenly things that are everlasting. Faith, hope, and love are the only remnants, and the greatest of these is love! We have been called children of God, and that is what we are. The World did not know Jesus, and it does not know us. We have been crucified to the World, and the World has been crucified to us (Galatians 6:14). The Life we now Live is done so through faith in the Risen Savior because we know beyond a doubt that there is no other way to the Father except through Him (John 14:6). Therefore, we must make every effort to confirm our calling and election. For if we were to neglect such a great salvation, one can only imagine horrible fire and torment as recompense.

For if we go on sinning deliberately after receiving the knowledge of the truth, there no longer remains a sacrifice for sins, ***but a fearful expectation of judgment, and a fury of fire*** *that will consume the adversaries.*

Hebrews 10:26-27 (ESV)

We know out of what we have been saved. But do the Dead know anything about this? Of course, they do not! The Zombie does not realize their dire state. They Walk around in the Darkness groaning and groping but never coming around to a knowledge of the truth. They are quick to proclaim the safety of their standing, all the while endangering themselves even further by their arrogance. They have unbelieving hearts, and as it is, their Sin springs to Life within them. They cannot separate sin from themselves. Their sin clings on to them closer than their very skin. Even though they are Dead in their sins, they animate Sin by giving it a vessel to carry out lawlessness. Tragic though it may be, this reality is all to familiar to us. Only the fool would regard sin without seriousness. For the ramifications of sin is tantamount to Death, but the free gift of God is true and everlasting Life expressed through a relationship with the Lord.

Take care, brothers, lest there be in any of you an evil, unbelieving heart, leading you to fall away from the living God.

Hebrews 3:12 (ESV)

The Saint Walks in the World all the while belonging to a World not yet known. Many of the Worthy Walkers have a deep awareness of a Home that they have never dwelled in but somehow have known. We sense that we belong somewhere else, or more accurately, that we belong to Someone else. The Saint is a child of God, but not all of the terms of their adoption have been fully made known or realized. Of course, the Zombie knows nothing about this, the Sleep Walker knows not what they ought to know, and the Worthy Walker bases their entire life upon this truth. These are wondrous truths that are so magnificent that even the angels long to look into these matters (1 Peter 1:12). How could it be that those blessed by such wondrous love could be halfheartedly considerate of such things? What shame is there for those who are Alive but somehow Asleep on the beautiful blessings of the Father? He blesses us with every good and perfect gift from above. He is not like our earthly fathers in that the gifts of our Heavenly Father are always perfect and exactly what we need. There is no shifting of character by temporal things, and there is no changing the quality of love that the Father graciously pours out for His Children. But we were not always Children of God, at one time, we too were children of disobedience. We were eager offspring of wickedness. We were caved in upon our greedy and selfish desires. Evil spiritual forces of Darkness led us astray in our former way of life. We were despondently and hopelessly Dead in our sins. Surely, we realize the great chasm that separated us from God, now that He has accomplished His saving work on our behalf? Yes, the Worthy Walkers are aware of this.

The **LIVING DEAD** Revival Guide

THE FALLOUT AND THE HALL OF FAITH

*And **without faith it is impossible to please God**, because anyone who approaches Him must believe that He exists and that He rewards those who earnestly seek Him.*

Hebrews 11:6

It is said that those who are in the Flesh, that is, Zombies, cannot please God (Romans 6). The reason for this is because they remain hostile towards Him. They will not obey Him, and they cannot obey Him because they obey a different lord. Their god is their Fleshly appetites that are catered to by the spiritual forces of darkness and the manipulation of the World. Consider for a moment how we might become more cognizant of the notorious and nefarious Zombies from the Old and New Testament. On the contrary, we should admire the steadfast faith of the Saints who have come before us. Perhaps we will join the ranks of those who turn many to righteousness and therefore shine like the stars in the sky. The obscuring gray area of these two groups can create be difficult to navigate. Like a fog that restricts our vision, we should approach with caution.

*Therefore, let anyone who thinks that he stands **take heed lest he fall.***

1 Corinthians 10:12 (ESV)

If we have come to know the Light and love and truth of God's Gospel Cure, then we will be able to identify who throughout the ages has been categorized as unfaithful or unfaltering. This represents my best attempt to understand what has been revealed to us through the inspired Word of God, and if in something I have made an error, I accept that this too God will reveal to me. This is by no means to say that I have any ability to determine the salvific state of another person. Rather this is an effort to identify the places where the Word of God declares a person either wicked or righteous. As we ourselves know, the blurry gray line that divides between the Living and the Dead is often too obscured to determine for ourselves clearly. However, there are other times when it is all too obvious that someone has denied the Lord God. What we can say for sure is that all those who call upon the Name of the Lord shall be saved. May He be glorified as we Walk ever closer to Him.

*I pray that the **eyes of your heart may be enlightened in order that you may know the hope to which he has called you**, the riches of his glorious inheritance in his holy people.*

Ephesians 1:18 (ESV)

A short list of notable biblical characters may help us recognize the means by which we can understand what kind of help we can offer to those who are in need. Our responsibility upon being brought to Life is to no longer live as the Zombies we once were but rather to turn our efforts away from ourselves only and onto others. This mindset reflects the light of the glory of God, which is displayed in the face of Christ (2 Corinthians 4, Philippians 2). The most use we can be to others is by speaking Life to them and being a representative of Christ Jesus unto those who do not know Him. We are the perfect ambassadors unto a Dead and Dying World. But only if we Walk in a manner Worthy to the calling that we have received. Who could know the tremendous value in the seed that we plant or water along the Way? We cannot clearly discern the effects of all our actions. We do not know how every way they may affect others. But we can be sure that it is the Creator who causes Life to Grow out of the Deadness.

There are a great many who, by their word and deed, can be known as Dead or Alive. The results of our actions are the Fruit that we produce. Only God will be able to divide between soul and spirit, joints and marrow, and even to the thoughts and attitudes of the heart (Hebrews 4:12). Regardless of our opinions, we must rely solely upon the truth made known to us in the Word of God and with the help of the Holy Spirit. It can be a difficult reality to comprehend even when it is of such limitless benefit to us. How is it that the infinitely holy God could be so kind and loving toward such undeserving creatures? Why would He do such a thing? Why would He willing lay His life down for our sakes? The only answer that we can cry out is that He loves us. Simple and powerful at the same time, the truth is that God loves us despite what we deserve.

> **We know God's love** *for us in this, that while we were still sinners*
> ***Christ died for us****.*
>
> Romans 5:8 (ESV)

The love of God is truly amazing. He has abundantly demonstrated the dimensions of His love (Ephesians 3:18-19) to us in saving wretched sinners like me. We do not know what is good without the help of God. Left to our own devices, we would surely bring about our own destruction. We have come to accept the wonderful truth that God is the One who gives us wisdom for how we should Walk. He is a wonderful counselor and a mighty God. He is always with us. Indeed, Jesus always Lives to make intercession on our behalf (Hebrews 7:25). He has divinely appointed us to succeed in bringing Him glory. All that is required of us has been simply laid out. We must do what is right, love what is merciful and Walk humbly with our God (Micah 6:8). His demands are not burdensome, His yoke is light, and He will certainly carry us beyond what we could bear on our own.

The **LIVING DEAD** Revival Guide

I tell you; he will give justice to them speedily.
Nevertheless, when the Son of Man comes, will he find faith on earth?

Luke 18:8 (ESV)

The following list is neither exhaustive nor comprehensive list but rather serves to help us see more clearly that the Zombie Apocalypse is indeed still upon us. But also let it be known that the Revelation of Jesus Christ in the Saints is coming quickly. May we not be found to be asleep upon the return of the Master. We do not know at what time or hour the Lord will return. We know not the specific details of the events but, instead, have a bigger picture in mind. The picture painted is that of a World overrun by the iniquity of sin and those who practice it. The World at the return of the Lord will perhaps be infested worse than ever before by the dreadful Zombies. Indeed, it may be eerily similar to the ways that it was during the Days of Noah. People will be so despicably evil as only to desire what is sinfully Deadly all the time.

Oh, the depth of the riches and wisdom and knowledge of God!
How unsearchable are his judgments and how inscrutable his ways!

Romans 11:33 (ESV)

DEAD WALKERS
(Condemned as Zombies and opposed to the Lord)

Cain, Lamech (the husband of Adah and Zilla, Genesis 4:19), Nimrod, Pharaoh, Korah's rebellion.

SLEEP WALKERS
(Confusing to identify as Living or Dead because we do not know the heart as God does)

Saul, Samson, Lot, Nebuchadnezzar, Demas, Simon, the sorcerer.

WORTHY WALKERS
(Commended as righteous, not because of works, but because of faith unto God)

Adam, Eve, Abel, Enoch, Noah, Abraham, Isaac, Jacob, Joseph

Talon Schneider

THE ZOMBIE'S APOCALYPSE

We know that we are from God, and the whole world lies in the power of the evil one.

1 John 5:19 (ESV)

Zombies have filled the earth from end to end. They cover the face of the earth and can be found in every place regardless of how isolated it may seem. They are found in the wilderness and in the cities. Despite the overwhelming numbers of the Dead, there is cause for great hope among the Living. Even though there are many more Zombies in the World than there are Saints, this should not be surprising. We know that the Way to Life is difficult and passes through the narrow gate. But the path that the Zombie is on is wide, and the great many of them follow it to their destruction. They take that path because it suits them. They are naturally driven to be their own demise. Their faithlessness and lawlessness are disguised as freedom, but they are slaves of their sin. Remarkably when we are given New Life and are Born Again into the Living Hope of the resurrection of the Dead through Jesus Christ, we can finally see that our Zombie existence has been put away to reveal Christ in us. God has always had a plan of redemption. But if the rulers at the time of Christ's sacrifice had known, then they would have never crucified the Lord of Glory (1 Corinthians 2:8). And while we were Dead in our transgressions and in the morbidity of our Flesh, God made us Alive by forgiving us of all our transgressions against Him (Colossians 2:13). That is the reason that we should be baptized, seeing that it symbolizes our sharing in the Death and resurrection of Jesus Christ. Because of Him, the forces of spiritual Darkness have no power over us any longer. He has nullified them because their power had to do with sin, but our power has to do with righteousness. The righteousness of Christ has covered us, and the sin that once was bringing about our destruction has been done away with once and for all.

He has destroyed what was against us, a certificate of indebtedness expressed in decrees opposed to us. **He has taken it away by nailing it to the cross**. *Disarming the rulers and authorities, he has made a public disgrace of them,* **triumphing over them by the cross**.

Colossians 2:14-15 (ESV)

Nothing could be more surprising than the truth about the Zombie and the Saint. At once, there was intense enmity, but now there is intimate family. Only the Lord could have enacted such a marvelous plan for redemption. What a shock it shall be to those who continually defy God! Many of us were, at one time, sinners in various ways. We were thieves, liars, murderers, sexually immoral, disobedient, and more. But despite these despicable beginnings, there was a love that feared nothing because it was perfect. The perfect love of Christ has cast out the fear of punishment that we had. He has saved us completely, and therefore there is now no condemnation for those who are in Christ Jesus (Romans 8:1). Only in Christ can the perfect love and justice of Yahweh be in full agreement. Only through the blood of Christ can forgiveness be received because it was through His death that we have Life. This mystery revealed to us by the Holy Spirit is considered foolish nonsense, according to the Dead. That is until they themselves are utterly changed by it! Until the Dead hear the voice of the Son of Man and are brought to Life (John 5:25). All those who have heard the voice are like sheep following after their shepherd. Praise the Lord who love His little flock so much that he would leave the 99 to go after the one sheep in need. Yes, there is great rejoicing in heaven when even one Zombie is converted into a Saint through faith in the Gospel Cure.

> *They only were hearing it said, "He who used to persecute us*
> *is **now preaching the faith he once tried to destroy.**"*
> *And **they glorified God because of me.***
> Galatians 1:23-24 (ESV)

Praise the Lord for his manifold wisdom! There is no other god like our God, who is mighty to save. Indeed, we were saved from the consequence of our sins by the sacrifice of His only son. However, it is all too easy to forget that it is His wrath from which we must be saved. His wrath against sin will be poured out either through Christ's sacrifice or upon the unrepentant sinner. Just as it was with the wicked servant whose great debt was pardoned, so too shall it be with us who believe. But God forbid that we would be wicked after receiving such a great salvation. Rather let us be good and faithful servants who seek first His kingdom and righteousness. For the time has passed for us to indulge in the ungodly ways of the Zombie. We have already spent too much time in the Darkness. We are no longer of the Darkness; we belong to the Day and, therefore, must align ourselves with the Light. The Zombie continues to hide in the Darkness because it thinks that it can hide its wicked deeds from the One who knows all things. And they are the ones that consider truth to be foolishness. They will be shown the error of their ways. But what will happen to them when they are made aware of their sin? For the Worthy Walker, it is essential to the conversion we have experienced. We must be made aware of our destitution before the Lord, for how else, could we come to recognize the significance of Christ's sacrifice? When we become aware of our endless sin debt before the Lord and are made conscious of our Dead condition before Him, there are only two real reactions. We may peer into that perfect mirror that grants freedom from sin to those who follow it, or we may perceive for a moment the truth of our nature but Walk away unchanged. The former are those that have been transformed by the renewal of their minds and the confirmation of the will of God in their lives. The latter are the Zombies who, despite hearing the Words of Life, have turned away to the continue in their Deadness.

> *"Therefore, judge nothing before the appointed time; wait until the Lord comes.* **He will bring to light what is hidden in darkness and will expose the motives of the heart***. At that time each will receive their praise from God.*
> 1 Corinthians 4:5 (ESV)

There is coming a Day when all things will be revealed. That which is whispered in the ear will be proclaimed from the rooftops. On that Day, when the Son of Man comes to be revealed in the World and glorified in His Saints, there will be Apocalypse like has never been known. Although this time, the Apocalypse will be upon the Zombie. They will no longer be able to deny that Jesus Christ is Lord to the glory of God the Father. For all the time that the Dead have Walked the earth, there has also been a remnant of God's faithful people. There may come a time when the World seems to have become so overrun with the living Dead and the effects of their influence upon the earth that the Saint may feel the loss of their footing. The Saint may be disheartened for a short time as they consider the prosperity of the wicked. Zombies feast and gorge themselves upon all that brings them pleasure. They become swollen with their feasting but never seem to stop. Meanwhile, the Saint experiences hardships and persecution, but the Zombie does not realize that their time is coming to an end sooner than they know. This is not something to take lightly; rather, it should motivate the Saint to reach out to the Lost with the message of salvation. In those times that the Saint is hard-pressed by seeing the prosperity of the wicked, they ought to go to the Lord with a worshipful heart and remember on what path they were before seeing the Light.

> *But when I thought how to understand this,* **it seemed to me a wearisome task***, until I went into the sanctuary of God; then I discerned their end.*
> Psalm 73:16-17 (ESV)

God has made known to us that the revelation of Jesus Christ will come at a time when people are not expecting it. His second coming will be as unknown as a thief that comes in the middle of the night. Perhaps He tarries so that the full number of Saints may take hold of the salvation that is offered. Jesus has already been lifted up and exalted and given the name above all names. We who know Him as both Lord and God have already committed ourselves to following Him in this life no matter the cost. All around the world, there are people who continue to seek for Him and find Him because their seeking is not in vain. It is great joy to know our Lord and Savior as soon as possible so that we might be able to Walk Worthy and please Him in our eagerness to do good. But the greatest good we can do is to Walk in the purpose for which He made us. Certainly, He has made us to be revealers of His truth. For that reason, Jesus came into the World to testify to the truth (John 18:37). The truth of Jesus is that He is the Word made flesh, being both God and man. He was willing to empty Himself to some degree beyond what I can fathom. We know that He condescended to us, His creation, and was willing to become like us by taking on the form of a servant. He showed us the way to the Father by becoming obedient even to the point of dying upon the cross. He became a curse for our sake to redeem us from the curse upon us. Although He never sinned, He was compassionate towards us and sympathized with our weakness. Because He laid His life down, doing the will of the Father, we have been restored. His atoning sacrifice is the propitiation for our sins and the means by which Zombies have become Saints.

> *"Therefore God has highly exalted him and bestowed on him the name that is above every name, so that **at the name of Jesus** every knee should bow, in heaven and on earth and under the earth, and every tongue confess that **Jesus Christ is Lord, to the glory of God the Father**.*
> Philippians 2:9-11 (ESV)

Now, if we know this, but are too fearful of the Zombies to tell them the truth, what will be said of us? What type of entry to heaven shall we receive? Surely not the rich welcome of those that likewise lay their lives down for the sake of the Gospel Cure! For those that lose their lives are the ones that find their Life in Christ. Those are the ones that exclaim, "For me to Live is Christ and to die is gain!" There is nothing to fear, seeing that we have been perfected in Love. Not a love of our own, but the undying Love of the Risen Savior who holds the power over death. So, what can stop the Saints? There is nothing that can separate us from His love. Nothing in all of creation can separate His love from us (Romans 8:38-39). Therefore, we have great boldness to be more than conquerors, not by might but by His Spirit, who Lives in us! We know He Lives because he Lives within us, and we have become intimately aware of Him. We have become so tremendously conscious of the Lord our God that we could not possibly remove this knowledge from our hearts. But that is the essence of the problem facing those that do not yet believe. They have lying hearts and deceptive motivations that are manifested as various sins. They are clouded and darkened in their understanding, seeing that they are alienated from God, just as we were. But the Revelation of Jesus Christ will come for a second time, and at that time, He will be revealed not to deal with sins as He did the first time but rather to bring salvation to those who eagerly await Him (Hebrews 9:28).

The time is short, for we are already in the Last Days. There is no time for us to wander aimlessly in search of fleeting vanities. Worthy Walkers must commit themselves to the Faithful Creator and continue in doing good (1 Peter 4:19). The Saints of God are looking for and hastening the return of the Lord Jesus Christ because we know that the more faithfully we do our job, the sooner the return of Christ will be. And who knows at what time it will be that He returns to us, but what we can say is that we have the choice to bow to Him now in humble adoration. Worthy Walkers willingly bend our knee and confess with our tongue that Jesus Christ is Lord to the Glory of God the Father! But the Zombie, too, will make this confession, even if they do not realize this truth now. They, too, will make that confession seeing that it is undeniable and true. But at that, it will be too late for them to be cured of the Death they have Walked in all their lives. The Zombie's Apocalypse will be the final realization that all their toiling in the earth has added up to an endless sin debt that will be paid for in Hell for all eternity. They will be judged accurately by the One who knows the beginning from the end and who declares things in advance as if they had already happened. The God of the Living will send them to their just punishment. Will the Zombie meet this realization in time? Will the Dead hear the voice of the Son of Man and Live? Or will the Dead neglect the Cure to Death and continue to violently quicken their fateful demise? We cannot say for sure; all that we can do is be faithful to the calling we have. We will see our Redeemer again, and He will be glorified in his Saints. At that time, it will be the Zombie's Apocalypse and the Revelation of Jesus Christ in His Saints.

> ***When he comes on that day to be glorified in his saints****, and to be marveled at among all who have believed, because our testimony to you was believed. To this end, we always pray for you,* ***that our God may make you worthy of his calling*** *and may fulfill every resolve for good and every work of faith by his power, so that the name of our Lord Jesus may be glorified in you, and you in him, according to the grace of our God and the Lord Jesus Christ."*
>
> 2 Thessalonians 1:10-12 (ESV)

The **LIVING DEAD** Revival Guide

The Zombie's Apocalypse is fast approaching. Even now, it is upon them. For just as it is with their identity, they have no awareness of the doom and wrath coming for them all. They have loved the Darkness for too long, and their hearts have been too calloused to recognize the seriousness of the charge against them. They have ignored the preaching of righteousness just as it was in the Days of Noah and others. But the time for their recompense will be at the end to display the enormous patience of the Lord. He has endured their disobedience for such a time as to display on the contrary His graciousness to those who have been brought to Life (Romans 9:22-23). There will be glory unto God both in His justice coming down against the unrepentant and in the Revelation of Jesus Christ in the Saints. We must hold fast to the confession of our faith without wavering. We know the one who doubts is tossed back and forth as one who is restless in their bed. They are tossed back and forth by the waves of errant teachings. These are the Sleep Walkers who Live in Christ but occasionally Walk in the Flesh rather than the Spirit. We who are strong must bear up with them for the sake of the Body. Worthy Walkers remain for this very purpose; that the weak would be strengthened, and the Zombie would be converted.

> But **there were** also false prophets among the people, just as **there will be** false teachers among you. They will secretly introduce destructive heresies, **even denying the sovereign Lord who bought them**—bringing swift destruction on themselves. Many will follow their **depraved conduct** and will bring the way of truth into disrepute. In their greed, these teachers will exploit you with fabricated stories. Their condemnation has long been hanging over them, and their **destruction has not been sleeping**.
> 2 Peter 2:1-3 (ESV)

We must remember to warn, wake, and alarm, if necessary, those who Walk in their Sleep. If they are Saints that Sleep, then we must pay careful attention to them, being sure to help them out of love and not out of disfavor. However, we may not be able to know for sure if they are truly Alive or have the appearance of Life but deny it by their actions. For there are already more than enough, who straddle the blurry line. Regardless, we have learned that the best approach for them and for us will be to administer the truth in love. They are idle when hard work is needed, and their focus is on their own gain rather than the needs of others.

Talon Schneider

And we urge you, brothers and sisters, **warn those who are idle and disruptive, encourage the disheartened, help the weak, be patient with everyone.**[1]

Thessalonians 5:14 (ESV)

TRUE SANCTUARY

Unless the LORD *builds the house, its builders labor in vain; unless the LORD protects the city, its watchmen stand guard in vain. In vain you rise early and stay up late, toiling for bread to eat—* **for he gives sleep to His beloved.**

Psalm 127:1-2 (ESV)

Where could we go to escape the Zombie Apocalypse? The spread of the sin and Death has reached to the ends of the earth. That is why we must, therefore, go to the ends of the earth with the message of Life through Christ. But what place can there be for safety among the Living? That place must be fortified with the strongest protection. Many have mistaken this to mean that we must hide ourselves away from the World and its Zombies. The unfortunately persistent fear of the Dead continues even among the Living. This should not be! We have been brought to Life through the death of Christ. We have partaken of His death and, in some way, have ourselves Died to the World. We consider ourselves crucified to the World and it to us. But if we harbor an incorrect sense of fear towards the Dead, then we will not be able to Walk as strongly in our purpose. Indeed, there is a difference between danger and fear. We are called to fear the One who is able to destroy the body and the soul in hell. We have no need to fear those who can only harm the body. The Lord will pay the harm they do to the Saints back, so we will leave room for His vengeance. On the other hand, we will not allow ourselves to be overcome by anxieties and fears that do not belong to the Saint but are more natural to the Zombie. They know fear and have decided to cover it up in various sensualities because they have lost sensitivity to what really matters. How could anything temporary compare to that which is eternal? We are now convinced that the meager and temporary suffering that we experience will be so short as to be not worth comparing to the glory that will be revealed in us. The Zombie's Apocalypse is coming down on them, not us! We will know the Lord, and He will be glorified as He is revealed in us. But let it be that we are found to be in Him as well. We must abide in Him, for apart from Him, we can do nothing.

The LIVING DEAD Revival Guide

And do this, understanding the occasion. The hour has come for you to **wake up from your slumber, for our salvation is nearer now** *than when we first believed.*

Romans 13:11 (ESV)

Our shelter and Sanctuary is in the Lord God, who protects us. He is able to save us completely (Hebrews 7:24-25). But the sacrifice for sins has brought complete atonement to those of us who have believed. There is, therefore, no longer any need for inferior sacrifices seeing that Jesus has given us propitiation before the Lord. He has perfected us not because we were worthy but because Jesus was worthy, and therefore those of us who are being sanctified can have great courage in the face of all these dangers (Hebrews 10:14). There are no limits to what God is able to do. Considering what a mighty work has been done on our behalf in the saving of our souls, there is nothing that is too difficult for our God. He is the Deliverer and Redeemer that we need. We will draw near to Him and rely upon Him for everything. This is in stark contrast to the way we were familiar with in our previous Walk. But what great joy it is that we could see such a difference. It is as different as Night is from Day! Admittedly it would be better for us to depart and be with the Lord right away. But we remain so that we may serve those who are to inherit salvation. Seeing that we cannot know who will believe our message, the best we can do is speak Life to any and all who would hear it with spiritual ears. As it was with us, so to it may be with them. But we will never know what would become of them if we do not do our part. The truth is that we are better off being within their midst, for then we are of greater influence. The type of Sanctuary that we need cannot be restricted to a single location. The time has come and is now here when the Lord desires those who worship Him in spirit and in truth, regardless of their location (John 4:24). So we can tell that our Sanctuary is not limited by where we are. The protection we need comes through faith in the Lord God Almighty. The Lord is mighty to save all those who call on His name. He is our safety and security. We have called upon Him, and indeed we run to Him, for He is our Life.

The name of the LORD is a fortified tower;
the righteous run to it and are safe.

Proverbs 18:10 (ESV)

Who is it that will raise an attack against the Lord's people? For even if you kill them, they are blessed! They are exalted in death because it does not separate us from God but brings us closer to Him. We have longed to see Him face to face. For a little while, we may have had to face various trials of many kinds, but despite it all, we rejoice knowing that the stronger our faith becomes, the closer our relationship with the Lord becomes as well. We would not be so brash as to seek the end of our own life by our own hands, for that prerogative belongs to the Lord alone. We know that He is in control, and we are under His will. We will trust that our life and our death is in the hands of God.

> *We always carry around in our body **the death of Jesus, so that the life of Jesus** may also be revealed in our body.*
> 2 Corinthians 4:10 (ESV)

We do not seek death, but if it is necessary, it will come. Just as it was said in times before, "Even if he kills us, we will not serve other gods." There are some who do not see this Sanctuary as the safety and protection that it actually is. The reason for this is because the only way to access its protection is through faith. We must Walk by faith and not by sight (2 Corinthians 5:7). The things that we can see with our eyes are fading away. Even the Zombie is under this rule seeing that they decay inwardly and outwardly every day that passes. Their decomposition is a difficult thing to behold, but we have not been trained to see them as we once did. When we hated them because we were like them, it made for no good result. But now, if we love our enemies and feed them when they are hungry, perhaps, we will see an opportunity to share the Gospel Cure. Even if they reject our kindness, it is not to obstruct us, for then we would be sharing in the experiences of Christ Jesus. A deeper understanding of Jesus' faithfulness will also increase our faithfulness. As that happens, we will be conformed to be more like Him in love. For that reason, we are called to be Living Sacrifices, always willing to lay our lives down if it would mean that somehow the Gospel Cure would be received.

There are those who would prefer to stay hidden away from the World. Their concern is for their own priorities, which is understandable in such a dire situation as this. We are already living in the aftermath of the Apocalypse that was brought about by Original Sin. But this seclusion has kept them safe at the expense of a lost ministry. Our ministry should not be lost because it is for The Lost. We cannot remove ourselves from the World because if we did, then we would no longer be able to effect change in the World. We are called to be in the World, but not of it. Therefore, we must purify those that are among us, doing so with careful evaluation of our own actions. There should not be perpetual and habitual sin found among the Body of believers. We will confront such behavior and alarm those that Walk in Sleep. But as we extend our efforts to those outside of the shelter that is Name of the Lord, we will undoubtedly see things which we would hope not to see. The Apostle Paul also observed this dilemma when he wrote to the Corinthian church, urging them to practice holiness in the fear of God. However, we cannot expect to remove ourselves from the sphere of evil behavior in the World because, in order to do that, we would have to be removed from the World altogether.

> *Not at all meaning the sexually immoral of this world, or the greedy and swindlers, or idolaters,* ***since then you would need to go out of the world.***
> 1 Corinthians 5:10 (ESV)

This will take place at the proper time. But while we await the Return and Revelation of the Lord Jesus Christ, we should be hard at work. The work that we do will be that of a simple life. We must learn to provide for our families and, if possible, for others as well. It is good for us to learn many traits and skills so that we can speak Life while at the same time offer the kind of assistance that all people need. These displays of godly behavior may just be the Light that is shined in Dark places. There it may be that the Holy Spirit works in the heart and soul of a Zombie. There are a great many things that will be required of us, but none of them will be in vain so long as we do them to the glory of God. For all that shines are itself a Light. Perhaps then we will be witnesses of the conversion of many Zombies who were Walking in Death and Sleep. At this, the scripture gives a great encouragement.

> *This is why it is said:* ***"Wake up, sleeper, rise from the dead, and Christ will shine on you.***
> Ephesians 5:14 (ESV)

Living Hope is handed out to those who have believed that Jesus Christ died for them and rose from the grave. Believing that we can have a risen Life as well. But clearly, we need a new Life; otherwise, why would it be referred to as being Born Again? Nicodemus did not understand this at the time that it was spoken to him. He wondered how he could be physically born once more. But the real focus of being Born Again is that the life we come into the World with is already Dead. We begin life not knowing who God is, and that is the reason that we must be renewed. But once we have been Born Again, our lives are never the same. We turn our perspective towards heaven and watch as the Lord works through us to will and to act according to His good pleasure. But may it be that we never cease to think of the needs of others. For the Dead cannot help but collect their fleeting desires as if hoarding them would cause them to remain forever. The one thing that lasts is that which is done for the glory of God. Therefore, the Worthy Walker can willingly participate in the suffering of others, knowing that the removal of our temporary possessions cannot compare to that which we are inheriting. We are receiving a kingdom that cannot be shaken, and therefore, our salvation is a better and lasting possession than anything this World could offer. So, let us not resort to those terminal efforts of the living Dead because they shrink back into their destruction. But we belong to the One who has redeemed us so completely that we are entirely protected under His will.

> *But we are not of those who shrink back to destruction,*
> *but of those who **have faith to the preserving of the soul**.*
> Hebrews 10:39

THE END OF THE WORLD

> ***The world is passing away**, and also its lusts;*
> *but the one who does the will of God lives forever.*
> 1 John 2:17 (ESV)

It has been made known to us who have come to Life that this World and its sinful desires are passing away. As yet, we do not see it because there is still time for those that the Lord draws unto Himself. There is time for them to believe, but the time is quickly passing away. This World is opposed to God, and its system of thought cannot continue forever. Those that abide by the will of the Lord can confirm more thoroughly that they will never Die. Jesus said that He is the Resurrection and the Life, and all those that believe in Him would Live in such a way that not even physical death would stop them from knowing what it was to Live (John 11:25). Even as we can now Walk with the Lord our God, we will be brought to an even deeper relationship with Him at the time that we finally surrender this physical life. We can know this with great certainty, but it is not a desperate or disappointing thing. For the Christian, there is the eager expectation of the consummation of our faith. The transformation from the Zombie to Saint is so drastic as to change the way that we see death. Before we were known to God, we were enslaved by our fear of death and the one who held its power over us. The spiritual enemy of God's people is called the "Prince of the power of the air" in Ephesians chapter 2 and the "god of this world" in 2 Corinthians 4. But he is enraged that his time is so short, and therefore he seeks even more tempestuously to bring about the end of the Christian. But what must be firmly gripped by the believer is that our Life of sacrifice is not in vain so long as it is done for the glory of God. We will offer our lives as Living Sacrifices knowing that our Lord Jesus Christ did so first on our behalf. He brought us salvation, and now we can overcome our fear of death, knowing that we will never be separated from our God ever again. This is of great disdain to those that oppose the Saints because for us to Live is Christ and to die is gain (Philippians 1:21). Even if we are to die physically, we are entirely confident that the departure from our bodies means to be united with the Lord.

> *So, we are always of good courage. We know that **while we are at home in the body, we are away from the Lord, for we walk by faith, not by sight**. Yes, we are of good courage, and we would **rather be away from the body and at home with the Lord**. So, whether we are at home or away, **we make it our aim to please him**. For we must all appear before the judgment seat of Christ, so that each one may receive what is due for what he has done in the body, whether good or evil.*
>
> 2 Corinthians 5:6-10 (ESV)

Knowing that both the Living and the Dead will appear before the judgement seat of Christ, we should be careful how we Walk in this World. We should Walk in wisdom as we evaluate the nearness of the End. We do not know at what time it will come to pass, but we do know that it will come with such rapidness as to catch many people off guard. They will be doing their everyday activities. They will be eating and drinking, and getting married, thinking to themselves that all is well. But there, in their ignorance, they will be confronted with the error of their ways.

> *But you are not in darkness, brothers, **for that day to surprise you like a thief**.*
>
> 1 Thessalonians 5:4 (ESV)

We do not belong to the Night or the Darkness because we belong to the Day and to the Light. We have been given new Life and will make every effort to confirm our calling and election. We do not want to be found lacking when the Lord makes His return. Rather we should seek to please Him with our Walk. For there are many, who are in need of seeing what kind of change can happen in someone who believes in Jesus Christ. For too long, there have been believers who have not made good impressions because of their bad behavior or apathetic approach. The time has come for us who believe to treat our salvation as a precious thing. And therefore, the salvation of others as an opportunity for us the do what would make the Lord pleased with His people. For what gain is there in this World? Why would we seek to gain even the whole World and run the risk of losing our souls in the process (Luke 9:25)? No, instead, we consider everything a loss for the greater worth of gaining Christ Jesus (Philippians 3). Having gained Christ, we can devote ourselves to the service of the Body.

NEW HEAVEN AND NEW EARTH

There is a river whose streams make glad the city of God, **the holy habitation of the Most High***. God is in the midst of her; she shall not be moved; God will help her when morning dawns.*

Psalm 34:4-5 (ESV)

Will we ever see an end to the current World? Yes, there will come an end to the miserable, corrupted, polluted, Zombie infested World. The physical World will experience great tribulation like has never before been seen. But likewise, the spiritual World will also undergo a great change at the End. As it stands now, there is much opposition to God being provoked by the system of thought in the World. Men are lovers of Darkness, rather than the Light because they have embraced their wicked ways and rejected the Way, the Truth, and the Life of Jesus Christ. Zombies cannot escape their own destruction because they constantly contribute to it. Their every deed is a Deadly disconnection from the Creator. Even the seemingly good works of the Zombie is merely a Dead act done in self-service.

There is coming a time when we will no longer be able to say, "Know the Lord" because all will know the Lord personally and intimately (Jeremiah 31:34 and Hebrews 8:11). That is not the time we now inhabit. Many do not know the Lord at all because none are righteous in their own merit. This has not stopped them from seeking to profusely justify their own actions. In toiling and strife, the Dead have prepared themselves only to enter into a further Death. But there are some who have turned from their wicked ways and have believed upon the grace of God.

Do not love the world or the things in the world. ***If anyone loves the world, the love of the Father is not in him***. *For all that is in the world—* ***the desires of the flesh and the desires of the eyes and pride of life****—is not from the Father but is from the world.*[1]

John 2:15-16 (ESV)

While we should have known the Lord our God from the moment of our birth, there has been a corruption upon the World System that has interfered with what should have been. As it was in the beginning with the World's Fallout, so it has continued. Where

The LIVING DEAD Revival Guide

Eve saw the temptation of the Forbidden Fruit as being good for food, pleasing to the eye, and desirable for making one wise, so it seems to have continued with all humanity (Genesis 3:6). We continue to fall into the same mistakes because that is our nature. Sin is natural to the Zombie. But where sin increased, God's grace increased all the more! Not that we should sin more to cause grace to increase but rather that we should lean on and trust in the Lord our God even more so when the temptation of this World seems too strong to deny. He is patient with us for our good so that we may repent and find favor with Him. Even if we are to be tempted in this World, we are not doomed to Fall into sin every time that we encounter it. Yahweh even counseled Cain when he was being tempted.

> *Then the Lord said to Cain, "Why are you angry, and why is your expression downcast? Is it not true that if you do what is right, you will be fine? But if you do not do what is right,* **sin is crouching at the door. It desires to dominate you, but you must subdue it***.*
>
> Genesis 4:6-7 (ESV)

Sin, like a ravenous beast looking to devour, was crouching at the door of Cain. Which is to say that he was being tempted by his desire to kill his brother. But instead of overcoming his sin, Cain was overcome with anger and jealousy so deep that it made him become like a ravenous beast as well. When he caved in on himself and his sinful desires, he showed how we give Life to Sin. We give a means for sin to be activated when we defy the commandments of God. The commandments themselves are holy and righteous and true, but in our defiance, we show the reason for why we need commandments. All the commandments being summed up in Love also reveals how desperately void of love the natural human really is. The Zombie does not know Love. But perhaps the Zombie can know love if God wills it. The time is running short, and there may only be a few meaningful moments that remain between now and the culmination of all things. It cannot be easily discerned at what time the Lord Jesus Christ will appear again unto us. It can be known that now is the time to believe and today is the Day of salvation. For as long as there is another Day, there is another time for the unbelieving to repent from their sins and receive forgiveness through Christ Jesus.

There was a time when Jesus was asked what the signs would be of His coming and of the end of the age. The answer that was given them began first with not being led the wrong way. The Living must not be led down the wrong path because they belong to the one who was and is and is to come. We no longer belong to the one who hates God and seeks to defame His Name. Nevertheless, many imposters will present themselves as the Savior, and those that accept a different Jesus and a different Gospel Cure will be deceived. Jesus informed His listeners that there would be wars and rumors of wars but that we need not be alarmed because all things are prerequisites to His return. They, however, are not the final signs of the end of the World. The horrible things that take place in the End, will only be the beginning of the end. Many of the Dead will simply go on with their lives, eating and drinking as if nothing new were under the sun. But the Saints will face much persecution, and they will be put to death. The Zombies will even think that they are doing God a service when they kill His Saints (John 16:2). There will be hatred in the End that comes with such zeal that the hateful will hate even themselves. This should not surprise us, seeing that we, too, were once as they are. We hated everyone and everything and were ourselves hated back (Titus 3:3). Some of us were the kind of Zombie who would do things we can only worship God for forgiving. We were among those who would take advantage of the weaknesses of others so that we could exploit them for our own gain.

> *For among them are those who **creep** into households and **capture** weak women, burdened with sins and led astray by various passions.*
> 2 Timothy 3:6 (ESV)

But we are not of that sort any longer. We have realized that these Last Days are causing many to realize how near the Lord's return really is, for He is drawing nearer even now. The End of the World will bring with it the kind of tribulations and threats that will bring hatred down on the Saints from all nations. We also know that there will be a terrible Falling Away of Sleep Walkers. Hatred and ever-increasing false teaching will motivate their apostasy. Sin in the Last Days will be so severe that the love of many will grow cold. Just as the hearts of Zombies are cold and callous as stone, so too will their love be towards one another.

We know that many antichrists have come into the World. There have been many who vehemently opposed the Lord and sought to kill those who vigilantly kept the faith that has been once and for all delivered to the Saints. But in the very End, it seems that one final antichrist will rise. The final anti-Christ will be regarded as the ultimate representation of man even though he is the worst of what we are. And that will be a problem that they cannot fathom. For man has been corrupted by sin to the deepest recesses of their being. This man of lawlessness will appear and cause many to believe that he has come to save them. The truth is that he has come as one that will lead many to a quicker destruction. Like animals that are caught and killed, the Zombies will put themselves into their own traps.

The **LIVING DEAD** Revival Guide

*Let no one deceive you in any way. For **that day** will not come, unless **the rebellion** comes first, and **the man of lawlessness** is revealed, the son of destruction, who opposes and exalts himself against every so-called god or object of worship, so that he takes his seat in the temple of God, **proclaiming himself to be God.***

2 Thessalonians 2:3-4 (ESV)

Fear nothing but God, my brothers, and sisters. For this End is necessary so that the Kingdom of God may be brought to culmination. We will endure, and we will be saved. Let us rejoice in hope, be patient in tribulation, and constant in prayer (Romans 12:12). The path of Life that God has prepared for us requires submission. Worthy Walkers have willingly submitted and eagerly confessed that Jesus Christ is Lord to the glory of God the Father. We are those that Walk by faith and not by sight because the Holy Spirit is with us. But the Dead Walkers can only act in hostility towards the Creator because that is their nature. It is no surprise to us who have been given heavenly wisdom that the final antichrist will exalt himself as a god under the power of Satan and the rest of the spiritual forces of Darkness. But let those who are Alive in those Last Days equip themselves with the full armor of God so that they may make their stand. If necessary, the Saints may die, but they will not merely die. They will gain Life eternal in the power of God.

*They have conquered him by **the blood of the Lamb** and by **the word of their testimony**. And they did not **love their lives so as to shy away from death**.*

Revelation 12:11 (ESV)

Whatever happens in those times, it is the prayer of all the Saints that the Lord God Almighty would be the Deliverer of all those who call upon His Name. He is faithful and true. He has never disappointed us because His will is perfect, and we have come to accept our lot in life as an opportunity to reflect the radiant glory of Christ. We will lay our lives down as Living Sacrifices, and when our sacrifice is finished, we will rise again to serve the Lord forever more. May we not become deceived, as Eve was, with the twisting of the Word of God. But with the purity of devotion that we have practiced in our Walk, may it be that God Himself strengthens, confirms, and establishes us. We know that there will come deceiving Zombies whose desire is to lead many astray, but we will stand together in the Spirit. We will not allow for the wool to be pulled over our eyes as if we had no Shepherd. We know the voice of our Master and will follow Him, only. There is no other Name given under heaven by which we can be saved except for the Name of the Lord Jesus Christ.

> ***Not that there is another one***, *but there are some who trouble you and want to distort the gospel of Christ. But even if we or an angel from heaven should preach to you a gospel contrary to the one, we preached to you,* ***let him be accursed.***
>
> Galatians 1:7-8 (ESV)

> *There is one body and one Spirit—just as you were called to the one hope that belongs to your call— one Lord, one faith, one baptism, one God and Father of all, who is* ***over all and through all and in all.***
>
> Ephesians 4:4-6 (ESV)

There is only one way to salvation, and it passes through the Body of Christ. He made a new and Living way for us through his body by offering himself as an atonement for our sins. We must now Walk as new creations, that is, if we are truly in Christ. For many false saviors will proclaim their own names. But we must not accept them. We cannot accept a different Gospel Cure nor a different Jesus Christ. We need only to know that the Lord will come to us as the lightning does in the sky. It will be with such rapidness and glory that all the sky will be illuminated by Him. And even if there is to be some kind of rescue or rapture for those who are Alive near the tribulation period, then they are blessed. But the believers must not allow for this to be the only hope nor a point of contention. Rather, we will be prepared to make our stand against the worst of times and maintain a Living Hope through the resurrection of Jesus Christ from the Dead.

> *For the Lord himself will descend from heaven with a cry of command, with the voice of an archangel, and with the sound of the trumpet of God.* ***And the dead in Christ will rise first. Then we who are alive,*** *who are left, will be caught up together with them in the clouds to meet the Lord in the air, and so we will always be with the Lord. Therefore encourage one another with these words.*
>
> 1 Thessalonians 4:16-18 (ESV)

We know that there is a significant difference between those who have died while being Alive in Christ and those who have died while being Dead to Him. Those that have Walked in faith will be with Him forever. Even the thief on the cross was welcomed into paradise by the Lord Jesus, who hung on the cross next to him (Luke 23:43). But we also know that those who die in their Dead Walk will by no means be given another opportunity to find salvation. There awaits for them only the fearful expectation of judgement. This judgment will be without partiality; it will be completely perfect because their Judge is perfect in all His ways. We would do well to pay heed to the lesson of the seasons. For we are aware when plants near their time for harvest, so let us be aware that these events are quickly approaching, and therefore the Saint may rejoice, even in the Darkest hours, knowing that the End of the World is the beginning of the Reign of Christ.

> *The saying is trustworthy, for: If we have **died** with him, we will also **live** with him; if we **endure**, we will also **reign** with him; if we **deny** him, he will also **deny** us; if we are **faithless**, he remains **faithful**— for **he cannot deny himself.***
>
> 2 Timothy 11-13 (ESV)

Even though we do not know at what time the Lord will return, we can remain faithful to Him. For we have considered ourselves Dead to the World - even crucified to it. We consider ourselves Dead to sin and Alive to God because of Jesus. We must endure because He himself endured the cross for the joy of bringing many Dead back to Life. Therefore, He was able to scorn its shame, knowing that his sacrifice was worth it. He sat down at the right hand of the Father, and if we find ourselves rooted in Him, then we too can be considered righteous in the presence of God. Though we have not done anything to earn this of our own effort, we know that what has been done for us is enough. He has reconciled us to Himself so that we could be made innocent of our transgressions. But we continue to bring to our mind that as we look for the return of Christ, there will be mockers and scoffers. They will denounce our faith just as it was for Noah in his days. Those people at that time were doing their daily routines even till the day that Noah entered the means of his protection that was provided by God. They remained unaware of their destruction until the flood came and swept them all away. Thus, it shall be when the Son of Man comes again. May we not be found as wicked servants who Walk in our Sleep instead of remaining vigilant in our service unto the Lord and His Saints. May we also regard the Zombies around us as needing to understand the seriousness of this predicament that is the End of the World as we know it.

> *Then **two** men will be in the field; one will be taken and one left. **Two** women will be grinding at the mill; one will be taken and one left. Therefore, **stay awake**, for you do not know on what day your Lord is coming. But know this, that if the master of the house had known in what*

part of the night the thief was coming, **he would have stayed awake** *and would not have let his house be broken into. Therefore, you also must* **be ready,** *for the Son of Man is coming at an hour you do not expect.*

Matthew 24:40-44 (ESV)

CHAPTER FOUR

RESISTANCE

KEEP YOUR EYES ON Z.I.O.N.

*And we urge you, brothers and sisters, **warn** those who are idle and disruptive, **encourage** the disheartened, **help** the weak, be patient with everyone.*
1 Thessalonians 5:14 (ESV)

There are Zombies In Our Neighborhood (Z.I.O.N.). They are everywhere. Zombies are in our homes, our schools, our government, our hospitals, our markets, and everywhere else. Zombies are our neighbors, but are we willing to speak to them the Words of Life and see them become our brothers and sisters? The call to share the Gospel Cure with the hurting and the lost rests in the hands of those who have been brought to Life by the Lord. We must do this, seeing that it is God's plan to use those that were formerly opposed to Him to bring glory and honor to His name now. But there seems to be a large number of the Saints who have become overly fearful of the Zombies In Our Neighborhood. Some feel that the best they can do is keep their eyes on them so as to be sure that they do not cause any harm or damage. We must not allow a fearful nightmare to overtake the Living Hope that is available to those that have been Born Again. It is right that we would keep a watchful eye upon those that have spent their time feasting on the Flesh. We cannot trust those that do not know the Lord Jesus as their savior. But that is what we can trust, that they are not to be trusted. We trust that they cannot be trusted - yet. So, if we keep an eye on those that may seek to cause us harm, then we will do well to Walk wisely among them.

> ***Whoever walks with the wise becomes wise**, but the companion of fools will **suffer harm**.*
> Proverbs 13:20 (ESV)

But we know that it is not those that can destroy the body that are to be feared but instead, it is the Lord who is to be feared because He holds the power to destroy both the body and the soul in hell. That is the destination of the Dead. They are on the path that will lead them to death and destruction. But their sins will not merely be punished and then forgotten. They have an infinitely offensive debt before the infinitely holy God, and without an infinitely worthy payment in blood of Christ, they will certainly suffer for all eternity. So we can see that is what we deserved and have been forgiven of, but we do not retain the motivation to save others from that, which was hanging over our heads. This should not be. We know the fear of the Lord, and therefore we will Walk in the wisdom of the Holy Spirit and persuade Zombies to turn from their sins and their ceaseless hungering after the Flesh. But there are many ways that we can go about this ministry. In fact, it would be best if we did not go about this alone. Paul sought trustworthy companions for his missionary work. For Paul, this was a way to not only have fellowship while in the often depressing and dangerous World, but it also served to strengthen both his faith and the faith of his friend.

> Yes, I ask you also, **true companion**, help these women, who have labored **side by side with me in the gospel** together with Clement and the rest of my fellow workers, **whose names are in the book of life**.
>
> Philippians 4:3 (ESV)

Likewise, Jesus did not send out His disciples alone but sent them out in twos. It is not good for man to be alone. Where one may fall and be unable to help themselves, two can help one another. We sharpen each other like iron so that we maintain a sharpness for the situations we encounter. Jesus knew His disciples needed fellowship along the path because the mission can be full of challenges. They were told to bring different things on different occasions. But in both cases, the glory of God was the result. When those that Jesus had sent out returned to Him, they were ecstatic because they had been conduits of the power of God. They exclaimed with joy, "Lord, even the demons are subject to us in your name!" And to that, Jesus replied that He saw Satan fall like lightning out of heaven. But he had a greater joy than the disciples display of power.

> Behold, I have given you authority to tread on serpents and scorpions, and over all the power of the enemy, and nothing shall hurt you. Nevertheless, do not rejoice in this, that the spirits are subject to you, but **rejoice that your names are written in heaven**.
>
> Luke 19-20 (ESV)

There is no greater joy than to know that the children of God are Walking in the faith. And at this, Jesus did rejoice and praised the Father because these things had not been revealed to those that were wise in their own eyes, but instead, the Gospel Cure came to those who knew they didn't deserve it. God opposes the proud and arrogant but shows favor to the humble. But these Zombies are hostile to God and His people. So, it is right that we Walk carefully among this wicked generation. We know that the days are evil.

> *Making the best use of the time, because the **days are evil.***
>
> Ephesians 5:16 (ESV)

We ought to ask ourselves if we really believe that the days are evil. For it would seem that some are in the habit of loving the World and the things that are in it. There is a limit to the liberties of Christians, but there are few that seem to remove from themselves the things that hinder them. The apathy that is caused by an evil World doesn't only come in the form of Darkness. At times it may seem that it is a Light or good thing that people can stumble over. We should be willing to cut off all the things that cause us to stray from the path. We should also be willing to remove from us those things that may seem like liberties to us but endanger those around us who are not yet strengthened in their faith. For the heart of a true believer should care more about the needs of others than their own pursuits. There is a need for Saints to embrace the counterintuitive. We are no longer bound to the way of the Flesh as we once were in our Zombie form. So why would we continue to embrace the dangerous behavior that caused us so much strife before? We shouldn't do that to ourselves or to anyone else for that matter. We can no longer live for our own selfish desires because to do so would reveal that we are indeed Zombies just as the scripture says:

> *… but [they] who [are] self-indulgent [are] dead even while [they] live.*
>
> 1 Timothy 5:6 (ESV)

If we are surrounded by the living Dead but continue to do nothing to evangelize them, then how can we expect to see any change? We should not expect change to take place where there is no cause. Those that remain in their sinful "Rest" will not be moved to rouse themselves unless they are given an alarm. But we come to them with the greatest alarm that could ever be given, and they somehow still refuse to respond. This is a mystery to us, but it must not stop us from our responsibility. We are not the cause of salvation, but we certainly are the means by which the message is distributed. Are we really going to simply stand aside as we see those that we know and love simply decaying because they are not being urged to receive the Gospel Cure? If we love someone, then we will tell them the truth. Even if it hurts them to hear the reality of their Zombified condition, we know that it will be for their good. Therefore, we trust that God will work in them even if we cannot see it with our own eyes.

Talon Schneider

Faithful are the wounds of a friend; profuse are the kisses of an enemy.
Proverbs 27:6 (ESV)

Who is it that feels so comfortable that they would deny the responsibility to speak Life to the Dead? Have we really become so sedated and seduced by pleasure in our World that we refuse to go beyond our comforts into the difficult places? The places we don't want to go are often the very place we are needed the most. What if it was ourselves who had received the Gospel Cure from a nervous and trembling servant of God who stood in the face of Death and spoke boldly, as he ought to have? What if that same servant had instead refused the call to Walk Worthy at that moment? Would that have affected our salvation? One can only fear the outcome of such changes to the story of redemption. We dare not provoke God by saying that we will address the issue with ourselves and others at the very last moment. Worthy Walkers are not prone to the dazed behavior of those that meander in their faith. We cannot abide in the false peace of reluctance, for that is the behavior of the Sleep Walker and the Zombie. They that disregard wisdom and make themselves into fools are only harming themselves.

*The fool folds his hands and **eats his own flesh**.*
Ecclesiastes 4:5 (ESV)

Somehow, it seems that even among the brothers and sisters, there is a tendency to fight and argue to the point of division. This should not be, for we have been called to unity. We are the Body of Christ. We remain in the World and operate under His Headship. But it seems that some behave as though they have become disconnected from the Head. To be severed from the Head is surely Death, for only through connection to Christ can we be considered Alive.

They have lost connection with the head, *from whom the whole body, supported and held together by its ligaments and sinews, grows as God causes it to grow.*
Colossians 2:19 (ESV)

*But if you **bite** and **devour** one another, watch out that you are not **consumed** by one another.*
Galatians 5:16 (ESV)

The LIVING DEAD Revival Guide
Z.I.O.N. UNIT

*Stay **alert**, stand firm in the **faith**, show **courage**, be **strong**.*
1 Corinthians 16:13

There is a need for the brothers and sisters to band together, particularly as the persecution of the Saints increases. But we can rejoice in our trials knowing that the strengthening of our faith likewise strengthens our shield. We must have a proper defense against the spiritual opposition that we experience in the World. We know that our Sanctuary is not in a physical building but rather in the Name of the Lord. All who call upon the Name of the Lord shall be saved. A those who run to Him will be safe, like one who has found shelter in a fortified tower. This battle that rages and roars is perceived by the Worthy Walker as not one between flesh and blood but with spiritual enemies.

> *For our struggle is **not against flesh and blood**, but against the rulers, against the authorities, against the powers of this dark world and against the spiritual forces of evil in the heavenly realms.*
> Ephesians 6:12 (ESV)

We do not fight with the weapons of this World but with spiritual weapons (2 Corinthians 10:4). The armory is well-stocked because its supplier is the Lord of Hosts. We must steel ourselves for this spiritual battle and commit ourselves to the rigorous training needed to hold fast to the truth we have received. Our aim is not to kill the dead, for that is not needed. They are killing themselves with their constant defiance and sinful activities. No, we must not kill them even if they are to kill us. I repeat we must not become like them! We cannot be overcome by evil; we must overcome evil with good (Romans 12:21). It has been entrusted to us to offer ourselves as Living Sacrifices even unto those that hate us. For if we feed our enemy and give them water to drink, then they will have what they need and may become more receptive to the Hope held out to them. Indeed, we may satiate their physical needs in such a way that causes them to hunger and thirst for righteousness. This is a great goal of the Worthy Walker that by the Light of God that we reflect, the Dead might see it and take notice of what is worthy. They may need just this demonstration in order to turn from their sins. What we need as followers of Christ is to maintain our steadfast discipleship in order that we may present ourselves as a worker approved by God. We should be ready for evaluation and examination in such a way as not to be disappointed. For we have a most sure victory over the Catalysts of Sin and Death through Jesus Christ, our Lord, and Savior. We will take up the call with a willing heart and be most confident that we have become more than conquerors through Him who loved us.

> *For though we walk in the flesh, we are* **not waging war according to the flesh.** *For the weapons of our warfare are not of the flesh but have divine power to destroy strongholds. We destroy arguments and every lofty opinion raised against the knowledge of God, and* **take every thought captive to obey Christ** ....
>
> 2 Corinthians 10:3-5 (ESV)

Our stronghold is the Lord, and nothing can defeat Him. He is a strong tower for the righteous to run to and find shelter. But even while we Walk in the physical world and the limited nature of our bodies, we will by no means be stopped unless it is the Lord's will. For His is the victory, and His is the glory. Our weapons are strong not because of the ones who wield them but because of what they represent. If we are good servants and Worthy Walkers, then the Lord will accomplish many victories through us and, in so doing, multiply His glory. Let all God's people coordinate themselves according to His perfect will as we press forward. We will demolish the lofty and arrogant lies of the spiritual enemies because those things cannot persist in the presence of God. We will take captive our own thoughts so that our sanctification may reach completion. We will also take captive the false philosophies of the enemy because many strongholds have been raised in an effort to ruin the faith of the brothers and sisters. We will not simply Sleep while these forces arise against us. We will put up a good fight; we will keep the faith. We will finish the race that has been marked out for us. We will do so not by our might or power but by the Holy Spirit Living in us. We will do so by the veracity of the Word of God, which like a sword, cuts through the lies so that we can proclaim the truth without wavering.

Training and Equipment

> *Moreover, we possess the prophetic word as an altogether reliable thing.* **You do well if you pay attention to this** *as you would to a light shining in a murky place,* **until the day dawns and the morning star rises in your hearts.**
>
> 2 Peter 1:19 (ESV)

If indeed Christ has been raised in our hearts, then we certainly know that which cannot be made unknown. We have been forever changed by what He has revealed to us. We have turned away from the Darkness and now reject our old ways. We cannot do so by our own power. There would only be futility in that effort. But so long as we cling onto the One who saved us from Death with reverence and love, we will not be denied. He has given us everything we need to fulfill our calling. But there are some who remain unaware of the great treasury stored up for the Saints. When we were in the Darkness and confounded in our hearts and minds because of sin, we were our own enemy. But now we have been aligned with God in the force of Light. His Light is the Truth, and it cannot be denied forever. For even that which is done in the Darkness will be defeated on the Day that Christ returns. In the meantime, we must commit ourselves to be well trained and equipped.

> *All Scripture is God-breathed and is useful for teaching, rebuking, correcting and **training in righteousness**, so that the servant of God may be thoroughly **equipped** for every good work.*
> 2 Timothy 3:16-17 (ESV)

How can one properly train without companions? We already know the direness of discipleship. We must not forgo the meeting together as some have because they risk losing what they have gained. We can be completely confident that the Holy Scripture has all that we need while the Zombie Apocalypse persists. Even till the very end, when Jesus Christ is revealed, there will be a need for the Saints to stand firm in the faith that has been once and for all delivered. The training of God's people is a constant practice; there is no time when we are not being refined into a more appropriate representative of Christ. That is partly what is so suspect when it comes to the behavior of the Sleeping believer. Not the believer who Sleeps in death but the believer who Sleeps in Life. These need oversight and assistance to reach maturity of faith. For the Body of Christ relies upon its members for many things. But where one member has become unreliable, the whole Body suffers. Likewise, if one member of the Body experiences pain, so too does the rest of the Body.

> ***The end of all things is near.*** *Therefore,* ***be alert*** *and of sober mind so that you may pray.*
> 1 Peter 4:7 (ESV)

The End is indeed near. That is cause for the Zombie to fear, but for the Saint, there is a strange hopefulness in it. We know that the End brings with it the Beginning of the rule and reign of Christ and, ultimately, the submission of all things under the Sovereignty of Yahweh. But for the time between now and then, we must be ready to give a defense for the hope that we have in us, knowing first of all that Christ is Lord and knowing secondly that we must defend the truth with meekness and respect. There is no need for the vehement behavior that is prone to the Zombie when we are those that have peace with God.

> The **night** is nearly over; the **day** has drawn near.
> So, let us lay aside the deeds of darkness and put on the **armor of light**.
> Romans 13:12 (ESV)

Armor of God

> But **since we belong to the day**, let us be sober, having put on the breastplate of faith and love, and for a helmet the hope of salvation.
> 1 Thessalonians 5:8 (ESV)

Do we realize how thoroughly well-equipped we are? God has not abandoned us to fend for ourselves with faulty equipment and broken weapons. We have not been left for dead. We have been left in the World for the sake of Life. Our charge is to help the helpless, defend the defenseless, and love the unloved. Praise the Lord for all that He has done for us! What a joy it is to fight this fight side by side with all the Worthy Walkers across the face of the earth! Take courage, O' Saint! Consider the Armor of God, and make sure not to put it down. God has provided us such a powerful resource, so long as we take action and lift it up! We must not let our Sword becomes dull, or our shield gathers dust, or our boots be untied.

> Finally, be strong **in the Lord** and in the strength of his might. **Put on** the whole armor of God, that you may be able to stand against the schemes of the devil. For **we do not wrestle against flesh and blood**, but against the rulers, against the authorities, against the cosmic powers over this present darkness, **against the spiritual forces of evil in the heavenly places**. Therefore, **take up** the whole armor of God, that you may be able to withstand in the **evil day**, and having done all, to stand firm. Stand therefore, having fastened on the **belt of truth**, and having put on the **breastplate of righteousness,** and, as shoes for your feet, having put on the **readiness given by the gospel of peace**. In all circumstances **take up the shield of faith**, with which you can extinguish all the flaming darts of the evil one; and take **the helmet of salvation**, and **the sword of the Spirit**, which is **the word of God**, praying at all times in the Spirit, with

*all prayer and supplication. To that end, keep alert with all perseverance, making supplication for all the saints, and also for me, that words may be given to me in opening my mouth boldly to **proclaim the mystery of the gospel**, for which I am an ambassador in chains, that I may declare it boldly, as I ought to speak.*

Ephesians 6:10-20 (ESV)

These spiritual weapons are the means by which we will stand firm against the schemes of the Devil, the Flesh, and the World. Although these Catalysts of Sin and Death seek to silence the Saints, it will not work. The Zombie Apocalypse may be upon us, but the Revelation of Jesus Christ in His Saints is upon the Zombie. There is a battle taking place in a realm where eyes cannot go. But we do not See these things with our physical eyes, rather we know them by faith. Thus, we Walk by faith and not by sight, knowing that the things that can be seen are passing away. But that which is unseen is eternal (2 Corinthians 4:16-18). We must continue to study the Word of God, gather together in fellowship, pray without ceasing, and remember Jesus through communion (Acts 2:42). The need for discipleship among the brothers and sisters is as important now as it has ever been. We are stronger when we stand together. We are strongest when we keep in step with the Holy Spirit. We are those that have crucified the Flesh through faith in Christ (Galatians 5:24-25).

*But I say, **walk by the Spirit**, and you will not gratify the desires of the flesh.*

Galatians 5:16 (ESV)

SPEAKING TO THE DEAD

You shall be holy to me, *for I the LORD am holy and have separated you from the peoples, that you should be mine. "A man or a woman who is a medium or **a necromancer shall surely be put to death**. They shall be stoned with stones; their blood shall be upon them.*

Leviticus 20:26-27 (ESV)

We are not called to speak to the physically dead. That is preposterous and completely pointless. For it is abundantly clear that the body apart from the spirit is dead (James 2:26). Rather it has been appointed once for men to die and then to face judgment.

Furthermore, there is no purgatory or limbo where a soul awaits the assistance of those who remain in the World as if there was anything that the living could do to help them. We are judged completely and unequivocally by the determination of our faith. If we have accepted the Gospel Cure that confirms the forgiveness of sins by grace through faith in the sacrifice of Jesus Christ, then we will be saved. If we have rejected Jesus Christ and the message of the Holy Spirit, then there is no hope upon death. It is not as though we have been called to be necromancers. The Bible specifically forbids that detestable practice. Even if the Zombies think that they can do such things, it is all in vain. They will be punished for their defiance and denial of the Living God. The pagans like to think that they can summon the dead as if they had any power to exert. But they will be judged for their actions even as the Saints shall be judged for how well they used their time and resources. The Saint will be judged, not condemned. Many of the Living will have a rich entrance into heaven and the presence of the Lord. But some of the Living will enter as though fire. They may suffer loss of some rewards and yet still have their souls saved from the fire (2 Corinthians 5:8-10). We are not Walking Worthy for the sake of the rewards, except for the reward of Life that is now ours through Christ. There is only one foundation upon which we may lay our efforts. That foundation is only the Lord Jesus Christ. Not that we add anything to Him, but we may offer Living Sacrifices or praise and patience and love for His glory. All that we do will be made known when the time comes. The quality of our efforts will be completely known by the One who evaluates them.

> *Now if anyone builds on the foundation with gold, silver, precious stones, wood, hay, straw— each one's work will become manifest, for* **the Day will disclose it**, *because it will be revealed by fire, and the fire will test what sort of work each one has done. If the work that anyone has built on the foundation survives,* **he will receive a reward**. *If anyone's work is burned up, he will suffer loss,* ***though he himself will be saved, but only as through fire***.
> 1 Corinthians 3:12-15 (ESV)

It should not surprise the Sleep Walker if they enter heaven with no reward other than that which is most important. They may not have made the best use of their time while they were in the World. And of course, this is not the main goal of the believer anyway. We do not fully know what the rewards will be, but we know what they will not be. They will not be temporary, they cannot be stolen, and they will not tarnish over time (Matthew 6:19-20). We have much to be gained as followers of Christ, and all the more as we make every effort to confirm our calling and election. Our hearts should be lifted even more so as we seek to hasten the coming of the Day. The aim of the Worthy Walker is to love like Jesus did in giving His life away. Although we do not know what the rewards will be, there is no greater reward than to be made like Jesus Christ in holiness. We shall be like Him when we see Him, for then we shall see Him as He is. In Him are all the treasures of wisdom and knowledge (Colossians 2:3). Because of Yahweh's plan of redemption, we are now found in Christ. Our identity is rooted deeply in who Jesus is. Jesus is to us the wisdom of God, righteousness, sanctification, and redemption (1 Corinthians 1:30). So, our focus is not on the things of this World, but our focus is on that which is above. We fix our eyes on things above, the unseen things, knowing that where our Lord is there also is our treasure—His name is Jesus.

> *Do not lay up for yourselves treasures on earth, where moth and rust destroy and where thieves break in and steal, but lay up for yourselves treasures in heaven, where neither moth nor rust destroys and where thieves do not break in and steal.* **For where your treasure is, there your heart will be also.**
>
> Matthew 6:19-21 (ESV)

But as far as the Dead are concerned, they have no interest in the treasure that is Christ Jesus. They have continually opposed Him. At times they have vilified the Saints for their adoration of the Risen Savior. They hurl insults at the Saints, but what they neglect to realize is how thoroughly they bless the Living when they do this. We are blessed if we suffer in a manner similar to that which Jesus suffered. It has been appointed unto us not only to believe in Him but also to suffer for His namesake (Philippians 1:29). Therefore, the Dead do their best to hurl insults at us, but we simply return blessings.

For this, we have been called so that we may gain a good report about our conduct among those that are perishing. Indeed, we must be careful how we conduct ourselves before Zombies. We do not know at what time they may be called to faith. If they happen to observe a Christian who stumbles in sin, what would that say about the power of the Cross in our lives? The message must not be tainted but must be preserved as it was from the beginning. There is only one way to be saved, and it is through Jesus Christ. No man comes to the Father except through Him (John 14:6). And even if the Saint makes a mistake, this may take place to make a way open for the Zombie to be reached even still. Regardless of the means by which we speak Life to the Dead, it is essential that the Gospel Cure be maintained as purely as possible. There must be no additive to the message, for if there is, it would likely cause much more harm than good. The Saints must be holy and cannot be conformed to the pattern of the World. The Lord is holy, and we must be made like Him. Therefore, we will reject the sinful ways of the Dead, but at the same time, we must not remove our influence from among them. It is a balance that must be maintained. Bad company corrupts good character (1 Corinthians 15), but perhaps by the Light that shines through us, they may see it and take heed as they ought, to the Source of the Light.

> *When you come into the land that the LORD your God is giving you,* ***you shall not learn to follow the abominable practices of those nations****. There shall not be found among you anyone who burns his son or his daughter as an offering, anyone who practices divination or tells fortunes or interprets omens, or a sorcerer or a charmer or a medium or a* ***necromancer*** *or one who inquires of the dead, for whoever does these things is an abomination to the LORD. Because of these abominations, the LORD your God is driving them out before you.* ***You shall be blameless before the LORD your God,*** *for these nations, which you are about to dispossess, listen to fortune-tellers and to diviners. But as for you, the LORD your God has not allowed you to do this.*
>
> Deuteronomy 18:9-14 (ESV)

Now let it be that the Saints speak to the Dead with the words that the Lord provides. There is no need for excessive emotions or overly strategic presentation of the Gospel Cure. It is a simple faith that is required. It is so potent that its mere conveyance has the power to heal at that very moment. The Cure to Death is placed in the hands of the Living. What will we do with it now? Will we treat it as a treasure that must be delivered to all those who would willingly receive it and keep it stored up in their hearts? Or will we disregard this wonderful gift of God, just as Jesus was scorned and hated and mistreated during the days of His earthly life?

Surely not! Worthy Walkers cannot contain the zeal that they have for the Lord, for thus it is to be truly Alive! We make Him known at every opportunity by our actions and our words. We know that our God Lives and that He will return quickly to bring us to where He is. So, we shall make it our aim to speak Life to the Dead in such a way as to not be ashamed at His appearing. We will be good and faithful servants. We do not expect to find Him where He is not, but rather we will make sure that He is brought to those places in our hearts. He is not the God of the Dead but of the Living. For all are Alive before Him. Therefore, when we seek Him, we find Him, for He is not far from anyone of us. If only we would reach out for Him.

The LIVING DEAD *Revival Guide*

And as they were frightened and bowed their faces to the ground, the men said to them, **"Why do you seek the living among the dead?"**

Luke 24:5 (ESV)

THE DIRENESS OF DISCIPLESHIP

And let us consider how we may spur one another on toward love and good deeds, **not giving up meeting together**, *as some are in the habit of doing, but encouraging one another—and all the more as you see the* **Day approaching**.

Hebrews 10:24-25 (ESV)

The issue of Discipleship cannot go unmentioned any longer. Perhaps the fear of the Dead really has gripped the Living by the throat. But there is no other way to fight back than to intentionally dedicate to that which the early Church likewise committed to keeping. They made it a habit to pray, to break bread, to study the scriptures, and to fellowship (Acts 2:42). Without these four simple practices, the early Church may very well have fallen under the immense pressure and persecution that they were facing. And maybe it was just that, the persecution that presses the Christian to the breaking point, and yet they remain intact and uncrushed. Their faith is made stronger by what they suffer, and for this, they rejoice, as it is right of those who have crucified the World and sin through faith in Christ. But as it is, there are many who are Alive that are yet wandering in their Walk. They should be roused to the mature level of faith that many brothers and sisters have died to present and preserve. But they somehow have found the cares of this World a little too entertaining. They have become distracted by the fleeting glimmer of things that perish with use. They have neglected to continue in their faith and by the power of the Holy Spirit so that perhaps they may finish what God started by means of the Flesh. To this, we must all be cautious to practice self-evaluation. However, it is no wonder that the Apostle Paul was so bewildered by the errant apathetic attitudes of those who had at one time suffered all things for the sake of Christ. For those same Believers to turn away to the side and become once again ensnared by the things that Christ has already defeated for them is perplexing, to say the least.

O foolish Galatians! **Who has bewitched you?** *It was before your eyes that Jesus Christ was publicly portrayed as crucified. Let me ask you only this: Did you receive the Spirit by works of the law or by hearing with* **faith**? *Are you so foolish? Having begun by the Spirit, are you now being* *perfected by the **flesh**? Did you suffer so many things in vain— **if indeed it was in vain**?*

Galatians 3:1-4 (ESV)

It was right for Paul to have such concern for those Believers who he had personally interacted with and seen their faith demonstrated. They were willing to suffer for him to great lengths. They seemed even willing to exchange their comfort for his peace. Even being willing to take the thorn that was in his flesh and exchange their very own eyes on his behalf (Galatians 4:15). They had given Paul such high regard that he was treated as good as the Lord Jesus Christ may have been treated. So, the question remains, what happened? How did such faithful men and women become so entangled in the things that hinder? Did they somehow believe that they could contribute to their salvation by means of their own works? Regardless of what they were thinking, it is clear that something went wrong. The answer for them is most likely the answer for us all. We must continue to serve each other as Living Sacrifices. We must not forgo our gathering together because we are weakest when we are separated from one another. We are at our absolute weakest when we distance our self from the Lord. But where one may fall and be incapable of rising, two can lean on each other and bear up under the other's burdens.

> ***Two are better than one***, *because they have a good reward for their toil.* ***For if they fall, one will lift up his fellow***. *But woe to him who is alone when he falls and has not another to lift him up! Again, if two lie together, they keep warm, but how can one keep warm alone? And though a man might prevail against one who is alone, two will withstand him*—***a threefold cord is not quickly broken***.

Ecclesiastes 4:9-12 (ESV)

It is a very lonely experience to have no friends while in the midst of the Zombie Apocalypse. But for the sake of the Living, there is one who sticks closer than a brother. There is one who comforts us at all times if we would still ourselves in His presence and listen to His encouragement. The Holy Spirit of God is forever with the Saint. By Him, we cry out, "Abba - Father!" The Holy Spirit empowers us so that we may do that which is commanded of us. God commands us and enables us to keep His commandments by His own power. We are weak, but He is strong. His power is made perfect in our weakness, and therefore we are all the more willing to rejoice in our suffering and to embrace our weaknesses. Because through our weaknesses, we become stronger in our dependence upon the One who is mighty to save. We can endure all things if it is His will, and we can do all things if it is His will, and we certainly will not be put to shame because our hearts have been lifted up by the One who never fails. Therefore, the fellowship of Believers suffers together, being connected, and united as One Body. We all participate in the suffering of the Saints, and we all are a great cloud of witnesses to one another. The Sacrifices of the Living will not go unnoticed forever. Just as the harmony of the Saint's worship will not always go unheard. But our focus, so long as we remain in the World, must be on how we can serve one another as we await the appearing of a great and glorious savior. They will wait upon the Lord, and we will wait upon the Saints. We will serve one another in love, just as the Lord Jesus Christ did when He gave His life for us.

*Bear one another's burdens, and **so fulfill the law of Christ**.*
Galatians 6:2 (ESV)

There is much gain to be had for those who abide by this law of love. It is the epitome of the Saint, seeing that there is no greater love than to lay one's life down for their friends. But how can one sacrifice for friends if they have closed themselves off from both the World and the Brotherhood of Believers? There are few greater joys in this World than to encounter a hitherto unmet brother or sister at a time that is most serendipitous. God knows all things, and all things work out for good unto those who love the Lord (Romans 8:28). But we must Walk in accordance with the will of God if we are to seek His blessing. How can we say that we are united to the Lord but have hatred in our hearts for those who are called according to His name? This is a most serious conflict. We cannot truly know God if we do not also love the brothers and sisters in Christ. Certainly, we are all varied in our personalities, but this is no excuse for there to be a bitter root of resentment that grows and causes division among the Body of Christ.

*See to it that no one falls short of the grace of God and that **no bitter root grows up to cause trouble and defile many**.*
Hebrews 12:15 (ESV)

An unfortunate reality persists despite the zeal of the Worthy Walker. There have always been scoffers, mockers, and the unreliable among the faithful. The Sleep Walker appears to be a fixture of the past, present, and future. But that is no reason to disregard them. Rather, for the Dead, the mission remains the same - to disseminate the Gospel Cure to all that would receive it. To those that Walk in their Sleep, they must be alarmed by their precarious standing, whether that calls for the breaking of fellowship for the sake of convicting their spirit or if it truly means the dismemberment of those that are infections among the pure and innocent. We must consider ourselves as children in regard to what is evil and as wise to that which is righteous. We must be innocent as doves but wise as serpents. We cannot afford to be innocent as serpents and as wise as doves. For that will only make matters worse. Some have become bitter over the abuses of liberties, and others have issues that only they can reveal. But whatever the case may be, the answer to all questions will be found in the Love of God which has been poured into our hearts through the Holy Spirit.

> *Not only that, but we also **rejoice in our sufferings**, because we know that suffering produces perseverance; perseverance, character; and character, hope. **And hope does not disappoint us, because God has poured out His love into our hearts through the Holy Spirit**, whom He has given us.*
> Romans 5:3-5 (ESV)

There is also a severe need for Discipleship to continue to grow. If we consider ourselves to be Alive in Christ, then we will certainly bear much fruit. And the fruit that we bear does not go to waste. The results that God produces in us are used for His glory and the good of His people. We are, after all, a strange people. Very strange indeed, seeing that we were once Dead and now have been brought to Life. He has determined to use us to exemplify His love. That love of His is most powerful when it is shared among the brothers and sisters of Christ. We must urge one another to grow in faith because, by this process, we grow stronger and more suited for the purpose that He has prepared us to complete.

> *But you are a chosen race, a royal priesthood, a holy nation, a people for his own possession, that you may **proclaim the excellencies of him who called you out of darkness into his marvelous light**.*
> 1 Peter 2:9 (ESV)

The chain of faithful believers must not be broken by the disobedience of apathetic children. Only together will we grow stronger as we all rely upon the Lord. United in our hearts and minds, we will be of greater impact on a Dead World. But divided, we will represent the tearing apart of what God has joined together. May that never be the case. May there always be a faithful remnant. Even if it requires that the Church find refuge underground and in unseen places, let it be that the Lord God has His way with His people. There are grave consequences for those who disobey Him, even if they have tasted the goodness of His mercy.

And with whom was he angry for forty years? **Was it not with those who sinned, whose bodies perished in the wilderness?**

Hebrews 3:17 (ESV)

We all have a part to play in the unity of the Body. We must be like iron that sharpens iron so that we may strengthen the faith of our brothers and sisters. Even if sparks fly when iron is sharpened in the end, it will be for the good if it produces the desired results. So long as Christ is preached and the Living Walk in accordance with the Holy Scriptures, there will be mighty things done among the Body of Christ. But may it never be that we begin to fall away as a group and find that our disgruntled grumbles are met with the same disdain as those who complained in the wilderness. We know our mark, and we must hit it with total accuracy. We will follow after Christ to the very end, even if it means the end of our lives. The fullness of Christ is the endless goal that our sights are set upon. But we know that we will not be justified by any means of our flesh or personal effort. Rather, our justification and righteousness come through faith in His finished work. Our Walk marches onward as we continue to trust Him with our lives. But even if our physical life is to come to its end, we will never stop serving God. We echo the message of those Saints of old in our resolution to serve our God only because we know he is able to deliver us from all peril. But even if he does not deliver us from physical death, we will not serve or worship any other gods (Daniel 3:17-18).

And he is not served by human hands, **as if he needed anything.** *Rather, he himself gives everyone* **life and breath and everything else.**

Acts 17:25 (ESV)

RESISTANCE IS FERTILE

I am the vine; you are the branches. Whoever abides in me and I in him, **he it is that bears much fruit, for apart from me you can do nothing.**

John 15:5 (ESV)

While we are in the World, there will be trouble. But as we know, the Lord Jesus has overcome the World, and therefore we too have overcome the World through Him (John 16:33). That is if we are in Him. Our identity must be rooted deeply in our connection to Christ. If it is not, then how could we truly say that Jesus Christ is Lord? The Zombie Apocalypse represents this identity problem on a large scale. There are a great many Zombies who are unaware of their condemnable condition before the Lord

God. They are like the soil that does not receive the Word that is planted, which can save their souls. For some of the Zombies, the Gospel Cure is quickly removed from them by the spiritual enemies of those loved by God.

Furthermore, they may, for a time, appear to have received the implanted Word only for it later to be revealed that the Gospel Cure was either choked out by the deceitfulness of this World's temptations or by the hardship brought about by the other catalysts of sin and Death. There is only one soil that can be definitively regarded as bountiful. That would be the soil that receives the Word of God and bears fruit. The kind of fruit that is expected can only be produced by the presence and power of the Holy Spirit dwelling within the Living. The Flesh counts for nothing; only the Spirit can accomplish the works of God. The Zombie sees ostensible good deeds done for what they think are the right reasons, but God sees the motives of the heart and is fully aware of the purpose behind the Dead works. Even as the body apart from the spirit is dead, so too is faith apart from works Dead (James 2:26). What we must learn to recognize as those who have been called to Walk in step with the Spirit of God is that He will never fail to bring His glory to completion through us.

> *Therefore, as you received Christ Jesus the Lord,* **so walk in him, rooted and built up in him and established in the faith***, just as you were taught, abounding in thanksgiving.*
>
> Colossians 2:6-7 (ESV)

There will come times when we are tested, and we must be prepared to be given more than we can handle. The saying, "God will never give you more than you can handle," is an incomplete saying, if not an outright false statement. The real experience is that God will place us in situations that push us beyond what we think we can handle, not to tempt us but to strengthen us. We know that God does not tempt, nor can he be tempted (James 1), but we also know that we are susceptible to many things in the World. We cannot allow the temptations we face to be greater than the opportunity they present for righteousness to reign. For we should not let our freedom be used for the sake of sin. But we should recognize that the testing of our faith is for our good, seeing that it produces in us a more resolute dependence upon the Lord. No matter the situation we will be aware that the Lord is always faithful and true and that His will for our life is ultimately good and glorious. Saints indeed take time to grow, and mistakes should be expected. But where sin may try to take us out, we know that God's grace is greater than our sin. Only God could take something that was so vehemently opposed to Him and render it nullified so that His supreme glory could be the only thing that remains.

The **LIVING DEAD** Revival Guide

How can the Saints learn to Walk with this mindset? We must make it a practice in our Walk to welcome that which challenges us so long as we maintain ourselves in the will of God. When we Walk in the purpose for which God made us, we will by no means be disappointed. He works all things together for good to those who love Him, but that requires that we love Him! And if we love him, then we will be willing to lay our lives down in a way that will produce in us righteousness and holiness that resembles the Lord Jesus Christ.

> *Since it is written, "You shall **be holy, for I am holy.**"*
> *1 Peter 1:16 (ESV)*

We must submit ourselves to God so that He may bring holiness to perfection in the fear of the Lord. We are indeed being conformed evermore into the image of Jesus Christ. This is what the Saints want to be made more and more like Jesus. Indeed, this is a worthy test for veracity in the claim of shaky Christians. Perhaps a man claims to be a Saint but by their actions deny the Lord who bought them. This is not to say that they are unbelievers and therefore Dead in their sins, but it should be a sign of trouble that someone would resist the sanctification process that brings all the Saints into a more perfect reflection of Jesus Christ.

> ***Submit yourselves*** *therefore to God.* ***Resist*** *the devil, and he will flee from you.* ***Draw near to God, and he will draw near to you.***
> *Cleanse your hands, you sinners, and purify your hearts, you double-minded. Be wretched and mourn and weep.*
> *Let your laughter be turned to mourning and your joy to gloom.*
> *Humble yourselves before the Lord, and he will exalt you.*
> *James 4:7-10 (ESV)*

The key to success in the testing of our faith is not to surrender so quickly under the pressure that we face. If we are tempted, we can know that Jesus was also tempted, but for our sake, He remained sinless. He is not unaware of our weaknesses, but having been tempted in all ways common to man, Jesus is able to help us in our time of need. Just as Jesus submitted Himself to the will of God and was therefore exalted, we can emulate the same kind of Walk. We know that if we draw near to the Lord, then He will draw near to us. That is the essence of the Life we have been given. He has drawn us to Himself in exalting Christ above the earth upon the Cross. But because Jesus humbled Himself to the point of death on the Cross, we now have Life! When we were Zombies, we rejoiced in the things that now bring us shame. In that time, the Lord was our enemy, and our god was our stomach, expressing itself through sinful desires. So now we repent from our sins and Die to our self-daily so that what remains may be the Life of Christ in us. This is the humbling truth of the gift we have received. We were Dead in our sins, but God has made us Alive in Christ Jesus, by grace through faith.

We will experience trouble in the World and under the animosity of the Devil and from the persistence of pestilent Flesh, but we need only to trust and obey the Lord our God. We should, however, be careful to keep in right standing with the Lord. For the enemy of the Saints of God seeks to steal, kill, and destroy us (John 10:10). That, of course, is merely a threat because the reality is that we are already glorified in Christ before the Father so long as we hold fast the faith we have in Christ Jesus. We must resist the enemy, knowing that his time is short, and his anger is stoked. But he will fail because God will not allow him to have victory over us. Furthermore, we are not alone in this struggle, and in The Resistance, we are surrounded by a great host of brothers and sisters suffering under similar circumstances. Therefore, with the comfort we receive from the God of all comfort, we are able to help those who suffer similar things. We will remain vigilant and watchful as we see the Day drawing near. These Last Days are evil, but they are temporary. The time is coming when we will dwell in the presence of the Lord forever. May that be as encouraging to us now as it will be then.

> *Be sober-minded; **be watchful**. Your adversary the devil prowls around like a roaring lion, seeking someone to devour. **Resist him**, firm in your faith, knowing that the **same kinds** of suffering are being experienced by your brotherhood throughout the world. And **after you have suffered a little while, the God of all grace, who has called you to his eternal glory in Christ, will himself restore, confirm, strengthen, and establish you. To him be the dominion forever and ever**. Amen.*
>
> 1 Peter 5:8-11 (ESV)

Futility in Faith

> *By which he has granted to us **his precious and very great promises**, so that through them you may become partakers of the divine nature, having **escaped from the corruption that is in the world because of sinful desire**. For this very reason, make every effort to supplement **your faith** with virtue, and virtue with knowledge, and knowledge with*

The LIVING DEAD Revival Guide

self-control, and self-control with steadfastness, and steadfastness with godliness, and godliness with brotherly affection, and brotherly affection with love. For if these qualities are yours and are increasing, **they keep you from being ineffective or unfruitful in the knowledge of our Lord Jesus Christ.**

1 Peter 1:4-8 (ESV)

It is right that the Saint grows in their faith. A problem sign would be the lack of growth over time. The Saint, who does not produce fruit, should be encouraged. They may need more help in their time of trouble. But with that comes the opportunity for their brothers and sisters to gather around them in prayer and fellowship. We know that the resistance we experience in the World can help us strengthen our faith. We also know that we have nothing to fear, seeing that our God has loved us with a love that is greater than the grave. Death could not hold Him, and likewise, it will have no more power over us. We have these promises from the Lord and are of great courage knowing that they are true and that He does not lie. Our Father is not like a shifting shadow that is difficult to locate or identify. He is known by us, and we are known by Him. But if we neglect our great salvation and the knowledge made available to us, we have done ourselves a disservice. For we will be responsible for what we know and what we teach to others.

Not many of you should become teachers, my brothers, for you know that we who teach will be ***judged with greater strictness****.*

James 3:1 (ESV)

We should expect to be judged, but we should also be encouraged, knowing that we have not been destined to wrath. We have been saved from the wrath of God now that Jesus has taken our punishment upon Himself. When we first believed, we knew very little, and as such, we were like spiritual infants. But now, having spent time in the Word and Walking with our God for some time, we ought to be able to teach one another. How do we know whether our actions will lead to the salvation of others? We cannot know the end from the beginning. We cannot know the ramifications of our choices but what we can know is that the Lord is faithful. We can trust that He does know the beginning from the end and the ramification of our choices. Where a spouse is unaware if their sacrifices will lead to the salvation of their unbelieving partner, we can have confidence that the Lord is good. Of course, it is better not to be unequally linked together, for Light and Darkness have no fellowship together. But in some cases, that is a willing mistake, and in other cases, that is the result of the effects of God's Holy Spirit calling the Dead to Life.

Talon Schneider

*We know that **we have passed out of death into life because we love the brothers**. Whoever does not love **abides in death**.*

1 John 3:14 (ESV)

CHAPTER FIVE

THE GOSPEL CURE

THE CURE TO DEATH

Therefore, if anyone is in Christ, he is a new creation.
The old has passed away; behold, the new has come.
2 Corinthians 5:17 (ESV)

Who could imagine that the cure to Death was so free and abundantly available? Furthermore, who could imagine that those in desperate need of it could willingly reject it? As unusual as it seems, that is exactly the case in this Zombie Apocalypse. The Dead cannot help themselves. They remain enslaved to sin, no matter how many ways they try to conceal it. They have all gone astray, every one of them. They fill themselves with everything but the answer to their problem and still cannot recognize their need for the Risen Savior. Their identity crisis is so prominent that it completely ruins them and many others around them. They are the ones who hear the Words of Life and disregard it. They see their reflection in the mirror that is the scripture and, to their horror, see that they are Dead. But they do not change. Instead, they Walk away and continue sinning. They mistake and abuse the patience of the Lord, thinking perhaps that at the very last moment, they could seek the Cure and be saved. But will it still be available to them when they want it on their own terms? One can only hope. Their sin nature must be dealt with before they face the Lord, or they risk serving the eternal penalty for their sins in hell. They may very well know at that time that they have been Zombies all along, but it will be too late. Would it be that fear would provoke the Dead to respond to the message? Perhaps it takes a mixture of fear and love for the Dead to finally realize what has been right in front of them all along. God does not will that any should perish, and He does not rejoice in the death of the wicked. But there is much rejoicing in heaven over the repentance of even one sinful Zombie. This is the heart that the Lord has for such a creature. We were the kind of creature that innately hates its Creator. This is the very creature that the Lord has loved. This says much about the Zombie, but it also speaks to the character of the Lord our God. He is patient, kind, and loving. He is long-suffering with a stiff-necked people. But His patience is for a time, and then, in the End, He will administer the judgment that has not been sleeping over the Zombies who have defied

Him for so long. Oh, that the Dead would turn to Him and be healed! They need not earn salvation; they merely need to accept the free gift of God in Christ Jesus.

> *For the wages of sin is death, but the free gift of God is eternal life in Christ Jesus our Lord.*
>
> Romans 6:23 (ESV)

This Life is a gift from God, but some treat it like a curse. The Dead often view this life as a curse rather than a gift. This Gospel Cure is mysterious, even to those who have received it. We who have been redeemed cannot help but marvel at the wondrous love of God. We are deeply convicted by His sacrifice because we know that we did not deserve it. We were the ones who deserved death, not Jesus. And this is what He has planned from the beginning. Even in the Garden of Eden, God had covered over the sin and shame of Adam and Eve (Genesis 3). But could we even fathom that this has been His plan from before the foundation of the earth?

> *Blessed be the God and Father of our Lord Jesus Christ, who has blessed us in Christ with every spiritual blessing in the heavenly places, **even as he chose us in him before the foundation of the world**, that we should be holy and blameless before him. In love, he predestined us for adoption to himself as sons through Jesus Christ, according to the purpose of his will, to the praise of his glorious grace, with which he has blessed us in **the Beloved**. In him we have redemption through his blood, the forgiveness of our trespasses, according to the riches of his grace, which he lavished upon us, in all wisdom and insight **making known to us the mystery of his will**, according to his purpose, which he set forth in Christ as a plan for the fullness of time, to unite all things in him, things in heaven and things on earth.*
>
> Ephesians 1:3-10 (ESV)

We now participate in His plan. We make it our aim to reveal Christ to the World in the hopes that the Dead, who still linger, would perhaps turn to the Lord in faith. There are many that we love and long to see converted from their Walk in Death into those who Live now and evermore. But of course, not all will be saved. Not all have faith. This is sad now and should motivate us to sacrifice what is necessary in order that our loved ones and those loved by others may somehow attain to the resurrection of the Dead. But we endeavor that their resurrection would be within Christ, not among those that are raised only to be judged and damned. How dreadful it is for those that die in their sins.

The **LIVING DEAD** Revival Guide

They will surely not escape from the wrath if they have not responded by then. They will experience the Second Death, which is a final separation from God. That is the great chasm that separates and cannot be spanned by anyone. It is the place where there is Darkness that can be felt. They may see themselves for the first time as they really have been all along, Zombies. In that place, they will weep and moan and gnash their teeth. They will go hungry and thirsty forever. Their insatiable appetite for sin will finally get the better of them, and they will be confined to a place of eternal torment. Is this serious enough for the Saint to be moved to compassion? Praise the Lord that He looked at us in compassion, for one can imagine that we all certainly deserved death. God should not have had mercy on us. But this is the mystery of the Gospel Cure. The mystery revealed in the death, burial, and resurrection of Jesus Christ from the dead. The mystery is that God loves us. And it will take quite some time for Him to make known to us the extent to which He has loved us in Christ.

> ***But God***, *being rich in mercy, because of the great love with which he loved us,* ***even when we were dead in our trespasses, made us alive together with Christ****—by grace you have been saved— and* ***raised us up with him*** *and seated us with him in the heavenly places in Christ Jesus, so that in the coming ages he might show the immeasurable riches of his grace in kindness toward us in Christ Jesus.*
>
> Ephesians 2:4-7 (ESV)

There is no greater truth than to know that God loves us. The Gospel Cure is that message to the World. That God loved us so much that He was willing to send His one and only son to die for the sin of the World (John 3:16). We know that Jesus had a will of His own. And even at one point sought for a different solution to the Zombie problem. Jesus asked for a different Cure to Death. But there could be only one way. The Death of Jesus Christ was the only means by which salvation could be offered to all these Walking Dead. Where we were once enemies, we have now been made to be friends who know some measure of His plans. We were Zombies and have now become Children of God. We hated Christ and have become His brothers and sisters. He is not ashamed of us. But rather, Jesus is proud to call us His family, and there is coming a time when He will make us known to all in heaven. There will undoubtedly be joy at the right hand of God. Do we believe all this? Can we believe all this? We must believe otherwise we are not accepting the Cure. And even if we do not feel as though He loves us because our body still resists, we can know that He does, in fact, love us!

Talon Schneider

*But God shows his love for us in that while we were **still sinners, Christ died for us.***

Romans 5:8 (ESV)

The Dawn of the Dead revealed that the Death that the first humans Died not only affected them. That sin impacted all humans after them. But God had mercy on them and has had mercy on us. God covered Adam and Eve. He warned Cain to do what was right or risk the punishment of being banished even further. Cain failed and became a restless wanderer. Noah found favor with the Lord and responded in faith to what he was told. Noah and seven others were saved from the Apocalypse of their Day, but the rest of the World was thrown under the deluge. That was intended to cleanse the World, but it was clear that sin would plague mankind from the beginning to the end.

Nevertheless, God had mercy on Noah. Abraham, Isaac, and Jacob responded to the Lord in faith. Despite the mistakes they made, God remained merciful. Joseph came into the World, and though he suffered for a little while, God used his suffering for the good of many. Even after Joseph was forgotten, and Moses became an important person in Egypt, God was still loving and kind toward a people who did not deserve to be loved as they were. They were freed from the enslavement of Egypt, and mightily delivered out of the hand of Pharaoh. Then they wandered in the wilderness for 40 years. And even when there was grumbling and uprising among those that had been freed from what they suffered in Egypt, there was a call to stand between the Living and the Dead.

So, Aaron took the censer as Moses had ordered and ran into the midst of the assembly. And seeing that the plague had begun among the people, he offered the incense and made atonement for the people. ***He stood between the living and the dead****, and the plague was halted.*

Numbers 16:47-48 (ESV)

Even after that, through the many adventures and expeditions, the need for a Cure to Death persisted. Even among those who had not sinned in the same way that Adam had sinned. It was overwhelmingly clear that Zombies were a part of this World. Even where the sin was different, the result was the same because the wages of sin all lead to Death. The separation caused by sin cannot be denied. We all know what it is to have a relationship with someone. But only the Worthy Walker can truly say that they have a relationship with the Living God and that not of their own effort. He is the One that brought us to Himself and performed the reconciliation necessary for the relationship to be made right. But we must ask ourselves if we are willing to make our stand between the Living and the Dead in order to see the glory of God and His kingdom advance. Will we Walk Worthy of our calling? Or will we stand aside and watch as the army of the Dead advances upon us?

DISPENSING THE CURE

*For what we proclaim is not ourselves, but Jesus Christ as Lord, with ourselves as your **servants for Jesus' sake**. For God, who said, "Let light shine out of darkness," has shone in our hearts to give **the light of the knowledge of the glory of God in the face of Jesus Christ**.*
2 Corinthians 4:5-6 (ESV)

Praise the Lord for what He has made known to us. He has saved us from a wretched existence that was devoid of His presence. It was as if a Light had cast out all the Darkness in our hearts and minds, and now, we can see clearly for the first time. When we believe for the first time, there is an incredible newness to Life. We experience the fullness that only comes from knowing God. And that is what is so important to us. We have experienced something that can never be forgotten. We have been given knowledge of Him in a way that can never be removed or made unknown. Even though we have not seen Jesus with our physical eyes, we love Him. Though we do not see Him yet, we believe in Him and are fill with a glorious joy so powerful as to go beyond expression (1 Peter 1:8). There has never been a greater thing done in all of human history, and there cannot possibly be anything that would compare. God has loved the unlovable with a love so powerful that it overcame death. Now having achieved Life for those that were once Dead, how much more willing should we be to make sure His Cure is known to all? We will treat this gift like the treasure it truly is!

*For where your **treasure** is, there will your **heart** be also.*
Luke 12:34 (ESV)

There is a treasure of such incredible worth that only God could have given it. It is not like the riches that the World seeks after that pass from one owner to the next and is never truly belonged to anyone for more than their time. The treasure of the Gospel Cure is a peculiar one because it becomes to those who possess it an even greater treasure when it is given away. We who have been saved should have no greater joy than to see the redemption of those who are being Born Again. Among those of us who have experienced the renewal of the Spirit, there is very little that can compare to how it feels. When we became conscious of our sin debt before the Living God, it caused us to be full of many conflicting emotions. There may have been a combination of fear, anxiousness, and dread mixed together with confidence, joy, and hope. But even if one cannot remember what it was like to be a Zombie, then their testimony is even more precious, for they have had more time in the Light than in the Darkness. They are given a gift of innocence that can only be known by a pure following after Christ. There are a great many who have spent more time in the Darkness of their closed minds and the enslavement of their sins who spend the remainder of their earthly Life in a constant battle. But even these are blessed because they are given an innocence that comes by faith. The same kind of innocence of all the saints who have been credited righteousness. But if we have been granted such a gift and have become like those who would hide their treasure, then what does that say about our hearts? Should we not be exhilarated to share such a treasurable knowledge? Yes, we should! Fearing the Dead is a foolish thing to do when they are the ones who need to be made fearful of their dangerous position before God. But if they respond to our warnings and are turned to the Lord, there will be the multiplication of the treasure stored up in all of the Saints.

Of course, Yahweh would make use of these jars of clay because He takes pleasure in the glorification gained through the use of a limited vessels such as us. We demonstrate by the fact of our weakness that it is His power at work in the Gospel Cure. The power is not of us. It is not as though we have discovered this Cure by our own means. We did not stumble into the realization by any mere happenstance. There is no coincidence before the Lord because He knows all things. But what we see is the careful execution of His plan for redemption from the beginning to the end. And the End has nearly ended.

Sadly, there are more and more Zombies that populate the World. They are blinded in their minds by the god of this World. The Catalysts of sin and Death will not surrender until they meet their own End. But they certainly will be put to Death in an eternal fire. Their judgment is already hanging over their heads because the victory of Jesus Christ was so powerfully exerted. He has completely triumphed over them. All that must happen now is for those that are to believe to come to their senses. The Zombie has no sense except for that which serves itself. They only know what it is to serve their pleasures. And so if the Gospel Cure is veiled to them, let it not be because it was not preached to them. But let every ear hear what the Spirit has to say in regard to the Life and worthiness of Jesus Christ. If they have heard the message and still refused to be healed by it, then they will have their End come upon them in their own way. But we that are Alive cannot allow for anyone to say that they have never heard of such a Cure to the miserable condition that faces Zombies everywhere.

*So, whoever knows the right thing to do and fails to do it, for him **it is sin.***

James 4:17 (ESV)

PRESERVING THE CURE

*Whatever happens, **conduct yourselves in a manner worthy of the gospel of Christ**. Then, whether I come and see you or only hear about you in my absence, I will know that you stand firm in the one Spirit, **striving together as one for the faith of the gospel** without being frightened in any way by those who oppose you. This is a sign to them that they will be **destroyed**, but that you will be **saved**—and that by God.*

Philippians 1:27-28 (ESV)

There have been attempts by the forces of evil to tamper with the truth of the Gospel Cure. This will not succeed but will only bring devastation upon their souls. Even though Zombies may attempt to ruin the faith of the Gospel, they will by no means be able to frustrate the plans of God. He laughs at their vain attempts to rise up against Him. Nevertheless, we who remain in the World must be ready and well equipped to make our stand against those that oppose the people of God.

There have been numerous false saviors and false gospels that have gone out to deceive. But they do not have any power. They are only making it more difficult for the true Gospel to be recognized for what it is. The true Gospel speaks of the means by which the Dead can be brought to Life. It is the hope that is held out to all who would accept it. Where there seemed to be no answer for us, that is the place where God has done His work. Jesus Christ, although He was sinless, accepted the punishment deserved by those who had sinned. We who have sinned now have access by faith to what should belong to Christ. The Gospel Cure must be preserved because, without it, we would become most pitiable among all mankind. If the Gospel we have received is not of God and is not true, then we have made false claims about God and endangered many others and ourselves. But we can know certainly that the Gospel Cure is the one true message about Jesus Christ and the forgiveness of sins through the shedding of His blood. We will not accept any counterfeit Gospel.

*For **false messiahs and false prophets will appear** and perform signs and wonders **to deceive, if possible, even the elect**.*

Mark 13:22 (ESV)

We must not allow ourselves to be deceived. It would not be easy to account for every lie concerning the truth. What we can do instead is familiarize ourselves with the complete comprehension of the true Cure to Death. The more that we know what is true, the better we will be at recognizing the erroneous renditions. After all, the message we have received is treated as foolishness to the World. They long for signs and powers that could be performed by a trickster or magician. But what we have experienced goes beyond the physical world. We have come to partake of the divine nature of God. He has made us blameless before Himself, even though we are not yet perfect in our own eyes. We certainly could not have done anything to change our own nature because that is what made us who we were. We were like the rest who had nothing but sin on the mind. Our bodies craved for the Flesh, but now that we have been changed, we cannot imagine ourselves acting any way like we once did.

It is not only for ourselves that the Gospel Cure must not be tampered with, but also for all those who would follow after us as we follow after Christ Jesus. The message about Jesus has been preserved for us so that we who have heard it and believed may be saved. Therefore, the Gospel Cure concerns those who have received it and those who are committed to maintaining its purity and veracity. This calls for a wise person. There will be many efforts in these Last Days to corrupt the message by various means. But they cannot overthrow the truth. Jesus Christ is both God and man, and He became like us in order to save us. Thus, the Word became flesh and made His dwelling among us. He came as it was foretold of Him. But even still, He was able to confound the "wise" who should have known what they were looking for at His arrival. There were some who knew of His coming, but the majority did not know Him nor receive Him.

We know that this World and all that is in it is fading away. All that can be shaken is being removed so that only that with is unshakable will remain. We must not be like those that shrink back, but rather we will be resolute in our faith. We can stand together on the firm foundation of Jesus Christ and be of absolute confidence concerning our souls. If we continue to Walk Worthy according to His calling, then He will finish what He started in us (Philippians 1:6). That is a great encouragement for us, even if we stumble in sin, we know that God is not going to give up on us. How encouraging it is to know that if God was for us when we were against Him, how much more will He be for us now that we are for Him? Now that we know what it is to be loved by Him, we have everything we need to Live a godly life.

There may be days when it would be needful to remind ourselves of what the Cure really represents. Those are the times when discipleship and communion are most advantageous. For in the remembrance of Jesus Christ sacrifice through the broken body and poured out blood, we can be strengthened again in our faith. Fortunately for us, His mercy endures forever, and therefore even when we have made great errors to the point of sin, He will not refuse a broken heart and a convicted spirit (Psalm 51:17). But God will make sure to bring about holiness in His people. This is part of the effect of the Gospel Cure on the Living. We should take no part of fellowship with those who make sin a habit. Those that practice willful sin are damaging themselves and others. They have not obeyed what is written and have run off to their own pursuits.

> ***Anyone who runs ahead without remaining in the teaching of Christ does not have God.*** *Whoever remains in His teaching has both the Father and the Son.*
> 2 John 1:9 (ESV)

Those that seek to peddle the Word of God for a dishonest gain should be terrified of what lies ahead for them. If they make God out to be a liar or, in some way, have twisted the text to suit their own motives, they will be paid back with the plagues written down in the Word of God. They will face the consequences of their actions. But we must do our part not to become deceived by departures from what is written. What we have written down for us is worth paying attention to, for by faith, those who believed in the past were commended. They relied upon the Word of God, and we, too, will do the same. The Holy Spirit uses the Scriptures to speak to us in a way that we can understand. He knows our inner being better than we know ourselves because all things are known by Him. He is the only immortal One and dwells in unapproachable light (1 Timothy 6:16). The Word of God will never pass away, many other things will rise and fall, but the Word of God will abide forever.

> *For whatever was written in former days was written for our **instruction**, that through **endurance** and through the **encouragement** of the Scriptures we might have **hope**.*
> Romans 15:4 (ESV)

EXAMINATION

> ***Do not be conformed to this world***, *but be transformed by the renewal of your mind*, ***that by testing*** *you may discern what is the will of God, what is good and acceptable and perfect.*
> Romans 12:2 (ESV)

The World will naturally try to squeeze out the Saints because they are no longer at peace with the World system as it is. Saints are children of God, and the reason it does not know us is because Jesus likewise was not known. The enmity we have with the World is just another proof that the spiritual condition of these generations is not in a good standing. In fact, anyone who loves the World is at enmity with God (James 4:4). But those that have committed themselves to the Lord will by no means be disappointed. Rather we have been appointed and chosen to be representatives of the Lord in this World. That is why we are not immediately taken up to be with Him upon our conversion from Zombie to Saint. For if we could have it how we would prefer, then many if not all of us would desire to depart from this World and our body and hence be with the Lord. But the reality is that it is more needful that those who were once Dead in the sins would likewise reach out to those that remain Dead. We no longer carry around in our bodies the desire to do what is evil. We no longer cater to the desires of the Flesh. Instead, we put down that which is Fleshly, Worldly, and sinful so that we could be better utilized by the Lord our God in this ministry of reconciliation. God, in his infinite wisdom, has been taking those that were formerly against Him and using them as ambassadors of His love. We have become compelled by His love for us, wherein before we know him, our primary compulsion was the desire to please ourselves. We were all too familiar with how to get what we wanted. The World facilitates that type of behavior, but all those who want to Walk Worthy will be persecuted and hated in the World. Nevertheless, we shall rejoice at the idea! Because we know that it is a great blessing to be hated on account of the Risen Lord and, therefore, further confirm our calling and election. This is a vital part of the process for the new believer, seeing that many old ways may still linger and cling to us. But all that we must do is trust and obey the Lord. For He is faithful and will not allow us to fall, but rather He will place our feet on stable ground so that we can run for our Life with the endurance necessary to finish the race.

> *Therefore, since we are surrounded by so great a cloud of witnesses, let us also lay aside every weight, and sin which clings so closely, and* **let us run with endurance the race that is set before us** *....*
>
> Hebrews 12:1 (ESV)

When Jesus made Himself known in the world, He was confronted in many ways. But His conviction never wavered. He had been manifested in order to heal the sick and save the lost. But on many occasions, those that were spiritually Sick and Lost were unwilling to recognize that they were in those needful positions. They were being overtaken by their pride, which would not allow them to humble themselves before the

The LIVING DEAD Revival Guide

Lord. Jesus proclaimed to them that it was the Sick who needed a Healer, and therefore if they deemed themselves as being healthy, then how could Jesus be of any help to them. However, there were many who came to Jesus realizing their depravity and their deep need for help. They came to Him in their weakness, and frailty, and infirmity, and He had compassion on them. But even as Jesus was performing these miraculous hearings, there was a level of doubt experienced by those who were there and hearing of these things. John the Baptist, while imprisoned, sought to know with more certainty if Jesus was indeed to promised Messiah. And the response that was given to him pointed out the nature of the Zombie Apocalypse being undone.

> *And said to him, "**Are you the one who is to come, or shall we look for another?**" And Jesus answered them, "Go and tell John what you hear and see: the blind receive their sight and the lame walk, lepers are cleansed and the deaf ear, and the dead are raised up, and the poor have good news preached to them. **And blessed is the one who is not offended by me.**"*
> Matthew 11:3-6 (ESV)

Jesus has come to undo what sin and Death had done in God's creation. But remarkably, God has given human beings the ability to choose for themselves whom they will serve. Even though there were many who heard the words of Jesus and believed it is still shocking to contemplate how many remained Zombies craving only the Flesh. The miracles were performed before their very eyes, and they were still weighed down by unbelieving hearts. Perhaps if they had examined their hearts motives and intentions just a bit further. Perhaps if they had been more willing to hear what the Lord God was speaking to them, then they would have been changed and truly transformed by the words of Life. Indeed, the source of Life had become visible to them, and they sought rather to kill Him. But Jesus was obedient even to the point of death upon the cross. He offered Himself willingly so that those who were called would hear his voice and be brought to Life (John 5:25).

The Living Hope that we now know will always be with us who have been Born Again into it. And yet we must be on the lookout for the corruption of those that would seek to infiltrate the brotherhood of believers like wolves in sheep's clothing. In times past, they sought to conform new believers into the old ways that were effectively Dead. They wanted the early believers to work and earn good deeds of enough merit so as to attain to salvation on their own terms. But this Gospel Cure cannot be earned; it can only be received. It is not for those that see themselves as having no need for it, but rather the Cure is for those who know that they need it. This message is hard to accept where there is pride, but that too can fall down in humility before the awesome power of God. The proud are opposed by God, but He will exalt those that humble themselves before Him. We must be careful not to hear the Word and not do what it says. Doing what the Word says is a confirmation of our faith and an essential part of obedience unto God. This is a Fruit of the Spirit that can be a reliable indication of a person's true position. But we must make an effort to not only evaluate the words and actions of others but more importantly, we should examine ourselves to verify that Christ is in us. And if Christ is in us, then we will be made more like Him with every day that passes.

> *For those whom he foreknew he also predestined to be **conformed to the image of his Son**, in order that he might be the firstborn among many brothers.*
> Romans 8:29 (ESV)

SELF EXAMINATION

> ***Examine yourselves*** *to see whether you are in the faith; test yourselves. Do you not realize that **Christ Jesus is in you--unless, of course, you fail the test**?*
> 2 Corinthians 13:5 (ESV)

It may become a necessary practice that the Saints begin evaluating their salvation on a more regular basis. For many deceivers have come into the world seeking to gain something by their trickery. But we have made efforts to strengthen our faith in such a way that we would not be led astray by the deceptive philosophies and cunning strategies of those that oppose us. We have anchored ourselves to the truth so that we would not be tossed back and forth by every wind of false teaching. But where we can know that the Bible has been preserved accurately for our sake, we must be more ready to test ourselves for any erroneous ways within us. When we were slaves of sin, we were free from the requirements of righteousness. We had no idea that there was a better way. But now that we can See what we were and, even better, what we are now, it is only right that we would continue to work out our salvation with the seriousness it deserves. For when we were Zombies, our thoughts and actions were evil. But now we have such a serious warning from Christ that it should make everyone shudder at the very thought of it.

> ***Woe to the world*** *for temptations to sin! For it is necessary that temptations come, but woe to the one by whom the temptation comes! And*

The LIVING DEAD Revival Guide

if your hand or your foot causes you to sin, **cut it off and throw it away**. *It is better for you to enter life crippled or lame than with two hands or two feet to be thrown into the eternal fire. And if your eye causes you to sin,* **tear it out and throw it away**. *It is better for you to enter life with one eye than with two eyes to be **thrown into the hell of fire**.*

Matthew 18:7-9 (ESV)

We must not act so emotionally that we would go too far with this admonition. But the point has been made aggressively clear. We cannot allow sin to rule our mortal body and make us its slaves once again. When we were Zombies, it did not surprise us so much when a sin would suddenly ruin us. We were aching inwardly and outwardly. But now that we have tasted that the Lord is good, we cannot enjoy those things that were bringing Death upon us. Now those sins we once committed have been put to Death. We have mortified the Flesh. That does not mean that it is necessary that we literally cut off our hand or pluck out our eyes, but we can see that those who would rather save their hand for sinning have no real desire to be with the Lord in His heavenly dwelling. That is a sad truth about the Zombie, they would rather carry around a necrotic hand and an evil eye than allow those things to become submitted to the will of God. But even in the Darkest of places, God is able to bring about His Light and His glory. It is up to us to examine and test whether the things that we are practicing are good or bad. We would do well to heed the advice of our brothers and sisters even if it is a hard thing to hear. The Word of God testifies in our favor that we should make thorough examinations of our thoughts and actions.

*But test **everything**; hold fast what is good.*

1 Thessalonians 5:21 (ESV)

But even if we test prophecies and find that our hearts are uneasy and unrested by what we discover, it may still be that we have room to grow. All things are permissible to the Saint because they have been set free. But not all things are beneficial. This calls for wisdom and patience. Some liberties are better off as Sacrifices made for the sake of those who cannot handle the newfound freedom of the Living. And even worse than that are those that offer wildly inappropriate teachings and call it Christianity. They lead many astray and will pay for their arrogant choices. The mature followers of Christ have made it a practice to evaluate what they see and hear, and do in order to have a closer Walk with the Lord.

*Beloved, do not believe every spirit, but **test the spirits to see whether they are from God**, for many false prophets have gone out into the world.*

1 John 4:1 (ESV)

We test ourselves to show that we are approved by God for sacrifice and service. And even if we are wrong on some point, if we are truly in Christ, then God will provide the answer to our misconduct. He will confront us by what the Spirit reveals to us so that we can change our choices and behaviors. Even as we are testing ourselves, we become more aware of the final testing that will prove the truth of our souls before the Lord. He will judge both the Living and the Dead, and nothing hidden will remain undisclosed. Therefore, we have reason to make ourselves right before the Lord right now. It is better to address the things that are hindering our Walk now than to never do anything about them. Who knows what we may miss out on because of disobedience in our lives? But if we train ourselves to respond in righteousness to all things, then we can be confident on the Day of salvation that we have not labored or ran in vain.

***By this gospel you are saved, if you hold firmly to the word**, I preached to you. Otherwise, you have believed in vain.*

1 Corinthians 15:2 (ESV)

REGENERATION

But when the goodness and loving kindness of God our Savior appeared, he saved us, not because of works done by us in righteousness, but according to his own mercy, by the washing of regeneration and renewal of the Holy Spirit, whom he poured out on us richly through Jesus Christ our Savior, so that being justified by his grace we might become heirs according to the hope of eternal life.

Titus 3:4-7 (ESV)

What we are has been made known to us in a greater degree now that we have believed in Him who calls us by name. If at some point, we considered ourselves righteous by our own deeds, we have had that misperception corrected. Our salvation is a gift, and by no means could we have earned it. We know ourselves now, as God truly knows us. The World does not know us because it did not know Him (1 John 3:1-3). We are the children of God and have been Born Again into a Living Hope through the resurrection of Jesus Christ from the dead (1 Peter 1:3-5). What was once Dead has now been brought to Life. What a miracle it is to see the transformation of the Zombie into the Saint. How compelling it is to see the believer stand before a crowd of Zombies and boldly proclaim the Gospel Cure to those that violently reject it. Even though it may seem like the Dead do not hear the message of Life that we proclaim, we can have confidence that God provides the increase to the seed that is planted and watered by various faithful followers. Indeed, God is able to make Life sprout up from the wilderness and can bring even the unlikeliest of Zombies to repentance and faith.

Our old self was experiencing that decay of the body and the spirit with every passing day. But now that we have been Born Again and regenerated, we know that we are not merely wasting away but rather are being renewed day by day. Surely, we know that we necessitated a new birth because of our previously Dead condition before the Lord. And perhaps it is worth bringing attention once again to that which we have already learned because it is easy to forget even the most important things. But the Gospel Cure will never be tiresome to those who have been redeemed. We will always find hope and encouragement as we remember what has been done for us. Even though we do not yet see Jesus, we are filled with a hope so glorious that it cannot be fully expressed because we are currently experiencing the Fruit of our faith, which is the salvation of our souls (1 Peter 1:8-9).

Therefore, Brothers and Sisters, if ever you or a fellow believer find yourself to have a downcast heart, do not forget to bring to mind that love of which you had at first. Rekindle the flame that first warmed your hearts at the mentioning of the Name of Jesus as we first believed. Be encouraged that the Day is drawing ever closer and is nearer now than when we first believed. For the Saint can always say, "To live is Christ and to die is gain" (Philippians 1:21). The Gospel Cure is not something we receive and then move on to something else as if there were anything greater to be gained. The greatest thing to be gained from the Gospel is not only the forgiveness of our sins but actually gaining Christ. We are receiving our true love! Indeed, we love because He first loved us with such a powerful love that not even the grave could hold Him back. He has loved us to the very end and is always living to make intercession on our behalf. He has promised us eternal Life. He has promised to Walk with us.

The Gospel Cure can be understood in so many different ways, but it will always center on the same essential points. We are saved by faith alone, through grace, according to the scriptures alone, in Christ alone, and all for the glory of God alone. We certainly can recognize the Gospel message in the undeniable facts shared in the scriptures.

*For I delivered to you as of first importance what I also received: that **Christ died for our sins** in accordance with the Scriptures, that **he was buried**, that **he was raised on the third day** in accordance with the Scriptures ....*

1 Corinthians 15:3-4 (ESV)

But we can also find the Gospel in the verses that expound on the truth of God's justice and love. We know God's love for us in that while we were still Zombies, Christ died for us (Romans 5:8). Furthermore, we have been given a message of reconciliation, seeing that God is able to present us before Himself as blameless and innocent (Jude 1:24). The means by which He has done this is by making Jesus, who knew no sin, to become sin for us so that we may become the righteousness of Christ (2 Corinthians 5:21). This divine exchange, vicarious atonement, and spectacular substitution all point to the fact that God must punish sin. God would not be just if He did not punish sin. The problem is that our sin is an infinite offense before His infinite holiness and therefore requires that an infinitely worthy payment be made. The Gospel recognizes this essential issue for the Zombie that stands condemned before God in their filthy rags of false righteousness. The Lord God has caused us to be made alive, even though we were formerly Zombies and alienated from Him even from birth. He did so by nailing our sins to the cross, and because of the victorious resurrection of Jesus Christ, we know that we too will rise from the dead. The Saint merely sleeps in death. But the Zombie must fear the sleep of death because it is impossible for them to turn away from their destruction once they have physically died. How desperate they should be! How they should cease their weeping and gnashing after all the sinful cravings of the Flesh and rather claw and grasp out for the Living God! If only they would be regenerated and confess with their mouth that Jesus is Lord and believe in their hearts that God raised Him from the dead and so be saved (Romans 10:9)!

We cannot know for certain what the condition of another person's soul may be until we have observed their lifestyle long enough to evaluate their Fruit. Not that we are the final judge, but we find ourselves in No Man's Land because there was no other who could have done what was needed in order to bring about salvation for the Lost. Jesus Christ Walked the very same earth that we have, and yet He did so without sin. He died for us so that we would no longer Live for ourselves but for the love of others. As we love one another, we practice what proves our new Life. The hallmark of the Saint is that we are no longer the Living Dead, but rather because of the mercy of God, we have become Living Sacrifices (Romans 12:1).

We are Alive! But the reason we Live is because we have received the Gospel Cure that causes us to always carry around in our bodies the knowledge of the death of Jesus on our behalf (2 Corinthians 4:10-11). As we do that, we exemplify what it means to be

Living Sacrifices and those who have been regenerated by God for a sacrifice and service that leads to the progress of faith and joy in others. Praise the Lord for such a wonderful calling. May He always work powerfully in those who Walk with Him who Lives forever.

BROKEN BREAD AND AN OVERFLOWING CUP

Jesus said to them, "You do not know what you are asking. ***Are you able to drink the cup that I drink, or to be baptized with the baptism with which I am baptized?"***

Mark 10:38 (ESV)

It may seem to the Dead that it is the Christian who is actually the cannibalistic animal. They also hurl insults at us in regard to our association with the death of Jesus. But every association with Jesus is a precious connection for the Saint. The Zombie does not know what they are doing. They think that they are correct, but they couldn't be further from the truth. The difficult teachings of Christ drove many of His Sleep Walking followers to depart from Him. They exclaimed that His teaching was too much for them to handle. But when Jesus asked Peter, one of His most endearing followers, if He too would depart from the Way, Peter's answer was like that of all the Saints.

*Simon Peter replied, "Lord, to whom would we go? You have the **words of eternal life**."*

John 6:68 (ESV)

The Saints know that there is nowhere else to go, and indeed we do not desire to depart from the Lord for anything else. We would rather suffer physical death than renounce our faith in the Lord. And that is just what many of the early believers experienced. They were willing to literally lay their lives down after they realized that Jesus Christ actually did come to die on the cross for their sins and rose from the dead on the third day, according to the Scriptures (1 Corinthians 15:2-3). That is the Gospel Cure, and to those who receive it, the Words of Life have become a treasure that is stored up in their hearts. Zombies scowl and moan at the mere utterance of this Gospel Cure. But there is no other name under heaven by which we must be saved, other than the name of Jesus Christ, our Lord, and savior (Acts 4:12). The way that we commemorate this truth is seen in two practices. They are ordinances observed for the purpose of association with Christ Jesus. The first is Baptism and the second is Communion. In both of these practices, there are abuses by those who do not know what they are doing. These abuses may have come to interfere with the true faith of those who are being saved from the damnation of their sins. But where the lies continue to rise up, the truth will rise to fight it even stronger. We must not let these most precious practices go to waste.

> *Now I commend you for remembering me in everything and for **maintaining the traditions**, just as I passed them on to you.*
> 1 Corinthians 11:2 (ESV)

Baptism

> ***Baptism**, which corresponds to this, now saves you, not as a removal of dirt from the body but as an appeal to God for a good conscience, through the resurrection of Jesus Christ ....*
> 1 Peter 3:21 (ESV)

Baptism is not what saves us. The Gospel Cure is the information that saves us. That is, we are saved by faith in Jesus Christ. And if we believe in Jesus and desire to live godly, then we will pledge ourselves to Him in a public way that can be attested to by many witnesses. This is the purpose of Baptism. It is for the submersion of our identity into the character and quality of Christ Jesus. Through our plunging into the identity of Christ, we can finally be cleansed of all our sins. Not because we have been washed with a physical cleansing but rather because Baptism symbolizes our association with the death, burial, and resurrection of Jesus Christ. Does that mean that after being Baptized that we should expect sin to completely disappear? No, it will remain until the End, but not any further. Does Baptism mean that someone is instantly saved? No, not unless the Baptism is true. Only those who understand its purpose and Walk in its truth can be saved in their Baptism because they do so in order to associate themselves with Jesus Christ. Therefore, the notion that one may be placed into water in order for them to be changed will have no effect. The only way to be saved is through the Lord Jesus Christ, and not by any works of our own.

Being baptized means that we have visibly and publicly dedicated ourselves to the Lord in such a way that it may be said that our old self was buried under the water. Our new self, who abides in Christ, is the one that came up from the water. Indeed, this practice is simply used to unify us with Jesus in an intimate way. This makes us responsible to all those who are witnesses to our pledge of faith in the forgiveness of our sins made available through the sacrifice of Christ. Therefore, the one who understands Baptism understands its significance to the Gospel Cure. We know that all who accept Jesus Christ as Lord and savior should be Baptized. But thankfully, we have the example of the thief on the cross to encourage those Saints who believed but were never Baptized. Because Jesus, the King of kings and Lord of Lords, said to the thief on the cross that he would be with Him on that very day in paradise (Luke 23:43).

> *What shall we say then? Are we to continue in sin that grace may abound?* **By no means!** *How can we who* **died** *to sin still* **live** *in it? Do you not know that all of us who have been baptized into Christ Jesus were* **baptized into his death***? We were buried therefore with him by baptism into death, in order that, just as Christ was raised from the dead by the glory of the Father,* **we too might walk in newness of life***. For if we have been* **united** *with him in a death like his, we shall certainly be united with him in a resurrection like his. We know that* **our old self was crucified with him** *in order that the body of sin might be brought to nothing so that we would no longer be enslaved to sin. For one who has died has been set free from sin.* **Now, if we have died with Christ, we believe that we will also live with him.** *We know that Christ, being raised from the dead, will never die again;* **death no longer has dominion over him***. For the death he died he died to sin, once for all, but the life he lives he lives to God.* **So, you also must consider yourselves dead to sin and alive to God in Christ Jesus.** *Let not sin therefore reign in your mortal body, to make you obey its passions. Do not* **present your members to sin as instruments for unrighteousness but present yourselves to God as those who have been brought from death to life***, and your members to God as instruments for righteousness. For sin will have no dominion over you, since you are not under law but under grace.*
>
> Romans 6:1-14 (ESV)

There was only one way for us to be saved. We could by no means save ourselves. We were at one time dire enemies of Jesus Christ. To demonstrate His love for us, He willingly went the Cross. Before he washed us and cleansed us from our sins, we were like all the rest, offspring of disobedience and doomed to die the Second Death. But at the right time, when God's loving-kindness was revealed, Jesus died on our behalf. Remarkably there are still some who cannot accept the love and grace of God. But we all must make an answer for our own lives. It is not as though we could answer for the life of another, but certainly, we will all be judged with complete veracity. And even if we had done good deeds, they would not have been able to save us. Salvation comes by one means only, and it is by the grace of God for those who believe it through faith.

> *He saved us, not because of works done by us in righteousness, but according to his own mercy,* **by the washing of regeneration and renewal of the Holy Spirit** ....
>
> Titus 3:4 (ESV)

Before He saved us, we were degenerate and decaying in our sins. We were wasting away, inwardly, and outwardly. We had only the tattered and bloody rags of our filthy false righteousness. We catered to the desires of the Flesh and observed only the rule that we would do as we wanted. We were utterly despicable. The only sway that held power over us was that of the evil spiritual forces that haunted us in the Darkness with the fear of death as the only sure thing. That fear caused many of us to store up for ourselves treasures on this earth that could only fade with each passing day. They were wearing out with every use. Some of them not even treasures but rather the source of our sinful enslavement. It was from this low point that He reached down for us. It was in that muck and mire and destitution that He came down to rescue us. He did this not because we had something to be admired, but almost more so because of our tremendous need for renewal. We were dying, deceased in many ways, and our days were numbered against us. But through the Washing of Regeneration that comes from the Renewal of the Holy Spirit, those that were once Dead in their sins have been raised up to be with Christ and made more like Him.

COMMUNION

> *Whoever* ***eats My flesh and drinks My blood*** *remains in Me, and I in him.*
>
> John 6:56 (ESV)

Similar to Baptism is the practice of Communion. This practice should be done with great seriousness and great joy. On one hand, we break the bread and drink the cup in order to commemorate the death of Jesus. It reminds us of the cost that was paid to ransom us. We were indeed bought at a price, not with perishable things like silver and gold, but with the precious blood of Jesus Christ (1 Peter 1:18-21). He is the lamb of

God who takes away the sin of the World. He is the Lamp who Lights the World and takes away its Darkness. But for some reason, even within this practice, there is a strange gathering of those who Walk in their Sleep.

> *These are hidden reefs at your **love feasts, as they feast with you without fear**, shepherds feeding themselves; waterless clouds, swept along by winds; fruitless trees in late autumn, **twice dead**, uprooted ....*
>
> Jude 1:12 (ESV)

How could it be that the Dead are somehow partaking of these precious events? Why are the Living allowing such a sacred ordinance to be so abused? Could it be so simple that the Living are afraid and reluctant to confront those that are making a mockery of our Lord and Savior? One should hope not! If the Dead are hidden among the Living, as indistinguishable as a dream to the Dreamer, then how ought we to feel when they eat at the Lord's table without regarding the One who bought them? Indeed, if He bought them with His blood, they should be there. And His blood was shed for the forgiveness of sins. But Zombies have no part in the brotherhood that comes through faith. They are faithless and instead should be fearful. Why are they not fearful? Are they getting their fill on the bounty of the Lord's people? They feast without fear, but if they knew what they were doing, then they would certainly fear. If they are fruitless, then Worthy Walkers should recognize the signs of their status. They should be warned and admonished. They should even be encouraged to take the plunge and believe once and for all that Jesus Christ is Lord. But unless they believe that, they have no participation in such a communion of Believers. This is not a new problem.

> *But in the following instructions **I do not commend you**, because when you come together it is **not for the better but for the worse**. For, in the first place, when you come together as a church, I hear that there are divisions among you. And I believe it in part, for there must be factions among you in order that **those who are genuine among you may be recognized**. When you come together, it is not the Lord's supper that you eat. For in eating, each one goes ahead with his own meal. One goes hungry, another gets drunk. What! Do you not have houses to eat and drink in? Or do you despise the church of God and humiliate those who have nothing? What shall I say to you? Shall I commend you in this? No, I will not. For I received from the Lord what I also delivered to you, that the Lord Jesus on the night when he was betrayed took bread, and when he had given*

thanks, he broke it, and said, ***"This is my body, which is for you. Do this in remembrance of me."*** *In the same way, also he took the cup, after supper, saying,* ***"This cup is the new covenant in my blood. Do this, as often as you drink it, in remembrance of me." For as often as you eat this bread and drink the cup, you proclaim the Lord's death until he comes.*** *Whoever, therefore, eats the bread or drinks the cup of the Lord in an* ***unworthy manner*** *will be guilty concerning the body and blood of the Lord.* ***Let a person examine himself,*** *then, and so eat of the bread and drink of the cup. For anyone who eats and drinks without discerning the body eats and drinks judgment on himself.* ***That is why many of you are weak and ill, and some have died.*** *But if we* ***judged ourselves truly, we would not be judged.*** *But when we are judged by the Lord, we are disciplined* ***so that we may not be condemned along with the world.*** *So then, my brothers, when you come together to eat, wait for one another—if anyone is hungry, let him eat at home—so that when you come together it will not be for judgment. About the other things I will give directions when I come.*

1 Corinthians 11:17-33 (ESV)

Revival

These are the matters that have provoked this Revival Guide. More than anything else, it seems to be the trouble that is presented in the lack of what should be evident. Death has come upon us because of negligence and pride. Where Adam should have served as a protector over Eve and all of humanity, he failed. But even if he had not failed, we ourselves surely would have. But there is One who is like Adam, but far better. He is the one who comes from above. It is the Lord Jesus Christ. The time has come for judgment to begin with the household of God. And if these are judged swiftly, what will happen to the ungodly? What will happen to the Undead? What about those that refuse to put their sin to death? Will they be allowed by God to also partake of the Wedding Supper of the Lamb as communion prefigures? Absolutely not! That would be so opposed to the entire message of the Gospel Cure that it would cause the entire nature of God to be brought into question. But that is not what should be questioned. The question hangs on those that claim Christ and those that do not. There are only two factions. And as it is written, there must be factions so that those who are genuine may be recognized. But what recognition will come down on those who call what is good evil and what is bitter, sweet? They must fear for their Lives. If we say that we are in Christ, then let it be so! But if we say we belong to Him and actually do not, may God have mercy on them by granting repentance before their time comes to an end.

The Revival of the Dead is the mission that is set before the Worthy Walker. If we carry out our calling, we will surely know what the joy of the Lord is. We know that it is not by our means that we are saved, and it is not by our means that those Zombies we encounter are saved. It all comes down to the Lord our God. And we praise Him for that because He took up a burden that no ordinary man could bear. This is the true God, and His love is real love. Perhaps, if it is His will, many more Zombies will turn from their sins as those that already believe, rededicate themselves to what we have already attained (Philippians 3:13-16). But even if the worst is yet to come, we can know that we have entrusted our lives to the one who can save us from death. If we, like Jesus, cry out to our God with faithfulness and reverance, we will be heard. And seeing that to be heard by God is more than we could even ask for, we can consider our request fulfilled even before we have seen it come to pass. We are beyond blessed. We should be dead. We were Dead, until the One who should never have died willingly carried His cross and suffered at the hands of men. But just as Moses raised up the bronze statue of a snake in the wilderness and all those who looked upon it in faith were healed, so too was Jesus lifted up above the earth on the cross so that all those who would lift their eyes to meet His face could be saved from their sins. That is, if only they would believe.

> *I tell you this, brothers: **flesh and blood cannot inherit the kingdom of God**, nor does the perishable inherit the imperishable. **Behold! I tell you a mystery**. We shall not all **sleep**, but we shall all be **changed**, in a moment, in the twinkling of an eye, at the last trumpet. For the trumpet will sound, and the **dead will be raised imperishable**, and we shall be **changed**. For this perishable body must put on the imperishable, and this mortal body must put on immortality. When the **perishable** puts on the **imperishable**, and the **mortal** puts on **immortality**, then shall come to pass the saying that is written: "Death is swallowed up in victory. O death, where is your victory? O death, where is your sting?" **The sting of death is sin, and the power of sin is the law**. But thanks be to God, who gives us the **victory through our Lord Jesus Christ**. Therefore, my beloved brothers, be **steadfast, immovable, always abounding in the work of the Lord, knowing that in the Lord your labor is not in vain**.*
>
> 1 Corinthians 15:50-58 (ESV)

AMEN, SO BE IT, COME QUICKLY LORD JESUS CHRIST.

About the Author

Talon Schneider was born in Lakin, Kansas. His parents are Scott Schneider and Gina Unruh. His step-dad is Todd Unruh. He has two sisters Tiana Schneider and Rian Unruh. His family has always been a source of help and hope.

In many ways, Talon is very ordinary, just a kid from Kansas with very little to distinguish him. But God, as He often does, takes the weak and lowly things to confound the strong and proud things. Through the advice of Talon's mentor, Mike Dicker, he thoroughly committed to the study of the scriptures and, therefore, the realization of God's love and truth. When anyone, great or small, is changed by the love of God, they are transformed and conformed ever more into the image of the Lord Jesus Christ.

While at college in Colorado Springs, Talon was Born Again into a living hope through faith in the resurrection of Jesus Christ from the dead. He tenaciously dedicated himself to following after our Lord and Savior. He soon finished college with his best friend and wife, Erika Schneider. Together they moved to Tribune, Kansas, to work on the family farm as fourth-generation farmers. This book was written primarily in the confines of a tractor. At other times, the writing was done late at night while holding one of his children. It is the beginning of the purpose for which God called him, namely that he would help others believe in God and Jesus Christ, whom He sent so that all of us together would know that we have eternal life through Him (John 17:3).

Follow Talon at:

crossperspectiveministries.com

Made in United States
Orlando, FL
06 December 2023